LEST WE FORGET

ALSO BY TESSA DUNLOP

Elizabeth & Philip
A story of young love, marriage, and monarchy

Army Girls
The secrets and stories of military service from the final few women who fought in the Second World War

The Century Girls
The final word from the women who've lived the past hundred years of British history

The Bletchley Girls
War, secrecy, love and loss: the women of Bletchley Park tell their story

LEST WE FORGET

War and Peace in 100 British Monuments

TESSA DUNLOP

with illustrations by Martin Hargreaves

Harper North

HarperNorth
Windmill Green
24 Mount Street
Manchester M2 3NX

A division of
HarperCollins*Publishers*
1 London Bridge Street
London SE1 9GF

www.harpercollins.co.uk

HarperCollins*Publishers*
Macken House, 39/40 Mayor Street Upper
Dublin 1, D01 C9W8

First published by HarperNorth in 2025

1 3 5 7 9 10 8 6 4 2

Copyright © Tessa Dunlop 2025

Tessa Dunlop asserts the moral right to
be identified as the author of this work

A catalogue record for this book is
available from the British Library

HB ISBN: 978-0-00-871314-0

Printed and bound in the UK using 100%
renewable electricity at CPI Group (UK) Ltd, Croydon

All rights reserved. No part of this publication may be
reproduced, stored in a retrieval system, or transmitted,
in any form or by any means, electronic, mechanical,
photocopying, recording or otherwise, without the
prior permission of the publishers.

Without limiting the author's and publisher's exclusive rights, any
unauthorised use of this publication to train generative artificial
intelligence (AI) technologies is expressly prohibited. HarperCollins
also exercise their rights under Article 4(3) of the Digital Single
Market Directive 2019/790 and expressly reserve this publication
from the text and data mining exception.

This book contains FSC™ certified paper and other controlled
sources to ensure responsible forest management.

For more information visit: www.harpercollins.co.uk/green

In memory of Cora Jarman

Stand and take pity beside the sign of Kroisos who had died, whom once in the front ranks rushing Ares destroyed.

*Epitaph for the deceased aristocrat Kroisos at the base of a kouros statue, c.540**

---

* Kouros means 'youth'.

CONTENTS

Introduction 1

PART ONE: OUTSIDERS

Chapter 1: Roman Hangover 11
    1. Boadicea and Her Daughters statue, Westminster Bridge, London, 1902
    2. Cavalry of the Empire Memorial, Hyde Park, London, 1924

Chapter 2: Viking Hell 18
    3. Viking Raider Stone, Lindisfarne Priory Collection, Lindisfarne, 800–825
    4. Alfred the Great statue, Market Place, Wantage, Oxfordshire, 1877
    5. Statue of Alfred the Great, The Broadway, Winchester, Hampshire, 1901

Chapter 3: Norman Conquerors 27
   6. Battle Abbey and Battlefield, Battle, East Sussex, 1070–94
   7. Richard Coeur de Lion (Richard I) statue, Old Palace Yard, Westminster, London, 1860

PART TWO: WARRING BRITANNIA

Chapter 4: Kill Thy Neighbour 37
   8. The De Montfort Memorial, Abbey Park, Evesham, Worcestershire, 1965
   9. Memorial to Llywelyn ap Gruffudd (Llewelyn the Last), Prince of Gwynedd, Cilmeri, Powys, Wales, 1956
   10. The National Wallace Monument, Stirling, 1861–69
   11. Sir William Wallace Memorial, St Bartholomew's Hospital, Smithfield, London, 1956
   12. Robert the Bruce statue, Battle of Bannockburn site, Stirling, 1964

Chapter 5: Hitting France 53
   13. Tomb of Edward, the Black Prince, Canterbury Cathedral, Canterbury, 1380s
   14. Statue of the Black Prince, City Square, Leeds, 1903
   15. Owain Glyndŵr statue, Corwen, Denbighshire, 2007
   16. Tomb of King Henry V, Shrine of Edward the Confessor, Westminster Abbey, London, 1431

Chapter 6: Family Feuds 65
   17. King Richard's Well, Bosworth Battlefield Heritage Centre, Leicestershire, 1813
   18. Tomb of King Richard III, Leicester Cathedral, 2015

Chapter 7: Tudor Wars 72
19. Battle of Flodden Memorial, Branxton, Northumberland, 1910
20. Langside Battlefield Memorial, Langside, Glasgow, 1887
21. The Armada Memorial, Plymouth Hoe, Plymouth, Devon, 1888

Chapter 8: Uncivil Wars 80
22. Naseby Obelisk, Naseby Battlefield, Northamptonshire, 1823
23. Statue of Oliver Cromwell, Cromwell Green, Westminster, London, 1899
24. Battle of Bothwell Bridge Memorial, Bothwell, Lanarkshire, 1903

Chapter 9: Breaking-in Britain 91
25. King William III statue, Carrickfergus, County Antrim, Northern Ireland, 1990
26. Massacre of Glencoe Monument, Glencoe, Argyll, 1883
27. Blenheim Palace, Woodstock, Oxfordshire, 1705–22
28. Black Watch Monument, Aberfeldy, Perthshire, 1887
29. Colonel James Gardiner obelisk, grounds of Bankton House, Prestonpans, East Lothian, 1853
30. Memorial Cairn, Culloden Battlefield, Inverness, 1881

PART THREE: LAND OF HOPE AND GLORY

Chapter 10: Nelson Mania 111
31. Nelson Monument, Calton Hill, Edinburgh, 1815
32. Nelson's Monument, The Denes, Great Yarmouth, Norfolk, 1819

33. Nelson's Column, Trafalgar Square, London, 1843
34. Collingwood Monument, Tynemouth, Tyne & Wear, 1845

Chapter 11: Waterloo   123
35. Waterloo Bridge, London, 1817
36. Holy Trinity Church, Kingswood, South Gloucestershire, 1821
37. The National Monument of Scotland, Calton Hill, Edinburgh, 1822–29

Chapter 12: Wellington   132
38. Statue of Achilles, Queen Elizabeth Gate, Hyde Park, London, 1822
39. Wellington Arch, Hyde Park Corner, London, 1846
40. Duke of Wellington statue, Round Hill, Aldershot, 1885
41. Statue of the Duke of Wellington, Royal Exchange Square, Glasgow, 1844
42. Duke of Wellington statue, Princes Street, Edinburgh, 1852

Chapter 13: The Crimean War   145
43. Crimean War Memorial, Bath Abbey Cemetery, Bath, 1856
44. Florence Nightingale statue, Waterloo Place, London, 1915
45. Mary Seacole statue, St Thomas's Hospital Garden, London, 2016

Chapter 14: The Boer War   156
   46. Boer War Memorial, Coombe Hill, Wendover, Buckinghamshire, 1904
   47. Second Boer War Memorial, Duncombe Place (opposite York Minster), York, 1905
   48. Statue of Horatio Herbert Kitchener, Khartoum Road, Chatham, Kent, 1960

PART FOUR: MECHANISED KILLING

Chapter 15: Unknown Warriors, Empty Tombs   169
   49. The Cenotaph, Whitehall, London, 1920
   50. The Tomb of the Unknown Warrior, Westminster Abbey, 1920
   51. The Belfast Cenotaph, Donegall Square West, Belfast, 1929
   52. The Bristol Cenotaph, Colston Avenue, Bristol, 1932

Chapter 16: Pillars of the Community   181
   53. Colchester War Memorial, High Street, Colchester, Essex, 1923
   54. The Response 1914 (Northumberland Fusiliers Memorial), grounds of the Church of St Thomas the Martyr, Barras Bridge, Newcastle-upon-Tyne, 1923
   55. The Crypt Chapel, Harrow School, Harrow, London, 1918
   56. The Alex Fitch Room, War Memorial Building, Harrow School, London, 1926
   57. Balmoral Estate Workers War Memorial, opposite the entrance to Balmoral Castle, Crathie, Grampian, 1922

Chapter 17: Empire's Heroes — 195
  58. Chattri Memorial, South Downs, near Brighton, East Sussex, 1921
  59. Muslim Burial Ground Peace Garden, Monument Road, Woking, Surrey, 1917

Chapter 18: Broken Soldiers — 202
  60. Machine Gun Corps Memorial, Hyde Park Corner, London, 1925
  61. 'Gueules Cassées': The Men With Broken Faces memorial, Queen Mary's Hospital, Sidcup, London, 2019
  62. Victory Over Blindness, Piccadilly Station, Manchester, 2018

Chapter 19: Female Heroes — 211
  63. East Window, St Mary's Church, Swardeston, Norfolk, 1917
  64. Edith Cavell statue, St Martin's Place, London, 1920
  65. Five Sisters Window, York Minster, York, 1925

Chapter 20: When Two Becomes One — 220
  66. Chatham Naval Memorial, Chatham, Kent, 1924
  67. Royal Artillery War Memorial, Hyde Park Corner, London, 1925
  68. Kinloch Rannoch War Memorial, Kinloch Rannoch, Perthshire, 1930

PART FIVE: AN EXCEPTIONAL WAR

Chapter 21: Readjusting to Peace   233
    69. World War II Avenue of Remembrance, The Tilt, Cobham, Surrey, 1946
    70. Portsmouth Naval Memorial, Southsea Common, Hampshire, 1924
    71. The Commando Memorial and Memorial Garden, Spean Bridge, Lochaber, 1952

Chapter 22: Great Men   245
    72. Winston Churchill statue, Parliament Square, London, 1973
    73. 'Monty' statue, opposite the D-Day Story museum, Clarence Esplanade, Southsea, Hampshire, 1997
    74. Alan Turing statue, Sackville Gardens, Manchester, 2001
    75. Freddie Gilroy and the Belsen Stragglers sculpture, North Bay, Scarborough, 2008

Chapter 23: The Greatest Generation   258
    76. The Overlord Embroidery, The D-Day Story museum, Clarence Esplanade, Southsea, Hampshire, 1974
    77. Kemble War Memorial, Church Road, Kemble, Gloucestershire, 1920
    78. Memorial to the Women's Transport Service (FANY), St Paul's Church, Wilton Place, Knightsbridge, London, 1948
    79. Special Operations Executive (SOE) Agents/Violette Szabo, Albert Embankment, London, 2009
    80. The Bevin Boys Memorial, The National Memorial Arboretum, Alrewas, Staffordshire, 2013
    81. The ATS Memorial, The National Memorial Arboretum, Alrewas, Staffordshire, 2005

Chapter 24: Blitzed — 277
  82. New Coventry Cathedral, Priory Street, Coventry, 1962
  83. RAF Bomber Command Memorial, Hyde Park, London, 2012

Chapter 25: Whose War? — 287
  84. Commonwealth Memorial Gates, Constitution Hill, London, 2002
  85. Sikh Troops War Memorial, Victoria Park, Leicester, 2022
  86. Gurkha statue, Princes Gardens, Aldershot, 2021
  87. Monument to the Women of World War II, Whitehall, London, 2005

Chapter 26: Collateral Damage — 300
  88. Kindertransport – The Arrival, Liverpool Street Station, London, 2006
  89. The Children of Calais, Dorset House Garden, Saffron Walden, Essex, 2015
  90. War Horse sculpture, Daisy Field, Shirehampton, Bristol, 2023

Chapter 27: Accidental Death — 309
  91. Eagle's Rock Cross, Eagle's Rock, Dunbeath, Caithness, 1946
  92. Memorial Cairn, Glen Loch, Forest of Atholl, Perthshire, 1994

PART SIX: PEACETIME BRITAIN?

Chapter 28: The Troubles — 321
   93. Bloody Sunday Memorial, Joseph Place, Derry/Londonderry, Northern Ireland, 1974
   94. Warrenpoint Massacre plaque, Warrenpoint, County Down, Northern Ireland, last erected 2020

Chapter 29: The Falklands War — 329
   95. The Yomper, Eastney Esplanade, Southsea, Hampshire, 1992
   96. The Welsh National Falklands Memorial, Alexandra Gardens, Cardiff, 2007

Chapter 30: Asymmetrical War — 336
   97. Maiwand Lion, Forbury Gardens, Reading, 1886
   98. Camp Bastion Wall, National Memorial Arboretum, Alrewas, Staffordshire, 2015
   99. Aaron Lewis Close, Hockley, Essex, 2014
   100. Basra Wall, National Memorial Arboretum, Alrewas, Staffordshire, 2010

Postscript
   The Armed Forces Memorial, National Memorial Arboretum, Alrewas, Staffordshire, 2007 — 349

Epilogue — 353
Acknowledgements — 357
Bibliography — 361

INTRODUCTION

Stella is crunched up in the front seat. Mine is a small hire car, poorly parked in a pool of evening light. She is well turned out, sunglasses to keep off the glare, dark polished nails and a navy two-piece suit. Neat with her words, she speaks when spoken to, but it is all there, just beneath the surface.

'Mum was a person who loved through actions. There was roast beef turned down low, vegetables off and ready, a tray-bake oozing caramel and she'd made an Eve's pudding. You know, the one with stewed apples.'

Across the road, a bronze sentinel soldier bends his head, silhouetted against an expanse of Irish sky out west, beyond County Fermanagh. 'Dad loved the uniforms and music and commemoration. It was common practice to be here on Armistice Day.' Stella shifts in her seat. 'He was of his generation, a disciplinarian but a kind man.' She shares an affectionate account of her father, Wesley Armstrong, a community-minded individual with a smallholding and a devotion to his local Methodist church. Wesley was someone who took pride in the unique military heritage of Enniskillen, probably the only town in the United Kingdom and Ireland which raised two distinct regiments, the Royal Inniskilling Fusiliers and the 5th Royal Inniskilling Dragoon Guards, in two World Wars.

LEST WE FORGET

Stella takes off her glasses. It was a while ago now. November 2027 will mark forty years and yet the feelings remain very present. Grief morphs and changes but it rarely fades. 'I remember a lot of kindness when we grew up. We helped each other. We had cows and hens and everyone mucked in. Then, like now, there were good folk and bad folk.'

And the story rolls forward again to Armistice Sunday 1987. Wesley and his wife Bertha were huddled from the rain beneath a dilapidated Catholic Church building, savouring the atmosphere inflected with military music. A day to remember the dead and give thanks for the living, before going home to Sunday lunch. 'I heard it from about a mile away, like a garage door slamming. I didn't think …' Stella stops. She didn't think, and nobody imagined, what came next. On Armistice Sunday, of all days. That lunchtime, Stella did not enjoy roast beef with her parents. The traybake went uneaten. She never again saw her mother and father alive. While commemorating the fallen in Northern Ireland's Enniskillen, Wesley and Bertha Armstrong were murdered by an IRA bomb. Stella trails off. 'I really loved my parents. My mum was my best friend.'

This is a book about commemoration. It focuses on bricks and mortar, bronze casts and stone inscriptions, and the delicate interplay of words, stories and memories. Monuments and statues are inanimate, static entities that depend on their relationship with human beings for relevance and agency. Enniskillen was a community where Protestants had long intermingled with Catholics; both are named in their hundreds on the local war memorial. Regardless, the IRA targeted Armistice Sunday, planting their bomb just yards from the soldier on his plinth. What happened next was a new level of terror: twelve innocents killed as they commemorated the dead.*

---

* In fact, eleven men and women died on 8 November 1987. A twelfth victim, Ronnie Hill, subsequently died having spent thirteen years in a coma.

INTRODUCTION

In the days that followed, Enniskillen became a byword for dignity and calm, matched by the town's silent soldier; an unwavering constant, head still bowed, leaning on his reversed rifle. Then, five years later in 1991, the memorial changed. Stella explains: 'They added eleven doves on the plinth to represent those who died that day, but they didn't consult the families.' Stella won't get out of the car; she refuses to look at the war memorial or have her photograph taken beside it. Symbols of peace, the doves cleaved to the flanks of this commemorative soldier in a country then still mired in violence. Compounding the grief, the names of 1987's dead were added to the reams of wartime fallen, with the additional inscription noting the victims had been 'killed'. For many, including Stella, the modification of a war memorial and the phraseology used gave the 1987 attack a grotesque legitimacy. Her parents and ten other innocent victims were murdered in an act of terror on 8 November 1987. Monuments and words matter.

In the immediate aftermath of the Enniskillen bombing, the British prime minister, Margaret Thatcher, visited the town. She picked her way up Belmore Street and faced down the memorial, a small black bag perched on her arm, a minimal black veil shading her brow. The images were beamed around the world. Thatcher insisted no stone would be left unturned in the quest to find the killers and bring them to justice. In fact, 'The Troubles' in Northern Ireland was not a fight she could 'win', but the martial prime minister had already learnt the value of binary language and military prowess.

Five years earlier, a decisive victory in the Falklands War had been closely followed by a defining moment at the Conservative Party Conference in Brighton. On 12 October 1984, just hours after a fatal IRA bomb attack in Brighton's Grand Hotel, Margaret Thatcher dusted herself down and delivered a speech to the party faithful. She closed with the words: 'The government will not weaken. This nation will meet that challenge. Democracy will prevail.' The oration was straight out of wartime leader Winston Churchill's playbook.

LEST WE FORGET

It is no coincidence that, during the 1980s, a decade studded with conflict and violence, Britain witnessed a surge in World War II commemoration. Legions of surviving veterans from that war entered the nostalgic twilight of their lives, just as Thatcher's Britain was searching for a broader military narrative, one that sought to move beyond the imperial abyss and posit good versus evil in the context of British military encounter. The result was a spate of memorialisation which has continued unbated through to the present day. In our cluttered remembrance schedule, it is hard to imagine the 1950s and '60s, when the masculine heroics of World War II were more likely to be recast in Hollywood japes than through sombre service and stone iterations.

These days, Philip Jarman is 101. As a teenager he served in the Pacific War, a cypher officer in the 26th Indian Division, Northern Burma, but after 1945 he didn't want to remember a conflict in which he lost a brother, a sister-in-law and a best friend. Philip insists that 'on 8 May, people celebrated, and why shouldn't they? They had borne the brunt of the struggle, including the civilian fortitude of night-bombing.' Immediately after the war, monument-building fell out of fashion; Philip's apathy some 80 years on is symptomatic of a cynical population who greeted the question of sculpture with a flat 'no'. In the words of one soldier: 'Let us have no more stone crosses or war memorials in the 1918 sense of the word.' Philip gives the comment context: 'A lot of Britain had been bombed in the war. We needed houses, not monuments.'

Then he pauses. 'In fact, there is one memorial I like. It's in Cobham where I used to live. After the war, the Women's Institute said "to hell with conventional monuments" and planted an avenue of cherry trees to honour the fallen. In May the blossom is quite lovely.' Philip's cherry tree avenue, subsequently replanted, is one of the 100 memorials in this book. *Lest We Forget* tells the stories behind monuments to war: the criteria for inclusion prioritise the act of remembering baked into their inception and its resonance in today's Britain.

INTRODUCTION

Ninety-nine-year-old Barbara Weatherill was integral to the arrival of the World War II monument that honours female service in London's Whitehall. She considers it 'ugly' and told the sculptor as much. Nor does she approve of the broad female canvass the memorial proports to represent: 'All we wanted was a monument to our local anti-aircraft girls.' Barbara quickly discovered that, once unleashed in the public arena, commemoration acquires a life of its own. The monument is indeed ugly (and some of its donors – among them, Jimmy Savile – questionable), but the sculptor, John Mills, had a difficult job. How to create a piece of art that spoke to all the women, from local do-gooders to cutting-edge 'gunner-girls', involved in World War II?

The visibility of certain wartime experiences over others has led to a recent, competitive scramble. Kindertransport children, animals and miners have all queued up at the altar of remembrance for a World War that has taken on fairy-tale dimensions. The last Conservative budget in 2024 opened with a pledge for a £1 million memorial to Muslim service in two World Wars, while a mooted holocaust memorial in central London awaits vital planning permissions. Inevitably, as a more inclusive commemorative script to a global war against fascism takes hold, earlier monuments celebrating imperial Britain have fallen out of favour.

Standing in Trafalgar Square, the bellybutton of the metropole, two Victorian military men were roundly dismissed in 2000 by the then London Mayor: Ken Livingstone declared he did not 'have a clue' who Major-General Sir Henry Havelock and General Sir Charles James Napier were. A couple of military giants from the vanguard of Britain's Empire caught up in today's febrile politics and prevalent cancel culture, an equivocal amnesia is the best they can hope for. Neither man made the cut for this book.

Amid a surfeit of heroes, the immortalisation of a select few in monumental form is a two-sided tale: the leader or conflict remembered intersects with the era and individuals that recast the chosen few. Ninety-eight-year-old Ruth Bourne was a Bombe machine operative at Bletchley Park; recollections of her own war in 1944–45 are jaundiced by the panoply of conflicts that scar the contemporary international landscape. She is sickened by what she sees: 'I remember when I went to school it was the first time I ever knew about war. There have always been wars. At school, you learn your history through wars, I don't really know why. It is something within men that they feel they have to have a war.'

Today, a fêted war veteran herself and a recipient of the Légion d'Honneur, Ruth insists that, 'apart from Boudica, I never learned about a war run by a woman. It's always been men, hasn't it?'

Certainly Boudica's vast presence as a warrior queen on Westminster Bridge is anomalous among a plethora of men who litter our streets. The ancient Briton provides a great start point for this book, just as she was the ideal (and ironic) pin-up for Victoria's imperial Britain. But Ruth is right: Boudica is not representative. Most monuments are to male heroes and fallen male soldiers. When writing *Lest We Forget*, my publisher insisted the readership would primarily be male. I thought about the legion of military and history men I have interviewed over the last year, the serving Commandos and majors who have broken down in tears, and the screeds of boys' names engraved in cold stone, and I disagreed. This is a book for both sexes.

Yes, as Ruth sagely observes, war is still predominantly the preserve of men, but the havoc it wreaks, and the lives it claims, are painful personal blows that transgress gender and detonate family life. Those left to pick up pieces and pray before lifeless art are so often women. As Helen Lewis, the mother of Aaron Lewis, a soldier killed in Afghanistan, eloquently explained: 'When I listen to the news, I hear people who have died and each one is like a stone in a pond. For every death, there are a thousand ripples.'

In World War I, 880,000 British service personnel died. The litany of subsequent monuments was just one manifestation of those ripples, a communal acknowledgement of the pain beneath the surface that continues to the present day. Lest we forget: every Israeli hostage has a family, ditto every Palestinian baby, and every soldier felled by a

INTRODUCTION

Russian bullet. For lasting remembrance, first the destruction and killing must stop. Enduring monuments require enduring peace.

Anniversaries are a recurring theme is this book: whether marking time in decades, centuries or (in the case of Victorian England's favourite, King Alfred) millennia, a significant watershed is the ideal excuse to galvanise wider interest and begin fundraising, both then and now. Heroes and epochs fall in and out of fashion, statues are erected and pulled down, but Britain's chronological arc remains the same. Although this book occasionally deviates from the narrative path (Reading's magnificent Maiwand Lion joins more contemporary memorials to yet another war in Afghanistan), most of the monuments tell a sequential story through time. Whether a recurring ancient form – statue, obelisk, empty tomb – or more specific local style, war monuments are silent communicators between a deceased majority and the nation's future generations. Which nation is yet more contested terrain – national heroes and identities are not formed in a vacuum. Scotland, England, Wales and Ireland slugged it out, often each against the other. Our statuary reflects that oscillating saga back at us, with Scotland's William Wallace and Wales's Owain Glyndŵr the medieval zeitgeists in today's feisty era of resurgent nationalism.

As the monuments gradually edge this book into the modern era, a beat change occurs. Universal franchise, unprecedented slaughter, and death within living memory all impact the tenor of remembrance: hero-worship morphs into the Glorious Dead. After 1918, mourning families, forbidden from retrieving the bodies of their fallen from abroad, flooded Britain's commemorative landscape. This book tries to honour their pain and pride and, in a reflection of their predicament, it too is firmly bedded on exclusively British soil. The space and place that a monument occupies are part of its power. To see is to believe.

I visited every monument selected here, from the memorial-cairn in Kinloch Rannoch, the Highland village where I grew up, to

LEST WE FORGET

Northern Ireland's Derry/Londonderry, home to the Bloody Sunday obelisk, a salient reminder that the British Army doesn't always get things right. The local voices I heard while criss-crossing the United Kingdom are at the heart of *Lest We Forget*. Kate Nash's brother Willie was shot in the Bloody Sunday massacre; she welcomed me into her home like a friend. Likewise, the Duke of Kent into Wren House, Kensington Palace; His Royal Highness was six when his father died, the last member of the Royal Family killed on active service.

A military man through-and-though, the Duke of Kent understands the power of commemoration and royalty's role as a symbol of state within that power-nexus. On my travels, I vicariously came across the Duke's name and title as someone who has unveiled umpteen monuments to war. He told me how those that impact him the most have a personal touch. 'I find them absolutely heartbreaking to look at sometimes.'

He is right, of course. Back in Enniskillen, Stella won't acknowledge the town's main war memorial, adapted to incorporate the murder of her parents and ten others in a way she does not recognise. It was thirty-five years after the IRA's attack when a separate memorial plaque was finally erected to commemorate those murdered in November 1987. Embedded in a wall, 'it is exactly where my mother and father were standing,' Stella explains, 'commemorating Armistice Day, when the bomb went off. Put a pin in the map and that is where they were.' In a constituency now run by Sinn Féin, there was resistance and prevarication before the plaque was eventually unveiled in 2022: a simple namecheck in black and gold to those killed by the IRA in 1987, including Stella's parents, Wesley and Bertha Armstrong. The memorial is a reminder of the truth: that, until the brokering of a fragile peace in 1998, there were decades of violence, slaughter and ugliness in Northern Ireland. Inscribed beneath the plaque, in the wall rebuilt after the bombing, are the words *Lest We Forget*.

PART ONE
OUTSIDERS

CHAPTER 1

ROMAN HANGOVER

Perhaps inevitably, Britain has no decent statue to the Roman Empire's conquering hero Claudius, a foreigner of questionable attributes. But today the streets are studded with Roman-style statues, including two of England's most enduring icons, both defined under the imperial yolk.

1. Boadicea and Her Daughters statue, Westminster Bridge, London, 1902

Boudica, Queen of the Iceni, c. 25–61

Who is Boudica?
 'Boudica is a fighter.'
 'Brudicca wasn't scared of anything.'
 'Don't know how Budicca diyed.'
 High on the top deck, armed with sharp pencils, florescent waistcoats and outsized packed lunches, Year 3 are on a day trip. They are off to find Boudica in central London. The Romans are baddies, they whipped Boudica. Eight-year-old Angelo insists, with Cassius Dio authority, that Boudica has red hair and a spear. The source materials for our hero haven't changed in two millen-

nia. (Much like Angelo, Roman historian Cassius Dio was just going on what he'd heard.) No matter, the Key Stage 2 curriculum loves a straightforward narrative and this ancient rebel is perfect Britannia fodder.

'What is resistance, Miss?'

It's like defending. Boudica was a defender, pushing against the Roman bullies. Boudica was an icon.

'What's an icon?'

Someone you look up to. By the time the bus arrives on Westminster Bridge, Boudica is a footballer, more specifically Bellingham, or Saka. Every generation has their pin-ups.

If Boudica did exist (nowadays some historians query even that, though most believe Tacitus wasn't a complete fantasist), we can be fairly certain she looked nothing like Queen Victoria, and neither carried a Persian spear, nor drove a Roman chariot. But this is the Boudica these children are about to meet.

'Is that Buckingham Palace?'

'No, it's Westminster. Look to your right! Can you see her? Beyond the souvenir stall! Look up!'

'Miss! Miss! I can see Boudica!'

We make our way to a defiant Boudica, her horses roaring towards the Houses of Parliament, her arms unfurled, unapologetic. This is empire personified.

'But I thought she was fighting the Romans, Miss.'

How do you explain to a class of eight-year-olds that the Boudica they are looking at belongs to the later British Empire?

'Miss, I thought the British Empire was bad.'

The children budge up on the steps beneath her statue. One boy won't sit down.

'It's dirty, Miss.'

'Do you think Boudica was afraid of the dirt?'

He still won't sit down. Boudica is standing in her chariot. Boudica and the children are trapped: the Thames below them, the tourists around them and, hovering beyond reach, the naked breasts

of Boudica's two daughters. The Key Stage 2 syllabus avoids details of the sisters' run-in with the Romans.

For adult learners, while failing to honour an agreement made with Boudica's late husband, the Romans also raped her daughters. Raging Boudica went on to destroy Roman-occupied Colchester, St Albans and London. As I write two millennia later, Hamas is accused of raping women in the 7 October 2023 attacks. Raging Israel is destroying Gaza and Lebanon. And only relatively recently has sexual violence been recognised as a weapon of war.*

'She was so angry that she burned down three cities. An ancient, blackened layer of soot remains. It is the only archaeological evidence we have of Boudica.'

'She doesn't look very angry, Miss.'

---

* The 1949 Geneva Conventions recognised sexual violence in conflict and in 1998 the Roman Statute identified rape and sexual violence as war crimes, in certain contexts.

LEST WE FORGET

The all-seeing children are right. Despite her raised arms, Victorian sculptor Thomas Thornycroft's statue wears a placid expression; her robes are loose, her hair flowing, her belly swollen. A fecund, youngish Victoria springs to mind. An early twentieth-century marble statue of Boudica and her daughters in Cardiff City Hall focuses exclusively on this maternal persona, but Thornycroft's Boudica works harder than that: his Iceni rebel is a domestic icon and an imperial warrior. No matter that Boudica rebelled (and lost) against the Roman empire in 60–61 AD. Here in London, she is the personification of victorious Imperial Britain. Stamped into her plinth, the children read Georgian poet William Cowper's heft of jingoism: 'Regions Caesar Never Knew/Thy Posterity Shall Sway.' Imperial Britain's reach went farther, much farther, than Imperial Rome's.

Inspired during the Great Exhibition of 1851 – and sculpted in Thornycroft's lifetime, but due to financial constraints not finally cast and erected until 1902 – Boudica is the link between ancient Britannia and Victorian power, a power mirrored in the Houses of Parliament she charges towards. The children write down the word 'power'. We talk about Boudica's fighting spirit, the black mark she left on early Londinium and how she inspired men and women beyond her Iceni tribe. A packet of Bourbon creams briefly distracts the troops.

'Are they vegan, Miss?' It's unlikely Boudica was vegan. But there is so little to go on, the field for interpretation remains open.

Within seven years of Queen Victoria's death, Boudica's statue became a staging post for a Suffragette march; rather than underlining British power, by 1908 she was riding on Parliament demanding votes for women. It is a lot for a class of eight-year-olds to take in, and conditions aren't conducive to learning. Italian Angelo has finished his biscuit. The children are ribbing him for his Roman ancestry. He likes the attention. 'Hey Miss! I am Caesar, and she is a petrifying woman.'

'Good word, Angelo. Write it down!'

2. Cavalry of the Empire Memorial, Hyde Park, London, 1924
St George, Roman soldier, d. 303

He beckons me with a white gauntlet. Thanks to John, I manage to dodge the police cordon and join the players and pensioners involved in London's St George's Day Cadet Parade. John is a senior standard bearer, and shows me what he did here, on King Charles Street, the day of the late Queen's funeral. Up came the wooden pole, out of its little bronze bucket, and down dipped his crested standard, crumpled like a bird.

John politely enquires after my purpose. I am writing about St George. 'Off the record, mind,' he mutters, 'George doesn't come from England.' But subsequent royal links are reassuring. Richard the Lionheart called on his protection against the Infidel; in the thirteenth century, Edward I stormed Wales in the name of St George; and, by the fourteenth century, against the French at the Battle of Crécy, the standard was raised, again to George. Safely back on English soil, the Order of the Garter was dedicated to St George in 1348. By the Tudor period, this Roman soldier was unquestionably England's patron saint.

'Attention!'

People shuffle into line; those without wreaths are stationed at the back. Around the corner, the dreamy white Cenotaph is stunning and a little sombre on this, a national day invented for St George. Flanked by hundreds of young military cadets, we march down Whitehall. A small crowd gathers beyond the barricade. I wish I had worn something smarter, a long coat perhaps, with a brooch.

'It's quite like Armistice Day, only instead of the monarch laying a wreath, it's the Royal Society of St George.' Gordon comes from the society's Pinner branch. 'We have a wheelbarrow race tomorrow at 3 p.m. It is unique in the country. We owe St George so much.'

LEST WE FORGET

Over the Tannoy, a reverend rediscovers a non-military George, the Christian martyr and patron saint. 'We look to our patron for prayer and protection ... And we ask St George to pray for us.' There is a nod to royalty, with a reminder that King Charles has yet to take up where his mother left off, as patron of the Royal Society. Has St George become too tainted, too thuggish for the royal brand?

On cue, three days later, a clutch of angry men sully 23 April. They crowd into Whitehall, craning unsuccessfully towards the Cenotaph. They don't bear the flag but rather wear it, a crusading cloak that marks them out as trouble. Public commentators tut; one presenter suggests hooliganism should come with a heavier penalty when perpetrated in an England flag. St George has been misappropriated once more, England's good name soiled.

But when did the misappropriation begin? Once a humble lad sticking up for the Christian faith, talking truth to overbearing power, St George (born somewhere in modern-day Turkey) died a martyr's death during Roman Emperor Diocletian's final wave of Christian persecutions around 303 AD. By the fifth century, a legend had started to crystallise. George acquired Roman soldier status; he was God's own superhero subjected to a super-death – tortured and thrice killed before finally succumbing to his own mortality.* Both ancient and medieval chroniclers rebirthed him with time-travelling superpowers; a Christian outrider accruing the artefacts and costumes of conflict: a dragon to slay, a horse to mount, chivalric armour to fortify. A Christian soldier for any age, and many countries.†

---

* According to legend, when St George refused to bow before the idols of King Dudyanos, the ruler of Persia, and instead confessed his Christian faith, he was killed and resurrected three times. On the fourth death St George was received in heaven.

† St George is also a patron saint in Aragon, Catalonia, Georgia, Lithuania, Palestine, Portugal, Germany, Greece, Moscow, Istanbul, Genoa and Venice (where he is second to Saint Mark).

ROMAN HANGOVER

The man and his myth remove horror from conflict. St George is an Ancient Roman trick, a Christian device to help men (they are predominantly men) transcend pain. Emblazoned and untouchable, a symbol of military purity, he appeared above World War I's killing fields early on, delivering good from evil at the Miracle of Mons when the outnumbered British held up Germany's advance in August 1914. The idea and image have endured. Gordon from the Royal Society stares at a bronze statue of St George on my phone and reassures me he has one very similar on his mantelpiece. I leave the Cenotaph and walk to find London's finest, full-sized Roman fantasy man standing in the shade of a maple tree, tucked into the south-west corner of London's Hyde Park.

Nothing has been forgotten: the sword is triumphant and upright, the crusading armour impenetrable, the gaze distant and the serpent-dragon skewered. Evil incarnate, the mythical beast sports a Germanic handlebar moustache and lies impaled beneath the hoof of an exquisite horse. It's a World War I monument, erected in 1924 to honour the Cavalry of the Empire – British, Canadian, Australian. International George has an international cast.

The sculptor was Adrian Jones, once a veterinary officer in the Royal Horse Artillery. His statue avoids direct reference to the merciless impact of mechanised death. (So many horses died in World War I that their utility on the battlefield died with them.) Rather, Jones's St George rides above the horror; his Roman identity, his legendary horse, his knight's disguise elevate him beyond relentless violence, onwards to chivalry.

England's contemporary marauders who storm the Cenotaph need a memo; someone must let them know they are charging towards the wrong monument. St George with raised sword and equine thunder awaits them in Hyde Park.

CHAPTER 2

VIKING HELL

Heroes need enemies and they didn't come much more lethal than the Nordic Vikings. Retrospectively, Victorian England couldn't get enough of Anglo-Saxon all-rounder King Alfred, but it requires a trip to Northumbria's Lindisfarne to understand what was once at stake.

3. The Domesday Stone, Lindisfarne Priory Collection, Lindisfarne, 800–825

Viking raid, Church of St Cuthbert, Lindisfarne, 793

Today, it feels more like an end point, a destination, a calling even, among the sand dunes and sea birds, before the tide insists upon a return to mainland England with its many humdrum demands. But for the Anglo-Saxons Lindisfarne was a start point, a liminal space between God and man, that inspired Oswald, King of the Northumbrians, to summon Aidan, an Irish monk from the sacred Isle of Iona. Under the guidance of Bishop Aidan, just off the Northumbrian coast, a holy island was established in around 635 and Anglo-Saxon England's Christian story grew wings.

Within three decades, St Cuthbert, northern England's principal patron-saint, was the island's abbot. After his death in 687, the cult of St Cuthbert took off, with monks and priests flocking to the tiny tidal island for contemplation, prayer and community. In Lindisfarne's sacred centre with its growing wealth, visitors and learning, Northumbrians discovered the word of God. Beneath the posthumous glow of St Cuthbert, this dedicated community created the Lindisfarne Gospels in all their bejewelled glory. Blessed was the word of God. Blessed was the Holy Island.

'It is a very special place.' Today's visitors lick ice creams, exclaim at the ocean vistas and check their watches. Like all special places, there are challenges. The only public toilet is hard to find and today's tide will flood the causeway from two o'clock. Peak season and Lindisfarne is not an ideal destination to be stranded. With only 150 locals, the remaining red sandstone cottages come at a high price, yet it's easy to get distracted. There is a castle, built in Tudor times to defend England from the Scots, and the ruins of a priory (another

victim of Henry VIII), peppered with numerous high stone crosses. This is indeed a holy place. Stare out to sea, drunk on the wonders of God's world and the sparkling superstition of early medieval Christendom, and then imagine the unimaginable: it is 793 and Viking ships pepper the horizon.

'Those were the first ships of the Danish men which sought out the land of the English race.'

Invaders. Raiders. Foreign killers.

'And they came to the church of Lindisfarne, laid everything to waste with grievous plundering, trampled the holy places with polluted step, dug up the altars and seized all the treasures of the holy church.'

Testimonies from the *Anglo-Saxon Chronicle* to Simeon of Durham record unconscionable terror. But it is an engraved stone that speaks a thousand words. Offsetting all the majesty baked into the religious glory of this island, one small extant tablet to terror still resides on Lindisfarne. English Heritage caution that there is no concrete proof the round-headed grave marker is a memorial to Viking brutality, but they have encased it in glass and named it 'The Domesday Stone'. Seven axe-wielding, sword-thrusting mad men all in a row, staring out from their safe space in the museum. Carved just years after the 793 Viking onslaught, and in a clear departure from the high crosses and name stones, this raider art speaks to Island Britain's persistent fear of the outsider. Its reverse is offset with a biblical story – sun and moon and desperate people in prayer before a cross. Judgement Day has arrived, when Christ admitted the godly to heaven, and the bad remained on earth to be consumed by fire. Or, in this case, by Vikings. Civilised Europe quaked and a letter from the court of Charlemagne lamented: 'Behold, the church of St Cuthbert spattered with the blood of the priest of God, despoiled of all its ornaments.' Murder most foul in the heart of early Christian England.

I hurry around the remaining exhibits; the museum is closing and the weather forecast is ominous. The cashier smiles. 'At least we have a causeway now. Back then, you had to chance it by foot or rely on ferrymen and small boats.'

Amen.

4. Alfred the Great statue, Market Place, Wantage, Oxfordshire, 1877

King Alfred, b. Wantage, 849

I have come a long way from Lindisfarne. Dropping across England, leaving ancient Northumbria behind, heading south west into what was once the Kingdom of Wessex. Wantage is a small market town just inside Oxfordshire. It is hard to reach – there are no trains – but Wantage likes to think it's worth the effort. Martin Farquhar Tupper, a minor Victorian writer, certainly thought so. In 1849, he organised hearty games and extensive cheer to celebrate the 1,000th anniversary of King Alfred's birth in this town. Otherwise known as Alfred the Great, or England's Darling, Tupper's Alfred bonanza was just the beginning of a full-on Victorian obsession with this Anglo-Saxon King of Wessex.

'He is England's founder' – or at least so I keep being told. I am standing on a flower box in Market Place to get a better look at Wantage's hero. He sports a cracked, chipped axe. It went missing in World War II, only to be lopped off again in the early 2000s. Having been muscled out of the twentieth century by legendary King Arthur, for some this Wessex King is just another man-statue with a (part-time) axe. But unlike Arthur, Alfred was definitely real.

Local church leader Neil Townsend uses Alfred as a rendezvous point. He is brim full of the Great King's unique selling points. 'In times when we lack identity, we look for identity figures. And Alfred is just that.' In Wantage, Alfred's Day has recently been reintroduced: locals dress up as Saxons, children burn cakes and Market Place is given over to early medieval games. Neil insists: 'Alfred arrived in a dysfunctional state with no army and no learning. And he was humble. He went around with a notebook, writing down the wise sayings of people he came across.'

'Like me now,' I say, stepping from the flower box to read the plaque.

ALFRED FOUND LEARNING DEAD, AND HE RESTORED IT.

EDUCATION NEGLECTED AND HE REVIVED IT.

THE LAWS POWERLESS AND HE GAVE THEM FORCE.

THE CHURCH DEBASED AND HE RAISED IT.

THE LAND RAVAGED BY A FEARFUL ENEMY FROM WHICH HE DELIVERED IT.

The real clue to his enduring legacy sits in the last line and ties our story back to Lindisfarne. Before Alfred imposed order on his Wessex kingdom, paving the way for his descendants to become future kings of England, he had to vanquish the Viking enemy. Those marauding heathens, gliding up rivers and beheading natives, never played by the rules; smashing into monasteries, raping and plundering. They were a problem. And also a solution. Nothing rallies hearts and minds like an external enemy – it was the Vikings who made Alfred great.

Cold-blooded Norsemen-murderers with their pillaging and prolonged winter stopovers grew ever more audacious. No Christian site was sacred: Northumbria's Lindisfarne, St Columba's Iona, the Northumbrian monastery at Jarrow, and then south to Mercia. By 870, the Danish conquest of the northern and middle Anglo-Saxon Kingdoms had begun. Alfred's Wessex was up next.

Jonathan Meakin works at Wantage's Vale and Downland Museum. He reckons Alfred is popular because he was the underdog. 'He burnt the cakes and hid in a Somerset marsh. And he had a terrible illness, probably Crohn's disease. His internal struggle was immense.' A bookish younger son who never expected to be king, Alfred not only triumphed over the Vikings, but then made good his Christian victory with a just peace, fortifications and learning. His is the acceptable face of Englishness.

As for Alfred's statues, they were a Victorian after-thought. London's came first; Southwark's Alfred disguised in peasant robes has a contemplative subtlety. Not so in Wantage where a Victorian military hero with money got things going. Alfred's patron, Colonel Robert Loyd-Lindsay, was a Crimean War veteran whose antics against the Russians find their reflection in the Anglo-Saxon King's prowess. At Inkerman, Loyd-Lindsay 'with a few men, charged a party of Russians, driving them back, and running one through the body himself'. A millennium earlier, Bishop Asser tells us that 'Alfred attacked the whole pagan army fighting ferociously in dense order'. He 'made great slaughter among them'.

Alfred went on to consolidate his realm. Local MP Loyd-Lindsay was awarded a Victoria Cross.* The latter's elevated standing and a military friendship with Queen Victoria's cousin, the sculptor German Count Gleichen, saw Alfred re-emerge from an 8-foot lump of white Sicilian marble in St James's Palace. The 1877 unveiling of this royal extravaganza in Wantage's Market Place involved Bertie, the Prince of Wales (who claimed Alfred as an ancestor). Even up close, standing on a flower box, it is hard to discern whether you're looking at an Anglo-Saxon King or a Victorian gentleman. A clue sits in the local museum, where a bust of Colonel Loyd-Lindsay with a bushy beard and an imperial stare shares uncomfortable similarities with marble Alfred.

All of which begs the question: who is the real hero of this piece? As Jonathan concedes, 'Without a statue, how many would know that Alfred even belongs to Wantage?'

---

* VCs were introduced after the Crimean War when press coverage gave the public a heightened idea of soldiers' bravery in action.

5. Statue of Alfred the Great, The Broadway, Winchester, Hampshire, 1901

King Alfred, d. Winchester, 899

If something started with Victorian Alfred in Wantage, it did not end there. That happened in Winchester, ancient capital of one-time Wessex, where Alfred died in 899 and where he was celebrated 1,000 years later with another statue.* Winchester is studded with Gothic splendour, including a storming cathedral (one of the largest in Europe) and Great Hall (boasting Arthur's Round Table). It is easy to get distracted. Unlike Wantage, where Alfred holds the number-one spot, here he competes in a different league.

My guide is Barbara Yorke, an emeritus professor of history. Alfred is her man. She explains that abundant sources, including those the king wrote himself, have sealed his place in history. But what about Alfred's place in Winchester? He was buried nearby, but it was the lack of a credible burial site that paved the way for an Alfred statue and a millennial celebration. A millennium on, Alfred's timing was impeccable. The high noon of imperialism looked to pomp and ceremony like never before, with historic tropes and characters plundered for revitalised ancient displays of Britishness. Cue impeccable performances of invented tradition at Victoria's Golden Jubilee, her Diamond Jubilee and then at the Empress Queen's funeral. At last, England was ready to celebrate its founding father, Alfred, in his final resting place – Winchester.

I visit on a Friday and the city is bustling, the market out in full force; I am tempted by beeswax candles, jars of honey, wind chimes and a bus tour. The latter is not required to find Alfred. His presence is inescapable from the end of the Broadway, pressed out in bronze against St Giles Hill – an enormous talisman to Anglo-Saxon resist-

---

* The Victorians got their dating wrong. The unveiling took place in 1901, rather than 1899, the 1,000th anniversary of the year he died.

ance, medieval fantasy and Victorian awe. Stacked up on two giant blocks of granite, he stands beyond reach, as was intended. Here in Winchester, Alfred's statue did not begin life as a local hero, rather an international celebrity.

Pressured into existence by a group of famous actors and writers including Henry Irving, Walter Besant and Arthur Conan Doyle, only the best would do. The sculptor of the age, Sir William Hamo Thornycroft, was commissioned to create him: a giant to the times, sword in one hand, shield in the other, Alfred the ultimate English warrior.*

---

* Son of Thomas Thornycroft, the famous Victorian sculptor behind London's Boudica, which was completed after Thomas's death with the help of his son.

But, over coffee, Barbara cautions against presumption. Yes, Alfred is dressed like a warrior king, but he holds his sword upside down, resembling Christ's cross. 'It symbolises Alfred's victory over the Danish King Guthrum who was obliged to become a Christian.' Victorian England made much of the link between evangelising Alfred and Britain's nineteenth-century imperial mission: Conan Doyle believed Alfred embodied the perfect Englishman – 'sturdy, resolute, persevering and formidable in action' – virtues that likewise demanded 'respect for law and order ... the distinguishing mark of every British colony'.

But, in 1901, the direction of British imperialism was not clear-cut, with the prolonged fight against Dutch farmers (and fellow Christians) in a dirty Boer War an uncomfortable backdrop. Under Alfred, Vikings settled and farmed in East Anglia. Were the medieval king's standards more advanced than Imperial Britain's? Barbara shakes her head. She has little truck with this idea of a compassionate Alfred, quietly pointing out that in Winchester the king hanged the captured crews from Viking ships. Not all Norsemen became East Anglian farmers.

On departure, Barbara hands me a paper she wrote about Alfred's millenary in 1901. It highlights a sizeable American presence at the event and their more forthright ideas around racial supremacy. A speech by General Rockwell at an Alfred lunch stands out: the Anglo-Saxons had 'been less changed than most by contact with other races and peoples ... is it too much to say that the Anglo-Saxons will be, if they are not already, the dominant race of the world?'

It turns out Winchester's Alfred the Great is a complex fellow. Unlike his chipped, off-white alter-ego in Wantage, he struggles with something of a superiority complex.

CHAPTER 3

NORMAN CONQUERORS

When it came to fighting, the Anglo-Saxons (incomers themselves) lacked a little savour-faire. The Normans quickly put that right. Within four generations, surplus energies were expended in the Holy Land, where marauding in the name of God was considered chivalric, as the Victorians were quick to remind us.

6. Battle Abbey and Battlefield, Battle, East Sussex, 1070–94

The Battle of Hastings, 1066

Matilda (not to be confused with William the Conqueror's wife) stands behind the till in the Gatehouse of Battle Abbey. 'Members go free,' she says, charging the Italian woman next to me £17. I admire Matilda's name. She smiles. 'It means Mighty in Battle.' Of course it does. A James (more Norman nomenclature) runs the show at Battle Abbey, but his rust beard gives him away. He laughs. 'Yes, my descendants were more likely Saxon!'

Nearly 1,000 years on and, these days, Sussex locals happily cohabit with their conquerors in the sleepy village of Battle, itself a memorial to the most famous year in the English calendar – 1066.

LEST WE FORGET

Before our journey south, my daughter cautioned: 'Remember, Harold would've won if only his troops had stayed on the hill.' The story of the Battle of Hastings reads like a political metaphor: don't let your opponent rush you into a snap contest, always maintain the high ground, keep some of your big hitters in reserve. But rather than pound the pavements, the Battle Abbey experience takes you off road. Like William, Duke of Normandy, we waited for the weather; seven months of incessant rain has finally given way to a glimpse of spring sunshine.

It is a curious experience, to walk carefree around the perimeter of a one-time bloodbath. Today, sheep graze and bluebells grow where once 'lethal missiles' – javelins, stones, even bodies – rained down on Norman invaders. Visitors are cautioned about the 'uneven surface' and a defibrillator is attached to a fence post. Risk-averse twenty-first-century Englanders wander through the green and pleasant pasture that briefly became a killing field in October 1066.

Jeopardy is rife in this tale. If only Harold had waited. If only he had advanced his shield wall. If only his brothers, Leofwine and Gyrth, had not died.* If only God had been on his side. The English Heritage narrator assures us that even Normans considered the Saxon king 'handsome, strong, courageous, eloquent, funny, confident, open and diplomatic'. This was a man capable of spurring his troops north, to take out Viking assailants (and his other brother, Tostig) at the Battle of Stamford Bridge, before hurtling south, goaded by incomer William's anti-social behaviour.

An hour of meandering through wild garlic and contemplating gruesome wooden statues and battlefield gradients, we finally near the summit. Harold is about to die. Perhaps it was an apocryphal arrow that killed the English king, or maybe Norman knights hacked him to death. Either way, the knock-out blow was fatal, and not just for Harold. The narrator assures us that the king's most outstanding feature was 'his love of England. But the England he loves was about

---

* Both men were killed during the Battle of Hastings.

to change forever.' This Anglo-Saxon land, already a recognisable political entity in the eleventh century, was defeated by an elite fighting force of Normans, French, Bretons and Flemish. The fourteenth of October 1066 was their day, and soon England their country.

And so onwards, dear visitor, to the Harold Stone, where the view is undulating, unthreatening, verdant. This, according to William the Conqueror, is the exact spot where Harold met his death. It is also the start point of a new England. King William insisted it was here that the High Altar of his abbey must be built. Today, beside the extant ruins of the Benedictine abbey that emerged over subsequent centuries, the foundations of the original Romanesque church are sketched in gravel. Next to me, the Italian visitor, Alessandra, sighs. 'Look at the way they have recreated the subtle footprint of history. There is nothing fake here. You English are very good at this sort of thing.' Which English, I wonder?

Back in Battle Abbey's shop, I discuss commemoration and the possible motives behind the erection of the Abbey. Was William atoning for all the death and destruction? Or constructing a statement of power and glory? A bit of both, site manager James concedes. When the Norman king discovered that builders tried to erect his victory church further downhill, he was outraged. They had to begin again at the summit. William's abbey was posterity's proof that God's will had been delivered, and with it a new form of radical monasticism in a new hierarchical England, under Norman rule.

Was it a better England? James won't be drawn. But even now, a millennium later, the after-effects are not entirely tension-free. If Battle Abbey is England's monument to what happened on that fateful October day, other memorials to our national story taunt us from across the Channel. The exquisite Bayeux Tapestry, embroidered by nuns in Kent, resides in Bayeux, the property of France. As for William the Conqueror, England's first French-speaking king, he is still riding high, wielding a papal banner in his birth town of Falaise, also in France. Touché England.

LEST WE FORGET

7. Richard Coeur de Lion (Richard I) statue, Old Palace Yard, Westminster, London, installed 1860

Richard I, Coeur de Lion, r. 1189–99

The close-fitting chain mail hugging a ripped, raised upper arm is a giveaway; 800 years after he took the fight to 'The Infidel', England's Crusader King, Richard the Lionheart, was objectified by the Victorians.

Or, more specifically, by Prince Albert and his middle-aged wife, Queen Victoria. Neither could resist Baron Carlo Marochetti's clay-cast incarnation which welcomed 6 million visitors to the Great Exhibition of 1851.* Within ten years, and part-funded by the royal couple, Richard had been recast in bronze and installed outside Westminster Palace's rebuild: a showy equine masterpiece which speaks to a camp-Italianate style favoured by Albert. Victoria was equally smitten, perhaps reminded of the young husband she'd once found irresistible. Having been married for as long as Victoria was by the 1850s, I confess to being equally susceptible to Marochetti's Richard. He works on many levels, but none quite right for the fresh horrors of 2024.

Today, inside Westminster's Houses of Parliament, Britain's new Labour government obfuscates about Israel's right to defend itself and equivocates over sending more weapons. Outside in the Old Palace Yard, Richard I is still charging forward, uncompromised. Our idealised version of the Christian soldier-king masks millennia-old religious and territorial atrocity in the Middle East. A happy ending remains elusive. As for the beginning, it is difficult to know how far to travel back. King Solomon perhaps? The Roman expulsion of the Jews? Christianity's genesis? Or maybe the Muslim conquest of the Levant? Heavily influenced by Sir Walter Scott's

---

* Marochetti was also the sculptor of Glasgow's Duke of Wellington statue that nowadays sports a traffic cone. See Monument 41.

storytelling (he was Albert and Victoria's favourite novelist),* evangelising Victorians plumped for the twelfth century's third Crusade and – hey presto – Marochetti's hero-king Richard.

Religious dark arts remain a favourite for writers in the twenty-first century. Just ask London's Temple Church which saw a surge in visitor numbers after it was featured in Dan Brown's literary phenomenon, *The Da Vinci Code*. I head east through the City of

---

* In 1825, Sir Walter Scott released *Tales of the Crusaders*, a series of two historical novels, *The Betrothed* and *The Talisman*. Richard I is one of the character statues on the upper tier of the south-east buttress on the Scott Monument in Prince's Street, Edinburgh.

LEST WE FORGET

London, dropping south of Fleet Street into the cobbled medieval Inns of Court; there, the Temple Church pre-dates the Inner and Middle Temples it serves. Despite extensive Blitz-bombing in World War II, the Round still stands, a circular structure modelled on the round Church of the Holy Sepulchre in Jerusalem. From 1185, the Knights Templar, soldier-bankers who financed and safeguarded pilgrims en route to the Holy Land, could experience Jerusalem when in London.

Inside the Temple Church, *The Da Vinci Code*'s Robert Langdon clocked 'the simplicity of the circle'; he eyed 'the curvature of the chamber's pale stone perimeter, taking in the carvings of gargoyles, demons, monsters and pained human faces'. The fictional professor was on a quest to crack an ancient code: 'you seek the orb that ought to be on his tomb'. I am looking for a crusader monument. Like Langdon, I pin my hopes on 'ten stone knights. Five on the left. Five on the right.' We are both sorely disappointed.

'The greatest knight that ever lived,'* William Marshal, First Earl of Pembroke, did go on a crusade; his effigy lies straight-legged among lesser mortals within the Round. I settle in for a lecture on his greatness. It is long and the stone floor unrelenting; I hold out for a story of Marshal in the Holy Land. Instead, the speaker trawls through the knight's feats in the negotiation of the Magna Carta under Richard I's successor, John I. The focus is English constitutional history and how it happened right here, in this chapel for the Inns of Court. Not one word is given to crusading. Today, the self-styled 'Mother-church of the Common Law' prefers to focus on the home front. This mysterious absence is explained on the Temple website: "The Round represented, during the crusades, the divisions between the Abrahamic faiths. The Inns and Church are now working hard to bridge those divisions, to promote genuine and generous encounters of respect and understanding.'†

---

* According to the then Archbishop of Canterbury, Stephen Langton.

† https://www.templechurch.com/temp/since-1163-3

Outside, in the real world, 2,000 walkie-talkies and pager devices blow up across Lebanon, killing at least thirty-two, indiscriminately taking out eyes and removing the fingers of thousands more. Within days, Israel announces further 'extensive' strikes. The nominally Christian West is unsure how to respond. Where does their culpability end? Again, it is difficult to know how far to travel back. Edward I's expulsion of the Jews? Russia's pogroms? Britain's imperial ambitions? Europe's Holocaust?

I return to Richard the Lionheart, outside Westminster Palace. He is still brandishing his sword. Miles from home, during the Third Crusade, this extraordinary warrior won almost every battle he fought (the siege of Acre, Arsuf, Jaffa). He committed appalling atrocities in the name of Christ, including the murder of 2,700 Muslim prisoners. But ultimately Richard recognised the need to compromise, signing a truce with Saladin, the great Ayyubid Sultan of Egypt and Syria. Christians and Muslims were granted safe passage to the Holy Land and Jerusalem remained under Islamic control, with Saladin extending tolerance to the city's Jewish inhabitants. For several years, there was peace. Imagine that.

PART TWO
WARRING BRITANNIA

CHAPTER 4

KILL THY NEIGHBOUR

When it comes to memorialising our medieval war heroes, a theme emerges – a love of the brave, defiant underdog. This equation sees England lose out to nascent Wales and Scotland in a narrative defined by that early colonialist king, Edward I. He first plied his trade at home in England against a French nobleman, Simon de Montfort.

8. The De Montfort Memorial, Abbey Park, Evesham, Worcestershire, 1965

Simon de Montfort, Earl of Leicester, c. 1208–1265

Despite the fate that awaits him, Phil Pembridge is in good cheer. As a seasoned knight, mounted and in full armour, the role of Simon de Montfort, the 6th Earl of Leicester, is hot, heavy work. By Sunday afternoon, he will have died twice at the Battle of Evesham Festival, two defeats interspersed with a victory (the home crowd need something to cheer). He bends to kiss my hand, a chivalric gesture restricted by chain mail. 'Research suggests medieval Percheron horses were smaller than mine,' says Phil. 'Full plate made mounting hard and, if a knight was knocked off his horse, he had to get on again.' His grey steed stares passively ahead, all too familiar with the drill. Phil has been in historical re-enactment for more than thirty years; he has lived its many ebbs and flows. Certain events, like the Battle of Hastings, are an annual fixture, with Evesham a muscular newcomer.

Here, in the heartlands of Worcestershire, interest in the thirteenth-century Second Barons' War is in the ascendant and silver-tongued, steely populist Simon de Montfort speaks to modern times. Insisting on constitutional reform and campaigning under the slogan of 'England for the English' (despite his French origins), this prototype Trumpian figure challenged Henry III's rule, resorting to violence when he didn't get his way.*

By 1264, de Montfort, renowned for the revolutionary Provisions of Oxford that subjected Henry III to a Council of Fifteen and regular parliaments, had led England to the brink of civil war. The king and his son Edward were taken prisoner, with de Montfort pushing to broaden his military support beyond the baronial class, most of whom he had alienated. Like many populists, the earl enjoyed more success among his followers than his peers. After his surprise victory at the Battle of Lewes, it was further north in Evesham, in August 1265, that the final showdown took place, with the royalist cause emboldened by Prince Edward's legendary escape from captivity. In Edward – renowned for his size; Longshanks was a later moniker – Simon had more than met his match. But Evesham remains unequivocal. De Montfort is their man.

A roar ripples down the high street. Simon, aka Phil, his trusty steed and hundreds of mercenaries clatter along cloaked in hallmark red lions.

'Hurrah!'
'De Montfort and Justice!'
'Bravo!'

---

* Plantagenet Henry III was the son of King John; he assumed the throne aged nine during the First Barons' War in a reign defined by civil unrest and piety.

'It's lovely, isn't it?' sighs Trevor Battersby, whose raison d'être is to think big for the Battle of Evesham Festival. Small children clutch de Montfort teddies, and medieval-style marquees hawk candyfloss and honeycomb, all below the backdrop of a majestic bell tower where Europe's finest medieval abbey once stood.

There is a memorial service on the one-time abbey's footprint. It was here de Montfort insisted that 'one should seek knights on the battlefield and chaplains in churches', before riding out to almost certain death against Edward's numerically superior forces. Some 5,000 men were killed; local abbots recalled that 'rivers of blood ran into the crypt'. De Montfort was beheaded and his testicles removed and hung either side of his nose. His hands and feet were severed and respective body parts dispatched to different parts of the realm.

Today, geraniums grow a rude red in his honour. They surround de Montfort's most recent memorial (two stand only 100 feet apart).* In 1965, stone taken from his birthplace – the French crusader castle in Montfort-l'Amaury – was fashioned into a rectangular block to commemorate the 700th anniversary of the Battle of Evesham, which proports to sit where what remained of Simon's body was buried.† In attendance at the unveiling were the Speaker of the House of Commons and the Archbishop of Canterbury. By the mid-twentieth century, de Montfort had a new following as the 'Father of Representative Parliament'.

A democrat for the modern age? Or a bloody-minded thug with timeless appeal? In August 2024, a wreath is laid, but the vicar won't be drawn on whether Simon was a 'good man or a bad man'. In 2015, another Speaker of the House of Commons, John Bercow, did not hesitate to mark the 750th anniversary, while Leicester's De Montfort University briefly swivelled over its nomenclature in light

---

* Also within Abbey Park is a 1930s stone cross commemorating de Montfort.

† Both memorials claim to mark the spot where some of de Montfort's remains were buried. After his death, the site became a makeshift shrine and place of pilgrimage, so much so that Henry III had de Montfort dug up and removed.

of the earl's brutal anti-Semitism. Simon had no qualms about murdering and expelling Jews, apparently.

Crucially, Frenchman de Montfort died an English martyr, his grizzly end in Worcestershire setting a precedent for a series of horrific super-deaths. At Evesham, the future Edward I learned the value of unapologetic brutality. Murder most foul ensured there was no King Simon, but today in the town his brand has never been so big. Trevor assures me 'since 2018, we've spent £70,000 every year on this festival and we always make a profit'.*

De Montfort and justice! De Montfort and Evesham! England for the English! Democracy! Reform!

9. Memorial to Llywelyn ap Gruffudd (Llewelyn the Last), Prince of Gwynedd, Cilmeri, Powys, Wales, 1956

The last Prince of Wales, Llywelyn ap Gruffudd, d. 1282

I crossed the Prince of Wales Bridge to get here. 'You mean the Prince Llywelyn Bridge.' I am corrected at Magor Roadchef. Once called the Second Severn Crossing, it was renamed after Prince Charles. Apparently the now-king did not green-light this 2018 decision. From his 1969 Caernarfon investiture, with its side of national militancy, to the early Welsh embrace of his young wife Diana (in 1981, the Princess delivered her first public speech to the Council Chamber in Cardiff City Hall), presumably Charles was aware that he had comprehensively failed to win hearts and minds beyond the Severn. It's unlikely William will fare much better (note the pointed silence around the subject of an investiture). To find a real Prince of Wales – that is, a Welshman fighting for the Welsh (which discounts the Tudors) – the journey back is long and treacherous: a thirteenth-century whodunit shrouded in romance, pain and lament.

---

* The surplus is reinvested to future-proof the festival.

Around 10 miles shy of the English border in mid-Wales, a rock rises to a jagged point, claiming to mark the spot where Llywelyn ap Gruffydd was killed in December 1282. If monuments can appropriate the language of architecture, then Llywelyn the Last's memorial stone is brutish. Next to the Prince Llewelyn Inn, it is the second twentieth-century Llywelyn monument to be erected in Cilmeri, a small village in Powys. The precursor was a traditional obelisk erected by the local landowner in 1902, a sign of changed times and times to come. By the turn of the twentieth century, a thrusting Wales, powered on coal's black gold, was pushing back against English dominance. While the UK was still seen as the union of three kingdoms, few could deny its contained four nations.

Welsh history is full of 'if onlys'. If only the Wales–England border wasn't so goddam porous and long. If only the English hadn't been overrun by generations of genius warriors – Romans, Saxons, Normans. If only Wales had enjoyed one centrifugal point, a definitive fertile lowland around which great minds and national wealth might have coalesced more readily. If only this westerly outpost of authentic Britons had held the line. If only Llywelyn, the last Welsh Prince of Wales, had lived.

LEST WE FORGET

In Cilmeri, beyond the ominous rock, there is a stream where story has it that the severed head of Llywelyn was washed and sent onwards to England's king (Edward I, who was crushing Welshmen further north). He promptly dispatched a messenger to Rome and, in record speed, the papacy was informed that the Welsh had been extirpated, their kingdom was no more. Llywelyn's head travelled to London for display on a spike, a ghoulish gift for the new capital of subjugated Wales.

Julian Lovell, a lay preacher who annually commemorates Llywelyn's death in the nearby ruins of Abbey Cwmhir,* shakes his silver head. 'He was the last true-blood Prince of Wales. What was exactly going on here is a mystery. Up until the 1270s the Welsh were in the ascendency. Quite what Llywelyn had to be gained from engaging with the English is unknown. We don't know why he was in Cilmeri in the middle of winter.'

Julian hands me a pamphlet, *Accident or Assassination? The Death of Llywelyn*, replete with documents and poems that take the reader into a tangled knot of history and myth: caves, reversed horseshoes, snowy trails, duplicitous Marcher Lords, elite bodyguards and one slain prince. The bigger geopolitical picture is easier to comprehend. There was the arrival of the Normans who subjugated the English within a matter of years, but made do with Marcher Lords and a fortified buffer zone along the Welsh border. For two centuries, this new status quo saw the co-existence of three broad entities: English Crown, Marcher Lords and Welsh Princes.

Exceptions stood out, among them Prince Llywelyn and Edward I. The former enjoyed a degree of precocious unifying success, alienating key players – both Welsh and English – in the process. Meanwhile, the latter learned the hard way during the Second Barons' War (when Llywelyn allied with de Montfort). The English king was in no mood for compromise. Irrespective of exactly who killed Llywelyn and under what circumstances (evidence suggests a

---

* Evidence suggests that Llywelyn was buried here.

Shropshire soldier impaled the prince without realising who he was), it's worth noting that Edward I, England's most powerful medieval king, had to commit all his kingdom's resources to crush the Welsh. Llywelyn was unlucky; ditto Wales.

Eight centuries later and change is finally afoot. Like everything else in modern Wales, Llewelyn's memorial stone is inscribed in two languages. Preacher Julian has been playing catch up, trying to master his mother tongue for the last forty years. Some things come easier to the young. My sister-in-law's family, who relocated from Guildford to Lampeter, were surprised to discover their children's education is primarily in Welsh. Today, the boot is on the other foot. Or, as they say in Wales, mae'r rhod wedi troi.*

10. The National Wallace Monument, Stirling, 1861–69

William Wallace, d. 23 August 1305

We are standing in Steven Hughes' back garden next to the swollen River Forth. His dream house has been flooded. Steven shrugs. He knew the risks. 'See there,' he says, pointing upriver. 'That's where the wooden bridge collapsed, trapping England's troops. It happened right in front of my garden.' Steven pushes his specs up his nose and grins. He doesn't just understand the importance of an origin story, Steven lives his own, daily.

We've completed a whistle-stop tour of Wallace monuments in Stirling's historic city centre. 'This is the top of King Street.' Steven straddles the cobbled kerb in his kilt, glowering down the hill. 'On the day of King Charles III's Proclamation, William Wallace had to look upon on all those paying homage to a successor of Edward I!' A mild-mannered Wallace, sculpted with Christ-like benevolence, stares out from beyond the clock tower, yet another Victorian reincarnation of Scotland's freedom fighter. We meet him again outside

---

* Literal translation: the [water] wheel has turned.

the City Council Hall, this time flanked by his successor, Robert the Bruce. And just beyond the medieval city wall stands Robert Burns, Scotland's bard who gave Wallace's story eighteenth-century wings. *Scots Wha Hae!*

Steven would like every story to be true. 'Some people swear that the sword found at Dumbarton Castle is Wallace's. Others say only part of it is. He would need to have been 6 ft 6 in to have swung it.' The contested sword is exhibited in the Wallace Monument, the big daddy of nineteenth-century Scottish monumentalism.

'A craig is a rock. Stirling Castle is on one craig, the Wallace monument on another – Abbey Craig. "He who holds Stirling, holds Scotland." Put that quote in your book. Stirling used to be the

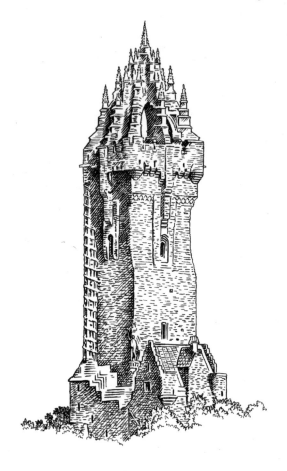

lowest crossing point on the Forth. No, the Wallace monument isn't my favourite …'

We swing into the car park. There's a tourist trail leading up the craig and a handful of Americans gravitate towards kilted Steven.* He shares stories about his city, his hero William Wallace and his Scottish identity. Steven believes in the idea of Wallace as a medieval democrat, a low(ish)-born freedom fighter who held out against English suzerainty and bullying. 'Scotland ruled by Scots' is the mantra he lives by, then and now.

We walk up the hill. 'It's 1297. Edward I had done well – he'd won the Barons' War, but then he clobbered Wales and tried to do the same in Scotland. He was an expansionist, which is regrettable.' Scotland looked like easy prey, facing down an interregnum after the sudden death of Alexander III. Victory at the Battle of Dunbar in 1296 put England on the front foot. In September 1297, Edward I's larger army headed north without their king to face a powerful Scottish military alliance: William Wallace in partnership with seasoned fighter, Andrew de Moray.† Here we get to tactics and Scotland's legendry schiltrons of pikemen, an England that doesn't know the terrain, and a bridge that falls into the river. Mel Gibson's biopic of Wallace, *Braveheart*, doesn't feature the Battle of Stirling Bridge on a bridge. Too dangerous, apparently.

The Wallace Monument is a behemoth to remembering and was built in the 1860s when Scotland flaunted its own Baronial style. I follow Steven's MacDuff tartan up the turret. He is climbing Scotland's past – or, rather, a version of its past. We arrive in the Hall of Arms, one of three viewing platforms built into the original design. There is an animation that simplifies Wallace's story. Steven tuts. We mount the stairs once more.

Respite next comes in the 'Hall of Heroes', a tantalising display of white male privilege in marble bust form. Sixteen famous

---

* Steven Hughes hosts Freedom Tours in Stirling.

† Estimates suggest the English had around 9,000 men, against 6,000 Scots.

LEST WE FORGET

Scottish men.* (Two women were added in 2019.)† Steven is unhappy. 'This is my least favourite floor. Why give over a quarter of the monument to other heroes? Why can't they go deeper into the Wallace story?' Steven is not alone; academics have likewise pondered Victorian Scotland's dilution of its own indignant past. The original winner of the architectural competition behind the monument included a 'rampant Scottish lion' triumphantly slaying a monster. (A metaphor for Wallace viciously skinning his enemy, Hugh de Cressingham?) Too anti-English was the Establishment's conclusion, with the design duly rejected. The monument needed to be more broadly national, the inclusion of other great Scots deliberately distracting from Wallace's violent phenomenon.

Worse still, these days there is no one to discuss this nuance with. A multi-million-pound revamp in 2019 saw the entire Wallace Monument experience become 'contactless'. We pay £11 to enter and are on our own, pressing buttons for nuggets of carefully curated information. 'It lacks the personal touch,' insists Steven. We've arrived at the contentious sword in its own glass case. One more flight of stairs to go.

At the top, the crown-styled spire is epic, the view magnificent, and the logic of trapping legions of English in the river's horseshoe bend immediately apparent. Two hundred and forty-six steps up, Stirling makes its own compelling case for forcing the English to think again. 'Wow,' I say. Steven smiles. There are some things that you can't argue with.

We head back down. Steven insists, 'Edward Longshanks was never going to let Wallace survive.' I nod; standing inside this monu-

---

* The first two busts were added in 1886, those of Robert the Bruce and Robert Burns. Fourteen more were added over time.

† A competition was held to find 'heroines' and, in 2019, busts of missionary Mary Slessor and co-founder of the Maggie's Centres for cancer care, Maggie Keswick Jencks, were added.

mental Victorian edifice it's easy to forget that Wallace was ultimately defeated and killed, the victim of a brutal English execution.

II. Sir William Wallace Memorial, St Bartholomew's Hospital, Smithfield, London, 1956
William Wallace, d. 23 August 1305

To those who knew and followed him, David Ross was a hero. At 6 ft 5 in, this passionate performer and nationalist was felled early by that contemporary Scottish killer – the heart attack. But not before he had walked the 450 ignominious miles that Wallace travelled 700 years earlier, from his capture near Glasgow to his death in London, having been betrayed by a fellow Scot, John Menteith. In August 2005, David undertook his own personal pilgrimage. Fans and fellow Wallace champions were urged to leave him to journey alone, before joining their charismatic leader at London's Westminster Hall.

'Aye, there we had a wee ceremony exactly where Wallace was sentenced,' Scotsman Ted Christopher explains. 'He was charged with treason, but Edward was never his king. The event took a bit of organising. We had some security issues to get in – they wouldn't allow the ceremonial swords and someone had to give up his pistols.'

Ted is a singer-songwriter. We catch up shortly after his return from Germany with the Tartan Army at the 2024 Euros. Scotland have just been thumped 5–1 in the opening match against the hosts, but Ted is unbowed. The Scots have form when it comes to managing defeat. *Scots, wha hae wi Wallace bled.* The road to victory is a long one, littered with great names and big characters. David Ross was Ted's pal. 'He was a great man. If he asked you to do something, you did it. He said "I am walking to London for Wallace and you're writing a song."'

The Scottish pilgrims walked the final circuitous 6 miles from Westminster to Smithfield together. This was the interminable distance along which a condemned, naked Wallace was dragged. 'We marched the symbolic coffin through the streets of London. There was no animosity. Some of the police were Scottish. A Scotsman came out of his hotel, discovered what we were doing and said, "To hell with my meetings. I'm joining you."'

A thousand Scots were headed to St Bartholomew the Great, a church that stood then, and still stands now, next to the site where a bloodied Scottish convict entered Smithfield's gallows on a holy day and was unceremoniously executed. The stories are legion. Wallace was castrated, disembowelled, beheaded. His body quartered and sent to Scotland's four corners.

One of the few hard facts in this gory tale is the cost of killing Wallace. The Executor's Roll of 1305 lists Edward I's finances: Wallace's execution bill was sixty-one shillings and ten pence – a mega death that created a superhero. In 1720, English poet Alexander Pope observed 'the Scots will fight for Wallace as for God'. That other English wordsmith, William Wordsworth, concluded: 'How Wallace fought for Scotland, left the name of Wallace to be found, like a wild flower, all over his dear country.' In the twentieth century, *Braveheart* spread his legend yet further still; I found two international fans standing in front of William Wallace's plaque embedded in London's 900-year-old St Bartholomew's Hospital. The memorial was erected in 1956, six years after four Scottish students stole the Stone of Scone from Westminster Abbey, originally swiped by Edward from Scone Abbey in 1296.*

Adjacent to the hospital is the church of St Bartholomew the Great where Ted performed his song for long-dead Wallace. The veteran singer is old now; his grey locks and comfy kilt lend his vocals a sage credibility.

---

* The Stone of Destiny was officially returned to Scotland in 1996. In March 2024, it arrived in Perth where the stone is the main attraction in the city's new museum. A year earlier, it had a stop-over in England for the 2023 coronation of Charles III in Westminster Abbey.

He tore apart my body so I could not rise on judgement day
What he did not realise is now I'll never go away.

Ted found the memorial service 'very emotional. We wrote down our thoughts and put them in the empty coffin.' I gaze at the plaque on the hospital wall. The coat of arms glitters gold, there are fresh flowers and a Saltire flutters in the breeze. 'Sir William Wallace … his example heroism and devotion inspired those who came after him to win victory from defeat and his memory remains for all time a source of pride, honour and inspiration to his countrymen.'

Wallace's demise hardened sentiment north of the border; the war was not over. And, for many today, the fight continues. Ted and I speak the morning after the 2024 General Election when the Scottish National Party was routed. He is unperturbed. 'The majority of Scotland wants independence. That is separate from the SNP's fortunes.' Like William Wallace, and David Ross, and Scotland's Tartan Army, Ted keeps the faith:

I'm coming home, I'm coming home, back where I belong
I'm coming home, I'm coming home, my spirit's coming home.

12. Robert the Bruce statue, Battle of Bannockburn site, Stirling, 1964

Robert the Bruce, King of the Scots, d. 7 June 1329

I am back in Stirling with Steven Hughes. Wallace is dead, his corpse food for the gulls. It is 1306 and Scotland has a new king, Robert the Bruce, a man who has already swapped sides twice in this prolonged Scottish war of independence, submitting to Edward I in 1302. Steven sighs. 'People always ask me which I prefer: Wallace or Bruce? They point out that Bruce crossed Wallace. I s'pose Wallace is Scotland's martyr, but Bruce got the job done.'

Bruce was a great warrior, a ruthless player whose eye on the prize saw him kill his main Scottish rival, John Comyn, in Greyfriars Kirk in Dumfries. Subsequently, he was crowned king of Scotland in March 1306, when he resumed the fight for Scottish independence. His now-enemy, that other warrior king, Edward I, responded in kind. Reprisals were extreme. 'Isabella MacDuff, who crowned Bruce, was held in a cage at Berwick Castle,' tuts Steven. 'A wee lassie, in a cage. Why didn't I learn about her in school?'*

Why have I not featured a monument to Edward I, one of England's finest warrior-kings? Steven shrugs. 'Me and my dog Molly, we've visited him in Burgh-by-Sands.' Another 700th anniversary commemoration, the statue is relatively new. It depicts a man in his prime brandishing a sword, which is a little far-fetched as Cumbria is where Edward met his death, succumbing to dysentery on his way to re-hammering the Scots. There is an obelisk too, on England's side of the Solway Firth. First erected in 1685, it collapsed, was rebuilt in 1803 and again in 1876, and most recently restored in 2000; it stands as a metaphor for Edward I's many battles in a war against the Scots he never quite won. The privilege of ultimate victory belonged to Bruce against a lesser foe, Edward II.

That is why I am back in Stirling, *Now's the day, and now's the hour*, on the site of Scotland's great victory over the English at the Battle of Bannockburn. *See the front o' battle lour*, eye-balling a giant statue of the Scottish king. *See approach proud Edward's power.*

Scotland's bard, Robert Burns, visited this site in 1787. Seven years later, he penned *Scots, Wha Hae*, a robust response to the horror of the French Revolution. Resistance! Or *Chaines and Slaverie*! The statue came much later, sculpted by Scotsman Charles d'Orville Pilkington Jackson for the 650th anniversary of the battle

---

* Isabella was married to the Earl of Comyn, who absconded to the English side after John Comyn III's death. In contrast, Isabella declared for Robert the Bruce and was the vital Clan McDuff representative at his coronation in Scone. Her late arrival necessitated a second crowning the following day.

in 1964. The late Queen Elizabeth II, Bruce's descendant through her half-Scottish mother, unveiled him: an armoured goliath, mounted with axe in hand, upon a mighty plinth.* The land was donated by another descendant, the Earl of Elgin, head of the Bruce family. These days, the earl stresses that 'we should not forget the message King Robert gave … he told his followers to go out and spread friendship over the land.' His Bruce is an Establishment figure. Steven speaks for a different Scotland, for whom Bruce is an inspiration. 'Here, at this monument, I get a feeling of what could be again. An independent country where the small folk make the decisions.'

---

* The statue was created using the actual measurements of Bruce's skull, re-discovered in Dunfermline Abbey in 1818.

LEST WE FORGET

Steven pulls up the Treaty of Arbroath on his phone. 'If he should give up what he has begun, seeking to make us or our kingdom subject to the King of England or the English, we should exert ourselves at once to drive him out …'

Did Elizabeth II know what she was unveiling? Faded in the mists of time, today's Bruce is who you want him to be. Steven comes alive here, confessing that there's an irony in his preference for King Bruce's monument over lower-born Wallace's, just 3 miles away. One is ticketed, the other is not. For Steven, it's all about freedom.

He strides away from the information board. The green-crested hills, and the Bannock Burn that trapped the English, frame his tartan silhouette. It's the first day of battle: an English knight, Sir Henry De Bohun, has spotted the Scottish king on his pony. 'Imagine you are Henry de Bohun,' says Steven. 'You're on a massive horse, you've locked your lance in tae position. Yer waiting tae hit Robert the Bruce. At the last second, Bruce turns his pony 90 degrees. Some say he gets it tae sit down.'

Steven is bending back now, on his haunches. 'As the lance passes, Bruce gets back up on his stirrups, he comes over the top and he smacks Henry de Bohun right in the face, smashing his skull. Some say he hits him so hard he breaks his axe. One-nil tae Scotland on day one.'

Someone claps. I say 'thank you'. Steven and I get back in the car for a break. He is still talking about Robert the Bruce. 'He was a good man, a fair man. He never lived in a castle after he became king …'

CHAPTER 5

HITTING FRANCE

National identity is rarely formed in a vacuum. Welsh nobleman Owain Glyndŵr made his name in revolt against the English. But, and here's the rub, the Celtic fringes were a relative sideshow in the Plantagenets' greater game plan: France. It was across the Channel that England discovered a gruesome new chivalric code and a raft of medieval heroes.

13. Tomb of Edward, the Black Prince, Canterbury Cathedral, Canterbury, 1380s

Edward of Woodstock, The Black Prince, d. 1376

It is important to set the scene. A goliath among medieval Christian Kingdoms, in the fourteenth century France vastly outstripped England on every front. Among its boasts were the glories of Paris, much the biggest city north of the Alps, the birthplace of chivalry, and the coffers of the Capetian kings. In contrast, little England combined an inferiority complex with an entitled French hangover that tracked all the way back to William the Conqueror.

Who was the mightiest of them all? In the Hundred Years' War (it actually went on for 116) the most significant figure who led minnow England to victory over France was unequivocally Edward, the Black Prince. Fêted celebrities do well to die young, and Edward proved no exception. Dying at forty-five and never burdened with kingship, this revered knight was equipped with a complete suit of armour at the tender age of seven. Onwards he went: adolescent Edward majestically won his spurs at the Battle of Crécy, before leading the charge for English glory at Poitiers and Nájera. Was it his blackened reputation for brutality or his black armour that saw his later Tudor reincarnation as the Black Prince? The question remains open.

Edward chose gilded bronze armour, not black, for eternity. To enter the Trinity Chapel in Canterbury Cathedral is to meet the man who has never grown old. The long Plantagenet face stares up into the perpendicular wonder of this magnificent Norman structure, his gauntlets pressed together, in prayer perhaps. But the image is not a peaceful one. To be 'fully armed', as if for war, was Edward's stipulation for his effigy 24 hours prior to death (diarrhoea, not a French longbow). To this day, chain mail flanks his face, a sword lies by his side, pointed spurs still shine in the holy light.

Indicative of the tomb's rarity, a team of researchers recently applied twenty-first century tech to uncover the ingenuity of this medieval royal art. A video probe, more commonly associated with intricate contemporary medical procedures, provided the first glimpse inside Edward's effigy for 600 years. The conclusions reaffirm the Black Prince's mastery in life and death. His son, Richard II, honoured his father's wishes and commissioned one of the Middle Ages' most sophisticated castings, including a collaboration with an armourer, to guarantee meticulous military accuracy and a state-of-the-art effigy for eternity. Edward was likewise clear about the location: he wanted an easily accessed tomb – maximum prayers for his 'rotting corpse' – and in Canterbury Cathedral that is what he got.

'The Black Prince came here on pilgrimage, before his campaigns in France.' Nathan Crouch's job is to be an unapologetic enthusiast of England's first cathedral and of Edward, its most famous long-term resident. Once upon a time, Thomas Becket's glorious shrine took centre stage in the Trinity Chapel, but the archbishop's reputation for challenging sovereign authority sealed his fate in life (a sword through the head) and in death, with Henry VIII's brutal destruction of Becket's shrine. Not so Edward's effigy and tomb, which survived the dissolution of the monasteries untouched. Nathan ponders this anomaly. 'I guess Henry VIII had no reason to destroy him.' Maybe he didn't dare. Bullies generally know when they have met their match.

As for the Black Prince, after seven centuries of prayer, he is still poised as if for war.

14. Statue of the Black Prince, City Square, Leeds, 1903
Edward of Woodstock, The Black Prince, d. 1376

It was a sunny August Bank holiday in 2006 and Channel 4's *Time Team* had been granted permission to dig up the emerald-green lawn in the middle of Her Majesty's Upper Ward in Windsor Castle. I was part of the on-screen team. Never before had archaeology felt so adrenalised. That weekend beneath the turf, we made contact with King Edward III (father of the Black Prince) and his Arthurian fantasy, uncovering the rubble-filled foundations of a circular building. Here, at last, was 'proof' of Edward's Round Table.

Imagine some 300 knights, a band of brothers, bonding together, feasting, dancing and jousting inside an enormous stone construct. The same Edward later established the Order of the Garter, with his prodigal son, the Black Prince, introducing the ceremonial white ostrich plumes, a glorious spoil of war. Hail England! Hail the new home of chivalry!

But the darkest arts in a knight's playbook are not for tournaments. The Round Table, always an ambitious building project, was never completed. Wars in France are not cheap and, ultimately, the

Round Table was pulled down. By 1350, the Black Prince departed England to penetrate deep into southern France: looting, burning, raiding. The accolades were unimaginable, with dead French peasants an essential by-product of gallantry. To brute force and chivalry! To the Black Prince, England's greatest knight!

Time Team duly grassed over the medieval foundations and I took respite in St George's Chapel, home of today's annual Order of the Garter ceremony, an infinitely more civilised affair. Queen Camilla and former prime minister Tony Blair are members. Likewise Prince Andrew, the Duke of York. Reputations come and go. The Victorians couldn't get enough of the Black Prince, but by World War I all the killing made people feel a little queasy and he fell out of fashion. This was unfortunate timing for Leeds city centre.

'A lot of people think the Black Prince should trot on, that he doesn't belong here.' Rachael Unsworth is a geographer and tour guide. She works in Leeds, where there is a thunderous equine statue of the Black Prince. On exiting the train station, he is impossible to miss, slap-bang in the centre of City Square. The enormous knight was erected in 1903, a decade after Leeds acquired city status, in the wake of Victorian England's obsession with chivalry, and just before Britain signed up to a new friendship with France. Edward never came to Leeds, but the city's first Lord Mayor, Colonel T. Walter Harding (an honorary title), was undeterred. He commissioned sculptor Sir Thomas Brock, a man renowned for thinking big.* Cue an Italianate piazza with a Black Prince so enormous he had to be cast in Belgium. No English foundry was large enough.

Rachael doesn't go a bomb on the obsession with warfare. 'All trumped-up in order for men to be heroic – and then to be reimagined centuries later to big up the elite of later eras.' Harding was a third-generation northern businessman (his firm made pins for textile machinery) and what he lacked in noble status, he more than made up for in money. Leeds, show-home of textiles and woollen

---

* Brock also sculpted the Victoria Memorial in front of Buckingham Palace.

cloth-trading, was duly bent to fit his vision. Today, the hulking Black Prince hogs the limelight; he is heading south on his steed, beyond a reshuffled cluster of four 'worthy men' in bronze and eight nymphs. The nymphs are a sore point; a naked, anonymous reminder that Leeds has no named female statues, with the exception of Victoria. Even the old queen has been displaced, along with the Leeds War Memorial, now outside the town hall.

Rachael shares a recent CGI of City Square reimagined without the Prince. The latest pedestrianised revamp was finished in May 2024, but the incredible hulk survived the refit. On his outsized plinth, perhaps he was just too big to move. Rachael is unsure. It's not as if Leeds doesn't have a military past of its own. 'Over the years, we've supplied a lot of soldiers, and military hardware, uniforms and boots.' The scarlet Irish Guards tunic Prince William wore on his 2011 wedding day was made by AW Hainsworth in Leeds. A link to a Prince of Wales, but not to *the* Prince of Wales, Britain's infamous medieval knight.

A week later and an alert pops up on a history WhatsApp group. An international fair – 'Making Leeds Medieval' – is pending. I scramble to make contact. Is the Black Prince having a comeback? Setting a northern trend? No. Apparently there is 'no connection to the statue'. The fair takes place in a different square.

Untouchable, the Black Prince rides on alone, an outsized reminder of England's addiction to its rich and violent past.

15. Owain Glyndŵr statue, Corwen, Denbighshire, 2007

Owain Glyndŵr, c. 1354–c. 1416

'Good luck getting in there.'

Wales knows a thing or two about mighty buildings as impenetrable instruments of power. Edward I subjugated their country with a ring of castles, imposing English power and Welsh humiliation. Cardiff City Hall is not a castle. Built at the turn of the twentieth century, 800 years after Edward's rash of fortresses, it flaunts an Anglo-dominant version of Welsh confidence and cooperation, funded by abundant coal. But, today, the locals don't have to let you in if they don't want to. It's not rebel forces but asbestos, apparently. This Edwardian jewel in Cardiff's crown isn't due to reopen for at least another year. Fortunately, I found an obliging employee, Geoff Cook. We slip in through the tradesman's entrance.

I have come in search of Owain Glyndŵr, a medieval visionary who turned the dream of an independent Wales into a brief reality. Ironically, Owain cut his teeth as a battle-hardened esquire fighting for England's cause against the Scots and French. Praise poems

abounded: a golden son, a fine soldier, 'an eagle, delightful beyond measure … mighty his stroke'. On either side of the border, Owain was a man to be reckoned with. Boasting an impressive lineage, it is no coincidence that he proclaimed himself Prince of Wales in September 1400, a year after the Black Prince's capricious son, Richard II, had been ousted by Henry Bolingbroke. Usurpation was contagious, and England's Prince of Wales, Henry, but a boy. In 1400, the future – both English and Welsh – was uncertain.

I climb the grand staircase to Cardiff's Marble Hall. 'The city exploded with the opening of the docks in 1907,' explains Geoff. 'They decided to have a hall of heroes voted for by the public. Except really the committee decided. Committees decide everything in Wales. It was going to be the ten greatest Welshmen, but eleven looked better, so they put St David in the middle. And it was the time of the Suffragette movement, so there had to be a woman. Boudica. Yes, she is English.'

Surrounded by spookily similar marble statues, Owain Glyndŵr isn't immediately apparent. Perhaps minister of munitions and later prime minister, Welshman David Lloyd George, did not want to be upstaged. However, by the time he unveiled the heroes in 1916, the politician needed Glyndŵr as a native repository for ideas of valour and liberty. Plucky Wales was framed in a World War I fight against the German oppressor, alongside little Belgium and smaller Serbia. The recruitment drive worked. In Alexandra Gardens outside the hall is Cardiff's enormous National War Memorial. Thirty-five thousand dead Welshmen. At least Owain Glyndŵr lived.

According to myth, he might still be in a cave; that, even in defeat, the Welsh never relinquished their hero speaks to his standing. But the marble man in Cardiff City Hall doesn't look like he has ever roughed it outdoors. Standing in a Robin Hood tunic with his Anglicised name (Owen Glendower), Alfred Turner's statue (yes, an English sculptor) is not resisting English occupation, rather posing in medieval costume. Geoff concedes the statue, like its location, is of its time. Cardiff City Hall's Glyndwr is the semi-mythical man in

William Shakespeare's *Henry IV, Part I*. The elegant marble statue coolly glosses over Owain's violent Welsh uprising. According to Geoff, 'for a long while in this city they weren't sure about him. You see, Glyndŵr sacked Cardiff Castle.' The self-proclaimed prince left much of his country in a worse state than he found it. How else to get the English out of Wales?

A statue that matches Glyndŵr's contemporary zeitgeist requires a trip north to Corwen, where Glyndŵr first raised his banner and sacked the surrounding towns. Gareth Jones will travel there in September, as he always does, for the anniversary of Owain Glyndŵr's first uprising, when the Welsh freedom fighter was proclaimed Prince of Wales by his followers. 'There's music, and flags with rampart lions, and children.' He pauses. 'A lot has changed in my lifetime.' Secretary of the Owain Glyndŵr Society, Gareth has seen his hero take off in recent years. 'As a child, I grew up knowing that Owain had sieged local Coity Castle at Bridgend. I could never fathom why he attacked a Welsh castle. Nowadays, those questions have been answered. It was built by the Normans, occupied by a Marcher Lord.'

So, in Wales, but not really 'Welsh' at all. Gareth is well versed in Owain's acme, his ability to capture and craft alliances with powerful noblemen. His Owain was no rebel; that is a title for Henry Bolingbroke, the English 'usurper' king. Rather, he sees Owain as a legitimate prince, with ambitions for a Welsh bishopric and two universities, a man who established Welsh parliaments, and at one point had most of Wales in his grasp. How long could it last? Ultimately, up against a country ten times more populous than his own, Glyndŵr was defeated. Henry IV's forces captured his family and hacked his henchmen to death, but Owain was never caught.

It is a long way to Corwen, a crucial north-Welsh stronghold, the starting point of Owain Glyndŵr's uprising and just a couple of miles from his hunting lodge. The rebellion was a 14-year, slippery, cross-country affair, but it started here, in remote, unforgiving geography that favoured local Glyndŵr. Beyond poverty and indignation, the Welsh leader tapped into something atavistic – a nascent national pride. 'That is why Corwen's first statue had to go. With drainpipe legs, it looked like one of the Seven Dwarfs. A lot of fun was made of it.' Gareth explains that the town is on its second Owain Glyndŵr statue in thirty years. The first, erected in 1997, mysteriously disappeared; a bit like the hero it tried to represent, no one knows where 'the gnome in wellies' went. Online traces of this embarrassing representation have also disappeared; the twenty-first century force is with an alpha version of Owain Glyndŵr.

Enormous, angry and in no mood to compromise, today's 'King of Corwen' roars at traffic from an 8-foot plinth of Welsh granite. Charging forward on a frisky steed, fully armed and brandishing a sword, the medieval hero has emerged from his cave and is still up for a fight.* I take a photograph in the rain and quietly explain that I was born in Scotland.

16. Tomb of King Henry V, Shrine of Edward the Confessor, Westminster Abbey, London, 1431

Henry V, r. 1413–22

In today's world, riven with identity politics, it matters where you are born – unless your nativity took place in the medieval Welsh Marches. It is early summer and I am walking the length of Offa's Dyke, an eighth-century trail that once separated Mercia from rival kingdoms in the west. My companion is Iolo Williams, famous for BBC *Springwatch*, all short trousers and flinty, Welsh good looks. There is no physical description of Owain Glyndŵr, but I like to imagine the middle-aged warrior shared Iolo's blue-eyed charm. Certainly, Iolo takes inspiration from this medieval hero. 'He was

---

* This second Owain Glyndŵr statue, sculpted by Chester-based Colin Spofforth, cost £125,000 and was erected in 2007.

the last beacon of hope for a united Wales. We celebrate his successes to this day.'

We have strayed from the ancient path to enjoy respite and an ale in Monmouth, nowadays a proudly Welsh border town. But for many in Wales, this destination is complex. Agincourt Square has a certain 'English' ring to it and, standing above us in the central recess of Shire Hall (itself a baroque statement of Britishness) is England's favourite warrior-king: Henry V. He was born here in 1386, but Iolo is unequivocal. 'Henry was an English monarch. He means little to the Welsh because Monmouth and Monmouthshire have flitted between England and Wales over the centuries.'

Henry's significance in Wales goes far deeper than the contested identity of his birth town. The young royal quickly became England's precocious teenage Prince of Wales, the warrior-child who cut his teeth helping his father thwart Owain Glyndŵr's rebellion. The relentless siege of Aberystwyth was hallmark Henry. Welsh dreams of independence wilted under this exceptional young man's unstinting counterattacks. Monmouth's 1792 statue with its kitsch crown doesn't capture the hero-king who later masterminded England's greatest victory in the Hundred Years' War. Iolo remains unmoved. 'Welsh longbowmen played a pivotal role in the Battle of Agincourt. I reckon they were probably mercenaries.'

To do him justice, England's hero needs an English champion.

'You want a monument to Henry? Outside the door there are piles of them.' Historian Dan Jones is a master of showmanship; his fat new biography, *Henry V*, cloaked in shiny red and white, is an effortless charge through the warrior-king's extraordinary assent to military glory on both sides of the Channel. The books are stacked Lego-like in the foyer, while their scribe sits on stage in Kent's Sevenoaks, waxing lyrical about medieval Henry. This man, the son of usurper-king Henry IV, championed the English language and was 'obsessed with building an English identity that is formed in opposition to other identities – Welshness and Frenchness'.

HITTING FRANCE

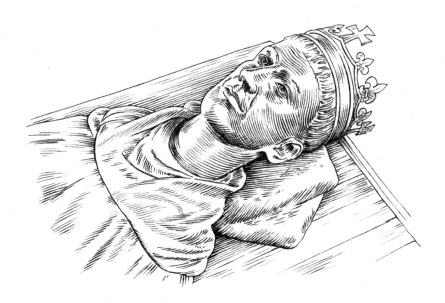

Dan's king doesn't just win every battle he fights, he is a devout nationalist and a visionary who pursues an integrated France on England's terms, with Jerusalem the ultimate dream. Beyond the shimmering success story that includes taking Harfleur, winning at Agincourt, the surrender of Rouen and onwards to Paris, there is strategic intent. 'The idea of a France in the fifteenth century stretching from Flanders to the Pyrenees, the entire western seaboard, was a nightmare for England. Terrible for business and a grave threat to national security. A deep plank of England's policy was to stop that at all costs.'

The audience are rapt. Henry has a nauseating baptism of fire – when fighting Harry Hotspur at the Battle of Shrewsbury, he received an arrow in the face that penetrated six inches deep (surely the prince's survival was God's work?). Dan follows this with an exoneration of the later king's relentless brutality. 'It is not a popularity contest,' he reminds his audience, with the slaughter of prisoners at Agincourt apparently the practical thing to do. After all, Henry was a man in a hurry; aged thirty-five, our hero would succumb to dysentery. Game over: France never to become England, the dream of Jerusalem unfulfilled. Regardless, the good men and women of Kent rally. There's a book signing to follow, with a king-sized queue.

After Dan's stirring rendition of God's chosen warrior, Henry's tomb inside England's most famous mausoleum was an anticlimax. On a quest for legitimacy, Henry's 1431 oak effigy sits within Edward the Confessor's chapel inside Westminster Abbey. Photographs are forbidden and the floor is weak, so access is restricted; I am allowed in but the hush is disarming and Henry's effigy robbed of its silver accessories. Henry VIII tried to ape his predecessor, while Reformation theft disfigured him. For centuries, just a block of wood; today, Henry V's polyester resin hands, head and crown are a 1970s refit.

The new Queen's Diamond Jubilee Galleries have further stripped Henry of his superpowers. The original shield, saddle and helmet no longer hang above their hero but are preserved separately, miles up an expensive flight of stairs. I press my face against the glass and try to imagine the hero-king reunited with his tools of war, leading England's men-in-arms. The image remains elusive, but the view from the abbey's exalted eves is breathtaking, a Westminster vista from God's house to the people's house. And between them both, Richard the Lionheart, his raised sword winking in the sun, charging onwards, to Jerusalem.

Among the pantheon of warriors, Henry has some way to go.

CHAPTER 6

FAMILY FEUDS

Victors invariably write their own history. In that context, the Tudors owe much to William Shakespeare. But, retrospectively, who erects the monuments? In a period when Christian concerns over the graven image inhibited most statuary, the tomb effigy remained all-powerful, a legitimising link between the mortal sovereign and the Almighty. More than 500 years later, Richard III had some catching up to do.

17. King Richard's Well, Bosworth Battlefield Heritage Centre, Leicestershire, 1813

King Richard III of England, r. 1483–1485

In October 2024, Penguin Random House published the paperback of Prince Harry's autobiography *Spare*. He did not change the text. Why would he? The hardback is the *Guinness Book of World Records'* fastest-selling non-fiction book of all time. Not bad for an intellectually ordinary prince in early middle age. But then Harry is both royal and centre-stage in an almighty family bust-up. Gold dust. Just ask William Shakespeare, the influencer of his day, who produced four plays about one dynastic squabble and, in doing so, gifted medieval Britain its most powerful brand: the Wars of the Roses. Long before the discovery of a king under a car park, this blood-fuelled psychodrama had enduring appeal. Here was a giant family feud in funny clothes that went on and on. 'The Cousins' War,' laughs Lynn behind the reception desk at the Battle of Bosworth Heritage Centre – only Henry Tudor, the exiled prince, was biding his time in Brittany, not Montecito.

Up on Ambion Hill, one-time camp for Richard III's army and now home to the heritage centre, it is imperative to choose a side in this brutal rivalry: Yorkist or Lancastrian? White rose or red? Richard or Henry? You are expected to 'vote' at the end of your experience. No matter if you can't decide which claimant should take precedence. These were not battles over ideas (that came later with the stodgy Civil War). They were dynastic power struggles; think recalcitrant 'spares'. The language is universal, whether in Shakespearian or tabloid English: 'And thus I clothe my naked villany ... and seem a saint, when most I play the devil.' Besmirched for allegedly killing his nephews in the Tower, ambitious Richard did not get a good press.

The trend for usurpations began early, in 1399, when Henry Bolingbroke, Duke of Lancaster and father of Henry V, grabbed the crown from Richard II. Against the backdrop of the Hundred Years' War, when the French throne was continually contested, challenging the English one was a natural next step. The royal family are past masters at bearing a grudge. By the mid-1400s, territorial losses in France fuelled vengefulness in England, with Henry V's heir, schizophrenic child-king Henry VI, exacerbating the problem.

I move into the heart of the heritage centre. John, a picture gallery assistant, is talking me through an involved family tree. There are many battles over decades that take place in a triangle somewhere between Gloucester, York and London. Yorkshire's Towton had the highest body count, a staggering 25,000 in one day, and the Cotswolds' Tewkesbury the best re-enactments, but none have the status or memorialisation of Leicestershire's Bosworth. John has been through this before: 'the winner takes it all.' Bosworth in 1485 has the dubious privilege of being the last battle in this gruesome killing game; upstart Henry's victory gave birth to the Tudor dynasty. 'Henry had a very, very ambitious mother back in England,' John insists. 'Margaret Beaufort. It was through her he had a claim to the throne.' (Our contemporary villains, Queen Camilla and Duchess Meghan, are part of a long-established female trope.) Back up the family tree we track, three, four generations, to John of Gaunt. 'Henry's claim to the throne was very weak' – hence the need for Shakespeare to denigrate Richard. Despite all their razzmatazz, the Tudors lacked legitimacy.

John points me towards a sundial on the brow of Ambion Hill. 'It includes all the battles in the Wars of the Roses.' Ringed in the heady aroma of lavender and sage, and looking out over fields of barley where the battlefield has recently been located, the metal sundial – with its respective thrones for Henry, Richard and Lord Stanley – is a modern, inclusive memorial.* The inscriptions remember the 1,000+ dead, they acknowledge Henry Tudor's 'unlikely' victory and they recall Richard 'slung naked across a horse'. Only a wreath of faded white roses laid for the August anniversary of the battle speak to recent, obsessive levels of Ricardian engagement. The genesis for that is to be found further down the hill.

A modest stone pyramid on the edge of Ambion Wood is an early nineteenth-century effort at Ricardian hero-worship. Fabled for housing the one-time spring from which fated Richard drank on 22 August 1485, it marks the beginning of a concerted fight-back for the slain king and his reputation. The pyramid was the endeavour of Samuel Parr, an English eccentric and teacher known for his devotion to grammar, unpopular causes and Latin epitaphs. Back in 1813, Parr was an outlier; more than 200 years later, we can hail him as a trendsetter. He scripted the Latin text to a gallant and fair king

---

* Lord Stanley's defection to Henry Tudor's side is considered a deciding factor in the battle.

on this limestone well, in front of which there is a plaque featuring Richard's emblem – the white boar. Erected by the 100-year-old Richard III Society, they celebrate their King for 'defending his realm and his crown against the invading army of Henry Tudor. He was 32 years old.'

Richard's life was as short as the journey to rehabilitate him has been long.

18. Tomb of King Richard III, Leicester Cathedral, 2015
King Richard III of England, r. 1483–85

Two words flash up on the screen: 'Her Story'. I'm settling in to watch a film about a lost king and the main protagonist is a woman. Acclaimed for her intuition and tenacity, and held up as the celebrated king-finder who led the hunt for Richard III, as a human receptacle for paranormal phenomena (or, rather, one particular phenomenon buried deep beneath an otherwise nondescript social services car park), historian and producer Philippa Langley is also highly strategic. She had to be. 'Shakespeare had done such a good job of denigrating Richard III, I needed something fairly major to overturn that.' We are back talking about the reputation of Richard as the hunchback king, twisted with sin and guilty of infanticide.

> My conscience hath a thousand several tongues
> And every tongue brings in a several tale,
> And every tale condemns me for a villain.

Philippa is an unapologetic Ricardian. 'Richard had four main pillars to his character: he was loyal, brave, devout and just.' She cites evidence to support her claim, reminds me of the Lancastrian king's northern powerhouse in Yorkshire and Cumbria, and reels off Richard's notable military victories (at the vanguard of the army at

Barnet and Tewkesbury in 1471 aged eighteen and, later, successfully resisting the Scots in the north). Hardly the feats of a hunchback. 'No, the discovery of his remains confirmed that he had scoliosis, a sideways curvature of the spine which would not have prevented him from fighting effectively. Richard would have done knightly training. He was fit as a butcher's dog.' She lightly adds, 'Usain Bolt has scoliosis.'

Richard III and Usain Bolt in one sentence – inconceivable just fifteen years ago, until Philippa came along with her legion of helpers, researchers and Richard experts around the world, who sent in the funds and saved her search for 'The King in the Car Park'. 'I knew the only way of challenging Shakespeare was to find the grave.' But Philippa's quest 'was always about more than the retrieval of old bones.' From the get-go, it was also about a reburial. 'You don't go looking for something unless you know what you are going to do when you find it.' Particularly important given that, in death as in life, Richard had some serious competition.

Westminster Abbey is heaving. It is unseasonably hot and the entire contents of the outside world have tipped themselves into London's giant burial chamber to take refuge from the heat, brandishing phone cameras and aggressive elbows (entry is £30 a ticket). I am carried by a tidal wave of humanity into the Lady Chapel where Henry VII is still in prayer, lying beside his lady wife, Elizabeth of York (marrying the enemy was a canny move). The chapel took a lot of forethought; by the time it was completed in 1516, Henry was seven years dead. A shaft of light strikes his golden face. The curator nods, as if in approval. The effect is intense, the axis of royal power lit up for all to see. Just feet away from Henry V, this first Tudor monarch's gold effigy lies above his own body, within a raised tomb, inside an exquisite chapel, inside Britain's most sacred home to the dead. Henry's quest for legitimacy continued long into the afterlife.

It is a relief to escape the capital's furnace and head north. In Leicester, the air is sweet and any tourists are only here to see one thing: Richard. Or rather, his tomb. The girl on the cathedral's reception desk smiles prettily. 'We have just reopened, but I don't believe the renovations would've happened if it weren't for Richard.' Floors have been levelled, the medieval beamed roof painted, plaster restored. What a difference a king makes. 'Head east to the ambulatory,' the receptionist tells me. 'Our Richard wakes up to the morning sun.'

Half a millennium is a long time. Richard's 2015 tomb is breathtakingly different from Henry's ornate, cherub-studded splendour. Here, there is no metal grill preventing intimacy. I walk right up to the Swaledale stone grave, scored through with a deep crucifix. I kneel beside the engraved base of Kilkenny marble, studded with two boars and Richard's motto. His royal coat of arms boasts 350 tiny semi-precious stones. I go online and watch the king's reburial and listen to a sermon that underscores the deep connection between a global audience and this young king who died on the battlefield. He was thirty-two years old, a perfect match for the bones they found. But I cannot take a picture beside his grave. In the words of a volunteer, 'this is an emblem of national mourning, not an "I was here" moment'. The good folk of Leicester are fiercely protective of their man.

'Richard was just inches away from killing Henry when he died. His skull was hit with an axe.' Philippa pauses. 'History turns on a sixpence.' So too the fortunes of a cathedral and a city – and a woman. I re-watch the burial, specifically to find Philippa. She looks imperial, in a tall, navy hat and high-collared coat, her ivory skin mask-like, her demeanour sombre. Richard, finally freed from his medieval purgatory; Philippa's own 'feelings' vindicated at last.

I am standing where the lead-lined oak coffin was lowered into the ground, carved by cabinet-maker Michael Ibsen, Richard's seventeen-times great-nephew whose DNA provided the conclusive match. The reburial was a serene spectacle, weird and wonderful to watch. All eyes were on this one-time parish church, since bumped up to the premier league of cathedrals. Royalty sat within its ranks, the Archbishop of Canterbury led the worship and Benedict Cumberbatch read a poem by the Poet Laureate. Not a bad cast, even for a king. Today, nine years later, the city still reverberates with his presence. There is the King Richard III Visitor Centre (where you can peer downwards into the relevant slice of excavated car park), a Richard III statue recently moved into the cathedral's footprint, and a Stephen Frears movie all about the king (and Philippa).*

In 1485, Richard was killed and the Battle of Bosworth lost, but when it comes to levelling-up England in the twenty-first century, no man has done more.

---

* *The Lost King*, 2022.

CHAPTER 7

TUDOR WARS

The Tudors are England's most famous sovereigns but, for obvious reasons, imperial Britain preferred to fête the Virgin Queen's seafaring heroes rather than recall early modern England's brutal interface with their northern neighbour, Scotland. This chapter seeks to redress that balance.

19. Battle of Flodden Memorial, Branxton, Northumberland, 1910

The Battle of Flodden, 9 September 1513

Google's response to the question 'Who was the last king to die in battle in Britain?' is unequivocal: 'Richard III at the Battle of Bosworth, August 1485.' It is quite wrong, of course. Some twenty-eight years later, on a foul day in September 1513, Scotland's King James IV was the British Isles' last reigning monarch to die in battle. Hardly an enviable title, but in Anglo-dominant Britain detail matters. It is one thing for the Scots to be defeated by the English; quite another for that defeat to be forgotten.

The Remembering Flodden project has been working hard to right this wrong; a small Northumbrian village (not Flodden, but neighbouring Branxton) enjoys the proud boast of being home to the world's smallest visitor centre. It's housed in a former BT telephone box with the disclaimer that they could not afford 'the £millions to rival the Bannockburn Visitor Centre'.

In 1513, Scotland was the aggressor, penetrating deep into Northumbria. This is reiver territory, a hyper-masculine region born of a centuries-long border conflict. Northumbrians and lowland Scots have much in common, including their dialect, diet and martial heritage. But today, Northumbria is consumed into a broader English identity, with the decisive Flodden victory reinforcing ideas of overbearing England against underdog Scotland in a battle that claimed 10,000 Scottish lives. The taint of English hubris holds back regional pride.

Derek is unimpressed. A Northumbrian who has brought his granddaughter, Rosie, to visit the memorial, he feels perplexed. 'I always support the Scots when they play football, but they never do the same for us.' English Derek speaks from experience; these days he lives on the Scottish side of border, in Jedburgh. But the Battle of Flodden was no football match, which perhaps explains why it took four centuries to memorialise. With a far bigger war just around the corner, Edwardian Britain finally honoured the respective legacies from this one-time bloodbath. In 1910, a forlorn stone memorial was erected, dedicated 'to the dead of both nations', with no word of winners or losers.

Today, this solitary cross draws the eye over fields of sun-baked barley. Derek is partially consoled. At least his native Northumbria is sporting its finest summer garb: rowan, sycamore and willowherb dress a now exclusively agricultural tableau. Together we wheel to the south where the Scots met their fate, forced from Branxton Hill to meet the Earl of Surrey's men in the bog below. The proximate ditch where Scotland's King James died gives pause for thought. The dead sovereign's body was subsequently taken to Newcastle; his sword and armour placed on St Cuthbert's shrine in Durham. Derek nods. This is his land, his people, his local saint.

Twelve-year-old Rosie is taking pictures. She prefers women's history. We consult the pamphlet that accompanies the trail. Neither saints nor women feature in this, the 'last major conflict in 500 years of border warfare'. Just battlelines, artillery positions and first and final encounters. Resilience in war comes with planning, but only if you hunt around in niche histories do you uncover Henry's (first) wife, Queen Katherine of Aragon, and her visionary assistance. Holding fort in England while her king chased down celebrity in France, she procured arms for the north, moved herself up to Warwick and helped temper the response to King James's early victories. Already on her second marriage, and older and wiser than her absent teenage husband, twenty-eight-year-old Katherine was a force to be reckoned with.

But, like Scotland's dead king before her, when the queen's womb failed to yield an English son and heir, Katherine's story is subsumed beneath the attention-grabbing antics of her revolting husband, Henry VIII.

I wave goodbye to my companions and head back into Branxton, where one stubborn St George's flag defies the muted mood. I stop at the telephone box and donate a tenner to the cause of Remembering Flodden – a contribution towards the next print run, in the vain hope Queen Katherine might make the footnotes.

20. Langside Battlefield Memorial, Langside, Glasgow, 1887

The Battle of Langside, 13 May 1568

'They're so bloody English!' was the grumpy retort of one Scottish historian when the BBC rolled out yet another Tudor series across their network. Channel 4 followed suit with *Elizabeth*, and Hollywood is never far behind. At one point, you'd be forgiven for thinking Cate Blanchett *was* the Virgin Queen. Certainly, neither actress Cate nor sovereign Elizabeth could pretend to be queen in

Scotland. And yet it required the fruit of a Scottish Stuart womb to unite Scotland and England's crowns for the first time in 1601. The birth of Mary I of Scotland's son James, north of the border, saw Elizabeth I reflect that 'the Queen of Scots is this day leichter of a fair son, and I am but a barren stock'.

Elizabeth had chosen her own course, opting for singledom and a dynastic cul-de-sac over the marital shenanigans that rocked Mary's reign in Scotland. Both women operated in a man's world where female rule came with invidious choices. Three marriages later, the Scottish queen – threatened, abused and imprisoned – ultimately sought succour south of the border, pleading with Elizabeth: 'I beg you ... to have pity on your good sister and cousin, and to be assured that you will never have a more near and loving kinswoman in the world.'

It is through the prism of more powerful, cold-blooded Elizabeth that Mary is so often judged – the one-sided game of cat-and-mouse, the cousin-queens swapping jewels and written words, culminating in Mary's imprisonment and execution, with Elizabeth signing off her cousin's brutal end. But that is not the story Glasgow's Langside Monument commemorates. Quite the reverse.

Reminiscent of an exclamation mark atop an urban hill, it is lovely. So was Mary. The monarch's coat-of-arms – the Scottish Thistle and French Fleur de Lys – are alluringly etched into blond local sandstone in a Corinthian column that is as tall as it is surprising. Erected in 1887 on the 300th anniversary of Mary's death, the Langside Monument commemorates the queen's battle for the Scottish throne in May 1568. Challenging her half-brother, the ruthless Earl of Moray, who pronounced himself regent to Mary's young son, the clash was the prelude to her captivity and eventual death in England. Elizabeth's subsequent posturing in the face of Spanish belligerence has seen the English monarch framed as the iconic, brave queen, but the elaborate Langside column, capped with a British lion resting his paw on a cannonball, helps to reframe Mary as the modern hero.

LEST WE FORGET

Iain Ross Wallace, convenor of Langside Community Heritage, is sitting with his service dog in the bus shelter opposite the column. More often than not he is in full costume – baggy brown pantaloons, surcoat, Tam o' Shanter and shepherd's crook – regaling people with stories from another time. 'When I do presentations about the battle, I say it is either a grossly underrated moment in Scottish history or a family squabble that got a bit out of hand. The truth is neither and both.'

The column marks the spot where the right flank of Moray's army faced down Mary's men as they advanced up the hill. The former, who'd quartered in Glasgow overnight, enjoyed the high ground and quickly pushed home their advantage. The battle took all of forty-five minutes with Mary watching on, above the trees, from Prospect Hill. In his motorhome, Iain and I track what happened next. The queen turned and took flight. It was the ride of her life, clattering on horseback through Scotland's lowlands, her head shaved to avoid recognition.

A canny, self-possessed woman who managed her role as a Catholic queen in a predominantly Protestant country as best she could, Mary was not a military strategist; that was the job of her commander, the Earl of Argyll, who lost the battle when he fainted and failed to reinforce his advance guard. The biggest take-away from Langside, which saw minimal casualties, was the indecisive result. If only Mary had not left Scotland. But history is full of 'what ifs'. And the queen, whose lived reality at the age of twenty-four included miscarriage, rape, abduction, depression and dethronement, can be forgiven for trying her luck with a female sovereign south of the border. It is ironic that in the #MeToo era, we hype up Elizabeth who, with Thatcher-style panache, insisted she had 'the heart and stomach of a king' while coolly condemning her cousin to death, when it was Mary who had the guts to live her truth with 'the heart and stomach' of a queen.

21. The Armada Memorial, Plymouth Hoe, Plymouth, Devon, 1888

The defeat of the Spanish Armada, 8 August 1588

I've spent hours trawling through men in ruffs online. Weaned as a young adult on the film *Shakespeare in Love* and the dashing delights of Joseph Fiennes, I'd anticipated joyous Tudor-tinged voyeurism with the seafaring brawn of the Elizabethan age. Hark now, 'my story starts at sea, a perilous voyage to an unknown land'.* But these days, that voyage has become something of a quagmire. Elizabeth's heroes – man-myths who successfully pitched Protestant liberty against continental despotism – are under siege. If, once upon a time, their English brand was the epitome of freedom in the face of Catholic absolutism, they now fight a pitched battle as erstwhile players in a modern culture war.

In 2020, with the Black Lives Matter movement in full swing, pirate and privateer Sir John Hawkins was the first to succumb. England's prototype slave trader had no chance.† Worse still, Hawkins' villainy implicated his younger cousin, the previously untouchable Sir Francis Drake. How the mighty have fallen. Previously caught in a love tussle between Tavistock, his place of birth, and Plymouth, where he was mayor and MP, with both submitting to the statue-scramble of the late Victorian period, nowadays Drake's position, if not imperilled, is certainly more equivocal.

High on his plinth in Elizabethan bib-and-tucker, the world he circumnavigated at his feet, the vice-admiral looks unperturbed on the promenade of Plymouth's Hoe, but panelling is being changed to flag up his early associations with England's slave trade. Drake's dark past has caught up with him. It's much safer to focus on the

---

* William Shakespeare in *Shakespeare in Love*, 1998.

† After a three-year legal battle, plans to rename Sir John Hawkins' Square as Justice Square are back on hold at the time of writing.

seafarer's combined efforts against England's arch enemy, Philip II's Catholic Spain. If Victorian Plymouth had to share Drake with Tavistock, not so their claim to the Battle of Armada, with Hoe's epic view of Spanish galleons eliciting his apocryphal line while playing bowls: 'there is plenty of time to win this game and thrash the Spaniards too'.* Matched only by his queen's cisgender lament: 'I know I have the body of a weak and feeble woman; but I have the heart and stomach of a king, and a king of England too.'

Five years after a bronze statue of Drake arrived on the Hoe, it was the turn of a classic Victoriana monument to commemorate the tricentenary of the Armada's defeat.† With sculptor Herbert Gribble at the helm, no expense was spared. Up popped a granite behemoth, studded with cannons, victory wreaths and bronze crests, all leading to a rotund Britannia (more Victoria than Elizabeth), replete with pet lion. Beyond the inscription 'He Blew His Winds and They Were Scattered', there is something effortful about the stodgy imperial symbolism of this piece; it is a mismatch for Drake's legendary equanimity in battle. Small wonder that Margaret Thatcher tried to light things up for the Armada's 400th anniversary when flaming beacons stretched from Cornwall's Lizard to Berwick-upon-Tweed. But no amount of remembering can reverse the direction of travel.

I arrived home from Plymouth to a message in my inbox. 'Tessa, re the Armada, are you going to the Sligo festival?' In one short sentence, a Tudor aficionado upended my Elizabethan journey. Forget anti-heroes and triumphalism, these days remembering the Armada has become an exclusively Irish-Spanish affair, with an annual festival exploring the shipwrecks, slaughter and salvage stories

---

* In their final showdown on 8 August 1588, it took the British fleet, under the joint command of Drake and Lord Charles Howard, eight hours to defeat the Spanish Armada. Bombardment of the 7-mile-long line of Spanish ships began on 31 July.

† He also enjoys Drake Memorial Park on the outskirts of Plymouth.

that crashed into the Irish coast in the wake of England's victory.*
Breaking off the battle against England after a change in wind direction, the Armada headed north around Scotland and Ireland, where it was hit by violent storms. In total, twenty-eight vessels made landfall on Ireland's west coast. News that the Spanish had drifted too close to the Emerald Isle's dissenting shores panicked England. Elizabeth ordered the hanging of all Spanish invaders – and of any Irish who helped them. Surviving accounts suggest that local 'savages' were infinitely preferable to the unrelenting English.

New focus came in the 1980s with the identification of three shipwrecks on Ireland's Streedagh Beach; 400 years earlier the vessels had been driven onto the shore, with the the loss of over 1,000 men. In September 2024 a new monument to the Armada was unveiled on that same beach by members of the contemporary Spanish Naval service. Together, these two European partners, Spain and the Republic of Ireland, celebrated Sligo's commemoration of 'our Spanish Armada heritage'. The history remains the same, but these days the story has moved on.

---

* Survivor Captain Francisco de Cuéllar's account is particularly vivid.

CHAPTER 8

UNCIVIL WARS

In 2021, a year after the death of George Floyd at the hands of a Minneapolis police officer, seventy-three Confederate statues were removed; 723 remain. These statue wars speak to a divided United States, where racial and political differences are played out in response to the iconography of the American Civil War. Britain's civil wars occurred two centuries earlier and were not defined by race and slavery but rather religion and politics. Regardless, the resounding paucity of commemorative architecture is significant and speaks to a broader continuity agenda in the retelling of Britain's historic story. How do we learn about ideological difference if we choose to pretend it never happened?

22. Naseby Obelisk, Naseby Battlefield, Northamptonshire, 1823

Battle of Naseby, 14 June 1645

London's Trafalgar Square bristles with statues and busts; it's like a free version of Madame Tussauds (with less diversity). The Roman trend for placing men on pedestals was rebooted during the Renaissance. Today, London's oldest free-standing bronze statue is of a mounted Charles I. He enjoys a prime position in front of The National Gallery, and was re-erected in 1675, twenty-six years after his execution, just down the road in Whitehall. A passer-by would be forgiven for thinking Britain's royal family really had reigned uninterrupted for more than 1,000 years.

The Romans used statues to consolidate power. According to classicist Dame Mary Beard, they 'spread the imperial face around the whole of the Roman world, like never before'. Likewise, in the 1670s Charles I's arrival in his London hotspot was a deliberate piece of Restoration propaganda during the reign of his son, Charles II. England's regicidal horror story, which had seen the removal of Charles I's head in 1649, is conveniently airbrushed out. Erected at the instigation of leading Tory minister, Lord Danby, bronze Charles, majestic in armour, reclaimed this contested space for monarchy.* As for a memorial to the other lives lost in a protracted series of civil wars, there is nothing to see. It was not in the country's interests to remember a domestic conflict which proportionally claimed more men than World War I. Easier to pretend it simply hadn't happened.

This curious absence of significant markers to the century of conflict that helped define modern Britain is replicated across the country. After extensive research (an unremarkable monolith at Marston Moor, a stone at Dunbar), I plump for middle England, more specifically Northamptonshire's Naseby, where a decisive showdown between Royalist forces and the Parliamentarians' New Model Army took place in 1645. But, even there, beyond commemorative road signage, you'd be forgiven for passing through the village none the wiser.

It's a damp day when I park up opposite (another) unremarkable obelisk. Appropriating the classical form that first militarised the

---

* Just south of Trafalgar Square, Charles I stands on the site of Old Charing Cross. Once home to a cross honouring Eleanor of Castile, wife of Edward I, and later destroyed by the Parliamentarians, after the 1660 Restoration this was the spot where eight men who signed Charles I's death warrant were executed.

LEST WE FORGET

Egyptian landscape, there is little ancient or wondrous about this monument, erected on what was once the rendezvous spot for the New Model Army. Built in 1823 (the Cool Britannia era post-Waterloo), it is the largest memorial across a site begging to be repurposed into a significant historical landmark. If, in the seventeenth century, irreconcilable world views saw the British Isles resort to arms, surely today's culture wars, replete with street violence, find an echo in those times? The conflict – more than 450 years ago – has much to teach us about nascent Britishness, when man's relationship with God and Parliament competed with his commitment to the king, pitching neighbours and nations, Puritans and Anglicans, royalists and republicans, each against the other.

Today, various interested parties, unable to garner the land or money necessary to create a visitor centre at Naseby, remember the battle online. The slogans are unequivocal: '10AM Breakfast followed by War. NOON, lunch followed by Democracy.' Needless to say, the devil is in the detail. It was here that Royalists under Charles I were routed by a disciplined, uniformed New Model Army led by General Thomas Fairfax and Oliver Cromwell. No longer did the Puritans depend on the Covenanting Scots (as they had for their victory at Marston Moor in 1644). Crucially, Naseby marked the beginning of the end for Charles I, who simultaneously lost the propaganda war when his papers summoning Irish Catholic assistance were captured and published.

Enthusiasts focus on this slice of central England as the birthplace of the British Army, a service which, unlike the Royal Air Force and the Royal Navy, has no regal appendage. Historically, the army's lack of reverence and recruiting appeal can be traced back to the mid-seventeenth century, a clear indication that monarchist Britain has never fully forgiven the New Model Army's success and Charles' subsequent beheading. This is perhaps why we would rather forget about the killing fields of Naseby. Too complicated. Too divisive. Even the obelisk can't make up its mind: the inscription claims the battle provided 'a useful lesson to British Kings: never to exceed the bounds of their just prerogative and to British subjects never to swerve from the allegiance due to their legitimate monarch'.

Wet and cold, I retreat into Naseby village, where the early medieval All Saints' Church has seen it all, including the civil war. Inside, there is a small showcase of pistol balls and battle memorabilia. Given the conflict's religious roots, it is perhaps appropriate that this house of God continues the campaign for a visitor centre. A large banner stands behind the pews, where Northamptonshire's most famous grandee has the final word:

'Some may think it's a shame that Naseby is not properly
marked on the map as a vital element of this nation's story.
I think it is a disgrace.'

– Charles, Earl Spencer

LEST WE FORGET

23. Statue of Oliver Cromwell, Cromwell Green, Westminster, London, 1899
Oliver Cromwell, 1599–1658

I'm sitting in the front parlour of a Tudor manor house in north-east Somerset, enjoying the company of a devout Catholic. Upon his mantlepiece, flanking the Blessed Virgin Mary, are two arresting ivory busts, one of Charles I and the other of his wife, Henrietta-Maria. Former cabinet minister and Conservative MP Jacob Rees-Mogg's effects also include a lock of the Catholic queen's hair (not on display).

Jacob is a proud champion of Charles I. He recalls the monarch's 'very romantic end. He went to the scaffold with such great courage and said "I am the better defender of people's liberties". And it was true. Cromwell cracked down on liberties much more.' This royal advocacy was broadcast live on the UK's self-styled libertarian GB News channel, with dour Oliver Cromwell, the killer of kings, predictably on the losing side.

I bid farewell to the Moggs' manor house and head west across Somerset to Over Stratton for a local ale in a seventeenth-century thatched inn, one of the UK's 401 Royal Oak pubs. The shared name offers timeless propaganda that has served to turn Charles II's ignominious 1651 defeat at the Battle of Worcester, when he hid in an oak tree, into a celebration of the Merrie monarch's restoration nine years later.

Heady though they are, these ideas of freedom and beer as the repositories of restored Englishness don't explain why the Civil War's most prominent monument, outside the Houses of Parliament, is a large statue of Oliver Cromwell, on a plinth, above a British lion. I visit him on his eponymous green; it is a searingly hot summer's day but, undeterred, historian Paul Lay joins me. He is fan-girl'ed by Rosalind at the security gate; she has read his book *Providence Lost:*

The Rise and Fall of Cromwell's Protectorate. Like Jacob, Paul is a monarchist, but his interpretation of the seventeenth century departs abruptly from the former's support of the Old Dispensation. During King Charles III's 2023 coronation, Paul mused that 'Cromwell would be happy with the settlement we have now, but not Charles I. Moderate Parliamentarians like Cromwell were appealing to the ancient constitution and fighting for a monarch, a House of Lords and a parliament. It was Charles' ideas of absolute monarchy, the apotheosis of which is Louis XIV, that were radical, not Cromwell.'

This liberalism speaks to the arrival of Cromwell's statue outside Westminster in 1899. Opposition had been considerable; the Protectorate's brutal crushing of Ireland in 1649 still lingered in the

public imagination, with Irish MPs joining High Tories to resist a statue outside newly built Westminster. However, what Paul describes as 'Cromwell's capacious religious liberty' ultimately won the day. Forget the cancelling of Christmas (more Restoration propaganda); according to Paul, Lord Protector Cromwell boasted 'a significant Catholic friend, and Quakers and Baptists were all free to worship'. But it was the Protectorate's resettlement of the Jews, expelled since Edward I's time, that set Cromwell apart and posthumously helped clinch his statue for Westminster. Stipulations insisted funding came from a single source: cue Lord Rosebery, former prime minister and prominent Whig, who was married to Hannah de Rothschild, of Jewish descent and heir to a Rothschild fortune. With the finances secured, sculptor William Hamo Thornycroft, considered England's best, was duly approached.*

Perhaps it's the heat, or his ungainly features, but I struggle to reconcile this liberty-loving giant, cavalry sword and bible in hand, with the regicide whose Ironsides brutalised Ireland. Seeking a middle way, I am stuck between what T. S. Eliot in *Little Gidding* termed 'the fire and the rose'. Paul references Europe's contemporaneous Thirty Years' War, insisting it was far crueller than anything Cromwell's military achieved. If Ireland was the reputational low point, what of Cromwell, the charismatic, disciplined soldier? The Fenland farmer who became an extraordinary cavalryman, fighting for the first time in his forties? The leader of a New Model Army that triumphed over the king at Naseby and won again in Dunbar against the Covenanting Scots? A sign from God, surely?

Cromwell's miliary force gifted England its first professional army, with the late Lord Protector's regiments, later the Coldstream Guards, marching out to restore Charles II, escorting him all the way south to London in 1660. It is a lot to take onboard: Cromwell, the monarchist who refused to become a king; Cromwell the regi-

---

* Hamo Thornycroft also sculpted Winchester's King Alfred. Statue, Monument 5.

cide who paved the way for Charles II; Cromwell the warrior whose painful victories in Scotland and Ireland presaged later political unions.

Memories of Jacob Rees-Mogg's parlour feel like a guilty pleasure: the large fireplace, the priceless royal busts, the old dispensation and a divided people. Before the sun gets too much, I ask Paul a final question. Is there a modern equivalent of Cromwell?

'I would say Margaret Thatcher,' he replies. 'Although a Conservative, she was not really Tory. Conservatives found it hard to live post-Thatcher – she'd turned them into a liberal party. And, like Cromwell, Thatcher was from eastern England, a very martial figure who had a difficult relationship with Ireland. And she misunderstood the British people as Cromwell did. While her mistake was trying to create a nation in the figure of her father Alderman Roberts, Cromwell's was trying to create a world where everyone was perfect and lived by their own bible.'

I thank Paul. The seventeenth century is tricky terrain, both hard to write about and hard to commemorate, which is why there are so few monuments. But I think there might be a middle way: in Jacob Rees-Mogg's Somerset parlour sits a portrait of Margaret Thatcher.

'And the fire and the rose are one.'

24. Battle of Bothwell Bridge Memorial, Bothwell, Lanarkshire, 1903

Battle of Bothwell Bridge, Lanarkshire, 22 June 1679

Peek through the curtain of historic Scottish resistance and romantic visions of tartan-clad Bonnie Prince Charlie hijack the senses; flamboyant Jacobites dominate Scotland's narrative within the Union for much of the eighteenth century. That irresistible defiance lies ahead, but ironically the resistance most extensively commemorated in stone is not Jacobitism, but its religious opposite, the Scottish Covenanters.

Dane Love is the secretary of the Scottish Covenanter Memorials Association. 'Most Scots are Presbyterian. Where I grew up in Cumnock, I was struck by the number of gravestones and monuments to the Covenanters.' Stranded in a local field, behind an iron railing, stood a stone to John MacGeachan, a Covenanter martyr, fatally injured in 1688 after an audacious attack on royalist forces. Armed with nothing more than the 1974 publication, *In the Steps of the Covenanters*, Dane's interest was piqued. Things have come a long way since then. Founded in 1966, the association now has charitable status and more than 400 members. I too have signed up. What is this extensive trail of commemorated resistance, dramatically branded 'The Killing Time', after the Restoration of 1660?

It is a difficult story with long roots, tracking back to Calvinist John Knox's protest-fuelled Protestant revolution in Scotland a century earlier. Unlike the state-sponsored Reformation in England, Scotland's was an act of rebellion from below. The result was unadulterated, self-righteous Presbyterianism; Scots believed theirs was the purest form of Protestantism – a direct covenant with God, based on Calvinist preachings, with no royal intermediary messing things up. When Mary Queen of Scots returned from France, she had to try to work with the majority-Protestant Establishment. Her son James VI (later also James I of England) spent much of the 1580s attempting to reassert royal authority over Presbyterians, with mixed success.

The intransigent Charles I had little truck with Scottish sensitivities. Ecclesiastical change, culminating in the imposition of an 'English' prayer book, saw Scots stream into an Edinburgh churchyard – Greyfriars Kirkyard – and assert, like the Israelites before them, their covenant with God in 1638. There could be no idolatry in Scotland. Two Bishops' Wars against Charles I followed, preceding two decades of civil war across Britain's three kingdoms.

Fighting first the king and then Cromwell, for the Covenantors this violent story did not end with the Restoration in 1660. Charles II reneged on his previous (opportunist) oaths guaranteeing the rights of the Church of Scotland, and the Restoration's Episcopacy re-introduced both bishops and royal supremacy. Presbyterian clergy were obliged to conform to the new regime; three-quarters did so, but more than a hundred refused to break their commitment to the covenant. The story oscillates between attempted compromise and violent retaliation, predominantly in the south west of Scotland, where today immaculately maintained memorials track the blood-letting.

There are so many that it's hard to choose. But if size matters, Bothwell Bridge Covenanter Memorial stands out. A prominent landmark on the northern bank of the River Clyde, hedged in by juniper and box (now a leafy glade for Glasgow's well-heeled), this obelisk marks a decisive defeat for the Covenanters in 1679 against government forces. The Duke of Monmouth led his troops across the bridge where they routed the ill-disciplined Covenantors. Hundreds died and over a thousand more were taken prisoner.[*]

'The rebellion went on for years,' explains Dane, 'but ultimately the Covenanters got what they were after. The King and the Church of Scotland are now separate. The established Church is free-standing.'[†] He is referring to the so-called Glorious Revolution of 1688 and the overthrow of the Catholic Stuarts. Today, King Charles III is the Defender of the Faith in England, not Scotland. The Covenanters' story is a reminder that the victors (in this instance Scottish Presbyterians) not only write history, they also build monuments.

Reverential in its messaging ('The righteous shall be in everlasting remembrance' is just one biblical inscription on the Bothwell obelisk), in their own dour way Covenanter memorialisation is the obverse of the Civil Wars' lack of monumentalism. And again, the

---

[*] The story can be tracked all the way to Deerness in Orkney where a dramatic tower overlooks the shipwreck of those captured post-Bothwell in 1679, en route to indentured service in the colonies. More than 200 drowned.

[†] The Church of Scotland is Presbyterian, as distinct from the Episcopal Church in Scotland which is Anglican and has bishops.

story is one-sided. Yes, Covenanters were brutally treated, 'The Killing Time' claimed thousands of martyrs, but what the 1903 Bothwell monument remembers as the defence of 'religious and civil liberty' had a radical wing. The Covenanters rebelled violently in 1666, and it was a successful (second) assassination attempt on Episcopalian Bishop James Sharp in 1679 that preceded the Battle of Bothwell Bridge.

Whether freedom fighters or religious martyrs, Covenanters crucially land on the right side of history. Their story, marked out in stone across Ayrshire, Lanarkshire, Galloway and beyond, is a neat reminder of Scottish truculence, best summed up by Sir Walter Scott in his Covenanter-inspired book, *Old Mortality*: 'It has often been remarked of the Scottish character, that the stubbornness with which it is moulded shows most to advantage in adversity, when it seems akin to the native sycamore of their hills, which scorns to be biassed in its mode of growth even by the influence of the prevailing wind, but shooting its branches with equal boldness in every direction, shows no weather-side to the storm, and may be broken, but can never be bended.'*

---

* The Battle of Bothwell Bridge is a central event in Walter Scott's novel.

CHAPTER 9

BREAKING-IN BRITAIN

Identity politics are not new. Responses to the arrival of Protestant King William on the throne in 1688 varied dramatically; the Dutchman's peaceful accession in England was not replicated in Ireland or Scotland, with commemoration of this period once again defining itself in opposition. Elsewhere, the benefits of the Anglo-dominant Glorious Revolution were quickly turned into British military advantage overseas. A feat worth building to.

25. King William III statue, Carrickfergus, County Antrim, Northern Ireland, 1990

King William III (William of Orange), r. 1689–1702

Iain Carlisle was seventeen years old at the unveiling of William III's statue in Northern Ireland's Carrickfergus. Today, he is the chief executive of the Grand Orange Lodge of Ireland; back then, he was an eager teenager. 'The monument is iconic for me. It was erected just where William came ashore and commemorates his arrival in 1690.' An unlikely hero, slightly hunched and dwarfed by his stone base, William is framed against a large Norman castle. This north-eastern corner of Ulster has been contested for centuries, but over the last 300 years it is Dutchman William of Orange who enjoys pre-eminence as the Protestants' saviour and protector. In 1990, Iain was just one among 100,000 who celebrated King Billy's historic anniversary on the streets of Belfast.

Iain regales me with a defiantly Whiggish interpretation of Britain's 'Glorious Revolution', one that reiterates ideas of the 1688 watershed inaugurating a moderate religious settlement in the wake of Stuart king James II's Catholic proselytising. William of Orange was invited to 'invade' England in 1688, subsequently landing in the Devon port of Brixham and acquiring the English throne from his ousted father-in-law without firing a shot. But this Calvinist stadtholder soon discovered that Britain's Celtic nations were considerably less amenable to both a new king and a Protestant settlement than England. By 1689, Ireland was engulfed in war.

In March of that year, exiled James II, supported by expansionist Louis XIV, had landed in County Cork to reclaim the English throne through Ireland's back door. As England's first colony, the seventeenth century had been a tumultuous one for Catholic Ireland. Rapid occupation and plantation under the Stuarts were compounded by Cromwell's ruthless put-down of an uprising in 1649, at the end of which more than 75 per cent of Irish land was owned by a small minority of Anglo-Scottish Protestants, predominantly settled in the north. Forty years later, James II arrived in Ireland and capitalised on a resurgent re-Catholicising process, with Ulster a Protestant outlier amid a sea of Jacobite dissent.

In 1689, Ulster strongholds Londonderry and Enniskillen were at the coalface of a Williamite–Jacobite showdown. The only missing player was England's new king. Given his hero-status among Ulster's unionists, it is ironic that William considered the prospect of going to Ireland a 'terrible mortification'. However, unimpressed by the progress of his general, Marshal Schomberg, he recognised that only the successful 'reduction of Ireland' would free him to focus on a broader European war.

BREAKING-IN BRITAIN

Today, Iain and his Orange compatriots are unfazed by the idea of a reluctant hero, preferring to restate their British pride. 'We actually went out and fought for the Glorious Revolution. We didn't just talk about it – we made sure it was secure.' This live interpretation of William's victory is key to understanding the community's oft-cited first 'blood sacrifice' for a greater British cause.

In Belfast, King Billy murals speak louder than words. Here, almost everyone has an opinion on the Dutchman's legacy. 'Well, it's a thing.' Eighteen-year-old Evan is phlegmatic but, when pressed, concedes that he climbs the Black Mountain to watch the bonfires burn across the province every 12 July, the anniversary of William's decisive victory at the Battle of the Boyne when James II fled, never to set foot in Ireland again.

Innumerable parades (over 3,000 of them), music, costumes and so many flags remain the proud emblems of this contentious history. Today, Belfast's only equine statue belongs to William: sword held high, he rides atop the Orange Hall on Clifton Street, implacable in the face of mooted Irish Home Rule at the end of the nineteenth century. It is fortunate this Victorian William is three storeys up; his equivalent in Dublin was detonated by the IRA. Compounding the problem, Belfast's original Orangeman is perched on an infamous intersection between two divided communities which, until recently, were defined by sectarian violence. William III's celebrated religious tolerance did not feel quite so tolerant for Ireland's Catholic majority; post-1690, their landholdings fell to a record low of 5 per cent. In Dublin, William III's victory treaty was quickly reinterpreted to favour Ireland's Protestant minority.

A century after equine William first lorded it over imperial Belfast, Carrickfergus's diminutive king, propped up between a stick and a sword, speaks to very different times. In 1990, fatigued after years of unrest and indiscriminate killings during The Troubles, the arrival of this King William embodied a battle-weary version of the province. More than three centuries later, the sectarian politics he inspires are no longer in the ascendant. New polling suggests Catholics outnumber Protestants and, as I write, Northern Ireland's first minister is the leader of Sinn Féin, a party defined by its desire to reunify the island.

But if Irish history teaches us anything, it is to take nothing for granted – and that includes defiant Orangemen. Today, north and south of the border, some resent the triumphalism baked into their marching season ('parading' is now the preferred word). Meanwhile, Iain works hard to ensure events have an inclusive, carnival vibe, or at least don't encroach on communities where they are not wanted. Like William before him, not everything is under Iain's control, but he does his best. In the Museum of Orange Heritage I am offered cups of tea and a tangerine bobble hat. Iain shares photographs of his parading attire: a bowler hat, a brolly and an orange sash, and he signs off his email with a Union Jack emoji and 'every best wish for a successful visit to this part of the United Kingdom'. I am charmed, but as a Brit, I would be, wouldn't I?

26. Massacre of Glencoe Monument, Glencoe, Argyll, 1883

Massacre of Glencoe, Glencoe, Argyll, 13 February 1692

Look down the black water from the far end of Loch Rannoch and, stretching into the distance, are the dark, sullen shapes of Glencoe. It is, and always was, evocative. The word, the geography, the songs, the association. As a child who grew up in Highland Perthshire, I could only wonder. We rarely went there. Just 35 miles over land and loch, but by road, the journey's more than double, slow and winding. Glencoe has never been readily accessible. Easy to pick off – or at least so they thought when the order was given for a massacre. Scottish writer John Prebble described it as 'the only recorded attempt at genocide in the history of the British peoples'.

Rosalin MacDonald shakes her head. She's had a lifetime to get used to the idea of the atrocity, but the more recent invasion of tourists is always surprising. 'I had to put the "massacre monument" sign up outside the house. Everybody was getting muddled with the First World War memorial.' Both Celtic crosses mark a loss of local life, but that's where the similarities pretty much end.

'It was murder under trust, that's what bothers me, makes me sad.' So sad that Rosalin has walked up to the Glencoe Monument to lay a wreath and remember the dead on her side (Rankin) and her late husband's (MacDonald) every 13 February for fifty years. Today, she busies in the kitchen, ever the hostess (like all good highlanders, I'm assured), producing a ham sandwich, a packet of crisps, a flask of tea. The historic echo is palpable. 'Campbell's soldiers had quartered with the MacDonalds for two weeks before they turned on their hosts. They played cards and drank together, fed them venison and beef from their black cattle.'

Prebble takes up the tale. Alistair MacDonald 'was standing by his bed with his back to the door, pulling on his trews, when Lindsay came in with a pistol in one hand and his half-pike in the other. He yelled, and the room was full of soldiers, melted snow black on their red coats, their bayonets cold in the flame of the night-light.'

MacDonald was murdered, and thirty-seven more perished.* No one under seventy was to be spared. I sigh. The clock chimes. Rosalin nods.

'Will we go up to the monument?'

Onwards to the iron railings, hand-painted black and silver, the Celtic cross picked out against an epic view. To the left is the Pap of Glencoe, shouldered by Bidean nam Bian and its famous climbing route, The Nose. 'The mountains saved some. The MacDonalds knew the passes, so Campbell's soldiers didn't kill them all. But many perished in the snow.' She shields her hand against the sun. On the horizon, more cars. The invasion keeps coming. The

---

* That is the number Rosalin cites. Other estimates vary between thirty and seventy dead.

Victorians fetishised the tragic landscape; the monument appeared in 1883.

What about culpability? William III wanted to focus on France. The Catholics in Ireland were bad enough without Scotland's Highlanders throwing in their lot with the dispossessed Stuart king, James II. Nascent Jacobitism needed snuffing out. A pacification was ordered. A deadline issued. A storm brewed. The Glencoe MacDonalds signed late. Poor, lawless, isolated. The chain of command is long. 'Foreign' King William signed the order to 'extirpate' them, on the grounds that the MacDonalds' rival clan, the Campbells, were to kill them. The youngest victim just five years old.

'I am sorry.' I finger Rosalin's MacDonald tartan. She smiles. 'I wish my husband had been alive to tell you more.' He stands on her wall, a fine dark-haired Highlander, a MacDonald framed against his mountains, beside his collie dogs. 'That was taken for the 300th anniversary in 1992. It was mad. Now, mind the cars on the road home.'

The mountains glower in the low light; vehicles pull over and shoot them. Eventually, the traffic calms, I am back on home turf, heading towards Schiehallion and the Central Highlands. At home, Ma is drinking tea with the local boatman. I regale Jim with stories of the day – how MacDonald hospitality was rewarded with cold-blooded murder from state-sponsored terrorists, the Campbells, who lived just over the hill in Glen Lyon. He shakes his head.

'Highland hospitality! Yae see that hospitality anyware. It's the decency of man, tae take the load aff yer feet.'

'But to murder them, Jim!'

'Aye, but they ware all lawless. MacDonalds were raiders. If they dinnae find livestock, they left wains without spoons.' He laughs. 'They knew what they ware doing when they asked the Campbells of Glen Lyon tae pay out justice. Yae huv tae see things frae a sides.'

27. Blenheim Palace, Woodstock, Oxfordshire, 1705–22

Battle of Blenheim, Blindheim, Bavaria, 13 August 1704

When we meet, the (now late) 11th Duke of Marlborough is already 80 years old. The production team insist I wear a skirt. I do what I am told, take a deep breath and walk beyond the prescribed tourist trail of staterooms and grandmasters into the private living quarters of Marlborough (as he signed himself).

'Hrumph.' The duke turns from his desk and looks at me with sad bug-eyes. He wishes I was not in his office, but needs must. He doesn't like television, nor does he have much time for nubile telly-presenters in skirts. But, he explains, 'although the Battle of Blenheim was won in 1704, the Battle for Blenheim, to maintain the structure of the building and finance, is on-going'.

The idea is that I will present a television series about Blenheim, for which the duke will grant us access, in the hope visitor numbers might increase. Hence the skirt. It is 2006; I've already spent two days at the palace (bewilderingly enormous, bigger than Windsor Castle and Buckingham Palace) and concluded the duke would never be happy. Telly success would mean more visitors stomping around the prime assets in his out-sized home, to pay for acres of

roof and neglected out-of-bounds rooms that sit forlorn and full of dusty bric-à-brac. And the duke didn't like visitors. He roared off in his Range Rover when they got too much.

Eleven Dukes after the first Marlborough and the British aristocracy had long since been knee-capped, their big houses mothballed or handed over to heritage trusts. But not the Marlboroughs' home. Their house is bigger than the monarch's and their heritage tied to more recent big hitters: Winston Churchill was born in Blenheim Palace, and Diana Spencer's bloodline is likewise part of their origin story. Aristocratic Britain enjoys less than six degrees of separation, and thanks to John, the 1st Duke, the Marlboroughs sit at the top.

When John Spencer Churchill penned a victory note from Blenheim to his good wife Sarah in 1704, its arrival marked a turning point in the War of the Spanish Succession and unleashed euphoria back in England. The hero of the hour, Marlborough's stunning victory in Bavaria was hailed the greatest military feat since Agincourt. The duke's capacity to marshal a broad church of allies (English, Austrians, Dutch) saved the Holy Roman Empire, smashed the French and realigned the balance of power in Europe. Marlborough's rewards were plentiful. Queen Anne insisted that a grateful nation build John, her favourite, a storming palace; the giant baroque pile, and much of its exquisite contents, are a testimony to English triumphalism.

However, long before Blenheim Palace was finished, Marlborough fell out of favour with his queen and the coffers ran dry.* But the battle, like the building, had a lasting impact. Victorious on the continent, emboldened England could hard-ball tetchy Scotland over their equivocation concerning the Hanoverian succession. Westminster declared that Scots south of the border would be deemed aliens unless there was political union. The Battle of Blenheim helped make the prospect of a politically united Great Britain a reality.

---

* Blenheim was referred to as a castle until the nineteenth century.

Scotland's elite quickly worked out that their best interests lay with the resurgent Protestant power on their southern border, not a Jacobite pretender who sat in France, a defeated Catholic continental power. The Treaty of Union, completed in 1706, was ratified by both parliaments the following year. Several Scottish regiments had played a vital role at the Battle of Blenheim, but it was always England's victory – Marlborough an English hero and his palace a giant English pad. Scotland's Union brokers were later derided by Robert Burns: 'bought and sold for English gold, what a parcel of rogues in a nation'. Meanwhile, in salubrious Oxfordshire, Blenheim Palace shone with ostentatious glory, every feature a manifestation of Marlborough greatness: the Victory column, the Blenheim tapestries and Capability Brown's gardens with the 'finest view in England'.

Back in the duke's office, we discuss his godfather and distant cousin, Winston Churchill. There is a picture of the war leader standing alongside young Marlborough, visiting a Blitz'ed site in wartime Liverpool. His Grace tells me that the opening of the Churchill exhibition inside the palace was his idea. It is a neat reminder that this family's story spans the arc of British dominance, from the inception of the union to the birth of Prime Minister Churchill with whom Britain had its last great military hurrah in World War II.

I bid the duke farewell and take my leave, unsure whether an exit requires a curtsey. We never meet again. The TV commissioner decided that stately homes had fallen out of fashion.

28. Black Watch Monument, Aberfeldy, Perthshire, 1887

First muster of the Black Watch, near Aberfeldy, Perthshire, 1740

How to police the Highlands? In the wake of the 1715 Jacobite Uprising, General George Wade was dispatched north to improve government control of Scotland's remotest regions. His solution was

LEST WE FORGET

250 miles of roads and bridges to facilitate troop movement; today, the finest extant example is Wade's Bridge as you enter the small Perthshire town of Aberfeldy. Look left from the bridge and you'll see a monument to what began as another Hanoverian response to the recalcitrant Highlands.

'He's a handsome bugger, isn't he?'

'Sure is.' I'm staring up at a muckle statue of a kilted warrior unsheathing his sword atop a dramatic Scottish cairn. My companion is Donald Riddell, a man who made his name offering tourists a unique blend of red squirrels, red deer, off-roading and captivating banter: 'Apparently, the statue at the top is Private Farquhar Shaw. You know the story. Sometime after 1715, clans loyal to the crown were recruited to guard the Highlands. They became the Black Watch and were ordered to march to London to meet the king in 1743.'

What comes next is a sorry saga of mistrust and murder in a turbulent post-Union, Jacobite-ridden period. The Black Watch, which had only ever patrolled in Scotland, became apprehensive when it was General Wade and not George II who materialised in the English capital. Rumours abounded that the regiment was destined for the disease-infested West Indies. No sir! One hundred and thirty-nine Scotsmen about-turned and began the long march home, only to be apprehended two days later. Three mutineers, including Private Farquhar, the regiment's best shot, were taken to the Tower of London and executed for desertion.

Farquhar Shaw is the grit in the Black Watch's otherwise loyal British story. Executed as a traitor, he has since become a Scottish hero. I press for more. Donald defers to his older brother. Roddy is a military man; he retired from the Black Watch a lieutenant colonel after thirty-two years of service and, when it comes to his regiment's monument, he tells a very different tale. It was here, in Highland Perthshire where Aberfeldy meets the River Tay, that six independent companies mustered for the first time in 1740. The monument was commissioned more than a century later to cele-

brate the Black Watch's subsequent outstanding service in Queen Victoria's Golden Jubilee year. Named after their dark tartan that underscored the force's intimidating distinction, and initially tasked to guard over their own, soon the Black Watch were conquering for Britain 'in every part of the world'.* Early success in the 1745 Battle of Fontenoy saw the French dub them the Highland Furies.

---

* Commonly known as 'Am Freiceadan Dubh' – Gaelic for The Black Watch.

Roddy talks modestly of his part in the Black Watch's later story, a life-long commitment inspired by his Uncle Ian. Serving with the regiment in World War II, Ian lost an eye to a mine in north Africa. Against expectations, and with the army desperate for experienced officers, Ian rejoined his battalion in spring 1945. Within a day, he was dead. Roddy pauses. The loss of an uncle, and his own subsequent decision to join the Black Watch, are testimony to a familial patriotism that many Highland regiments inspired. Close-knit communities yielded generations of young men and none more so than the Black Watch, with Perthshire an essential recruiting ground.

'It's all changed now.' When Roddy was commissioned from Sandhurst in 1973, the British army was 155,000 strong; today, it boasts fewer than 73,000 soldiers. The Black Watch regiment was disbanded in 2006, its current status as a battalion within the Royal Regiment of Scotland further impacting recruitment. 'But at least they've kept the red hackle.'*

The one-time Highland Furies are a diminishing force, a reality that casts Aberfeldy's warrior in a new, poignant light. For Roddy, it really matters. 'Since our old regiment disappeared in 2006, we have a get-together and a church service there every two years.'

It is the Black Watch's history that speaks to Roddy's idea of the monument. He has no truck with the notion that Private Farquhar Shaw stands at its top. He dismisses his brother's romantic association, and cites the sculptor, William Rhind, who wanted to build 'a colossal statue 10 foot high on the summit of the cairn, representing one of the original Highlanders … in the act of drawing his sword, suggesting that he is going forth to fight the battles of his country.'

Which country? Britain? Or Scotland? Rhind certainly made no mention of a Farquhar Shaw, the Highland martyr killed in London who most Google searches link to the statue. Bar a little weathering, the Black Watch statue has not changed in over 150 years, but the

---

* A distinctive short spray of red feathers worn in the bonnets of the Black Watch.

identity of Scotland has. Roddy sees the Black Watch's history baked into its stone, but Aberfeldy, these days more quaint tourist town than military recruiting ground, leans towards contemporary ideas of a restive, insouciant Scotland. Farquhar fits that bill nicely.

Beyond his Black Watch identity, Aberfeldy's warrior is whoever you want him to be.

29. Colonel James Gardiner obelisk, grounds of Bankton House, Prestonpans, East Lothian, 1853

The Battle of Prestonpans, September 1745, Prestonpans, East Lothian

Read the headlines and you'd be forgiven for thinking all Scots opposed Brexit, when in fact – and despite their Auld Alliance with France – 38 per cent voted to leave the European Union in 2016. The country remains in the 1707 British Union, but the 44.7 per cent who voted for independence in 2014 shout the loudest. Like most nations, Scotland is a complicated place.

I've come to The Pans. As its colloquialism suggests, Prestonpans is a downbeat town that sits on the North Sea coast, east of Edinburgh. Today, the fight is between two high-street bakeries: England's Greggs and Scotland's Baynes. Baynes are winning. They sell steak and haggis pies.

'I wish I was writing a book,' says the woman serving.

'I wish I could find the Prestonpans war memorial.'

'Have a pie on the house.'

I'm looking for a war memorial to the Battle of Prestonpans, the Jacobites' greatest military success against government forces in 1745. A Highlander on a stone, perhaps. But the only man in a kilt is adjacent to Baynes and he stands for Prestonpans' fallen in Britain's two World Wars. Scarce local money has seen this memorial spruced up: new wooden benches and bedding plants border open-air windows that look across a celadon blue sea, and a supplementary plaque has been added, dedicated to those 'who laid down their lives in the defence of democracy. Spain 1936–39'.

Disconsolate, I return to the Jacobite Museum over the road, housed in the town hall for a peppercorn rent. Volunteer Maggie shrugs. The World War memorial is the only one she knows. A plastic doll of Charles Edward Stuart, better known as Bonnie Prince Charlie, the Young Pretender, sits on the stage, drinking wine. He doesn't hold the answers. Like the second Jacobite Rising, my mission looks destined to end in failure. But, in Prestonpans, the story was one of military success.

Bonnie Prince Charlie was a gambler. Buoyed by continental hopes of tripping up new Britain's war machine through a Scottish back door, he landed in the Outer Hebrides in July 1745, with a few companions, arms and gold coins. Disregarding warnings that French back-up was required, Charlie hurried south, gathering an army of 2,500 men and capitalising on General Wade's infrastructure designed to quell the Highlands. Hurrah for British investment.

Onwards to Edinburgh, which the Young Pretender took at lightning speed. Highlanders were exceptional soldiers: hardy, loyal and mobile, but, by 1745, the Jacobite cause relied on more than the north. For every covenanting Presbyterian Scot appeased by the Settlement of 1688, marginalised Episcopalians flocked to the Stuart cause. Perthshire, Angus, Forfar … the line cut through the heart of Scotland. Great lairds were moved to fight; Glamis Castle had already lost one earl in the 1715 rising. (The late Queen Mother came from Stuart-supporting Episcopalian stock, not Hanoverian.)

Dynastic and religious motives were powerful and, after 1707, 'No Union' was added to Jacobite banners. Britain's expansive European wars and failed crops encouraged rebellion; Scotland was having a cost-of-living crisis. General John Cope's Hanoverian troops were routed by the Jacobites, right here on the coast. Briefly, Charles was master of Scotland.

So where is the monument? On the outskirts of town, I park up at a sports centre, beyond the coal slag that proports to be a battle-site viewpoint. Apparently, somewhere here there is a memorial to a local man who died. It takes me a while to find. The pin is wrong in Google, the track overgrown and the monument blackened with time and neglect. Erected in 1853, the apogee of Victorian Britain, it is an obelisk flanked by lions, paid for by public subscription and now obscured by railway lines and sports fields. Today, few in Prestonpans care to remember Colonel James Gardiner, an experienced soldier who made his last stand here, within sight of his own house, long after his troops had deserted the field. A brave Scotsman who died fighting for Britain's Hanoverian cause.

Like I said, Scotland is a complicated place.

30. Memorial Cairn, Culloden Battlefield, Inverness, 1881

The Battle of Culloden, Culloden Moor, Inverness, 16 April 1746

The Very Reverend's black cassock is flapping angrily. The wind has picked up and is carrying the piper's mournful mewl beyond us to the stragglers at the back. 'I have celebrated mass with a chalice found on this field, a sacrament performed here, history connecting us physically, emotionally with the Passion of our Lord.'

I want to stop, to write down the Reverend's words (Scottish Episcopalism is nuanced, like so much in the tangled Jacobite story), but this is not the moment. We are marching across the moor towards the cairn. It is mid April and the 278th anniversary of the Battle of Culloden. Hundreds of people have amassed near Inverness to pay respects, a colourful hotchpotch of tartan breeches, bonnets, white roses, biker leathers and belted plaids.

Having established that Episcopalism (not to be confused with Anglicanism) was the driving theological force behind Jacobitism (not Catholicism), the Reverend is now tackling the tragedy of Culloden head-on. 'It was disproportionate. This was the first time grapeshot was used by government forces. It killed nearly 2,000

Highlanders in minutes. And then, afterwards, the disproportionate response, the executions, the deportations. With all the warring at the moment, we can learn from this battle.'

In 1745, Bonnie Prince Charlie's surprise Jacobite force had stormed south, committing atrocities, slicing through men with their claymores, besting their foe. The Jacobean victory at Prestonpans proved a wake-up for government troops. In early 1746, notorious Hanoverian redcoats, ingloriously dubbed Sassenachs, caught up with and overtook their internal enemy. In Inverness, on an exposed piece of moorland, they wreaked their revenge with a pepper spray of grapeshot and, later, punitive retribution. Where does the parallel lie today? Gaza and Israel?

'Yes, something like that. Disproportionate.'

We arrive. The nineteenth-century cairn is large, a stout pepper-pot with a tuft of yellow whin for hair. A man is reading a Gaelic prayer in front of a microphone; another, a MacLeod from Skye, reminds us of Bonnie Prince Charlie's dramatic escape, bravely assisted by Flora MacDonald, and the heartache behind these popular heroes – the fate of the Kingdom of the Gaels, their tragedy, their dissipation, their lost language. For them, no more tartan, no more bagpipes. My Episcopalian companion takes shelter from the driving rain and I duck to read the inscription. 'The Battle of Culloden … The graves of the gallant Highlanders who fought for Scotland & Prince Charlie …'

Like all inscriptions, it is a simplification. The Saltire at the entrance of the battle site is only part of the story. Disaffection with the 1707 union fuelled the Jacobite cause, but as many Scots profited from it and fought for the Hanoverians under the Duke of Cumberland. Lining the route to the cairn, red Hanoverian flags flutter – an apologetic corrective for the nationalist mythmaking that Culloden gave birth to. I stand next to Steve Lord from the 1745 Association, an Englishman wearing the association's tartan. His colleague lays a wreath of white roses and sea holly, and, one by one, the clan representatives step forward: Chisholm, MacDonald,

MacGregor, Cameron. Ms Maclean is too small to reach the microphone, but her message is clear: she is here to honour her forebear. It has been nearly 300 years and still the injustice burns.

'This is for all the government troops that fell on that day.' Another wreath, this time for the fallen Hanoverian soldiers. 'That's a first. I've never seen that happen before,' mutters a man beneath his bonnet.

A Gaelic chorus strikes up and rain defeats the less committed. I join them, walking back across the moor, away from the site of the last battle fought on British soil, 278 years ago. We jostle together in the visitor centre. I buy a claymore brooch and give it to my Sassenach mother waiting in the car. 'Once upon a time this was a terrorist weapon used to kill your ancestors.' She laughs and pins it on her anorak.

PART THREE
LAND OF HOPE AND GLORY

CHAPTER 10

NELSON MANIA

The 1805 Battle of Trafalgar killed Vice-Admiral Lord Horatio Nelson and created Great Britain's first superhero. Protracted warring at sea against Revolutionary and Napoleonic France spanned decades and Imperial Britain's overbearing obsession with the need to eliminate the French threat defined Nelson's naval career. The monumentalism that followed his victorious death speaks to the significance of that Great British achievement.

31. Nelson Monument, Calton Hill, Edinburgh, 1815

Horatio Nelson, 1st Viscount Nelson, 1758–1805

The night I was prepping to write about Horatio Nelson in Scotland, comedian Jack Dee cracked a joke on a Radio 4 panel show. 'You join us today on a visit to Edinburgh, the city known throughout the world as the England of Scotland.' The audience guffawed. The Scottish capital enjoys a somewhat refined reputation, with Glasgow commonly seen as the hotbed of dissent and anti-British sentiment. History moves fast up here. Not so long ago, Glasgow was the second city of empire – a great hub of industry and shipping that oiled Britain's sea lanes and supplied the men to secure them. And in

the wake of his hero-death, it was this giant Atlantic-facing port that commemorated Horatio Nelson first.

Even on a dreich day, the city's Nelson Monument is unmissable, a commemorative obelisk that glowers upwards in the centre of Glasgow Green, a construction mission completed in August 1807, within two years of the Battle of Trafalgar. The message was clear: Nelson's success story was Scotland's success story. His mission was their mission and England's victory Scotland's victory. (Dublin quickly followed suit in 1809 with a pillar.*) Great Britain, with its new Union flag, was on a roll.

But Glasgow is just the start point of Nelson's end game in Scotland. The bog-standard obelisk, irrespective of its height, doesn't

---

* The Pillar on Sackville Street was severely damaged by Irish Republicans in 1966 and subsequently entirely demolished. In 2003, the Spire of Dublin was erected in its place.

capture the admiral's complexities, his star qualities, his attention to detail, his startling bravery. That required time and money – and a forty-five-minute train journey east across Scotland's Lothian belt to Edinburgh.

Ian spent fourteen years serving in the Argyll and Sutherland Highlanders. He's a former military man whose trade is now rope access. 'My boys hang off ropes. You can get up the stairs, but to pass material up you need ropes. We'll built a crow's nest at the top, a working platform. The ball will come down in a couple of weeks.' Completed in 1815, Nelson's Monument on Calton Hill is renowned for the large mechanised timeball that's visibly lowered each day when Edinburgh's one o'clock gun is fired, a signal to the shipping in the harbour at Leith. The sychronised device was added later in 1852, but surely the precision would have pleased Nelson, the man who kept a weather log every day, including on that fateful morning of 21 October 1805. How else could he be sure of the surface upon which his fleet had to fight?

Ian pulls his beard. 'It is very hard, working on a listed building. Everything has to be precise. But it's important. This building is important.' Ian's accent is from the north of England, but he is working in Scotland and he served in a famous Highland regiment. He is a former British serviceman, part of the historic legacy that triumphed under Nelson, long-famous for his diverse crew and their universal love of the vice-admiral. During the Napoleonic Wars, Britain's military band of brothers was broad and included Scotsmen. In January 1806, London sensibilities were affronted when Highland soldiers of the 79th and 92nd regiments swung down Horse Guards Parade in all their tartan splendour for Nelson's state funeral. Proscribed for much of the eighteenth century, here was the kilted warrior reincarnated on the streets of the capital as a symbol of British exceptionalism.

The post-revolutionary French enemy represented all that Nelson reviled: republicanism, Jacobitism, anti-royalism. In contrast, British Scotland came of age in an Edinburgh that was readying to welcome its first monarch since Charles II. By 1822, George IV, swathed in tartan, was playing his part in Sir Walter Scott's new-look Scotland – a visual embodiment of a northern force that bent its neck to imperial Britain and international gain. Edinburgh's monument, redolent of an upside-down telescope (Nelson's other eye), is a reminder of Scotland's part in this celebrated story.

'I will be a hero,' exclaimed young Nelson, 'and confiding in providence I will brave every danger.' He expected his men, irrespective of their birthplace, to do the same. Britain's numerous Nelson memorials are about more than the heroic death of one triumphant man; they symbolise a unity of purpose. I stare up at the workmen, climbing towards the tower's 105-foot summit on their precarious ropes. Is it not dangerous? Ian shrugs. 'They know what they're doing. I have a good team. The ball will drop again by the end of summer.'

32. Nelson's Monument, The Denes, Great Yarmouth, Norfolk, 1819

Horatio Nelson, 1st Viscount Nelson, 1758–1805

There is something 'world's end' about Great Yarmouth. First, it's necessary to navigate Norfolk – 'Nelson's County', according to the signage – where, beyond the quaint splendours of Norwich, lies a seaside town that time forgot. Recent tourist ambition ingloriously capitalises on an extraordinary seascape; the result is a higgledy-piggledy quayside with big dippers and neon lights built just beyond the ocean's vast expanse. Amidst the clutter, the town's astonishing pillar is easy to miss.

We are somewhere south of the amusements and my local guide, Anthony Oliver, is apologising for the location. Where once artist J. M. W. Turner captured the exquisite Doric column between grassy dunes and a wide aqua-blue sea, nowadays a post-industrial sprawl traps its architectural ambition. A true seafarer's beacon, the 144-foot monument (or Norfolk's Naval Pillar) struggles upwards regardless, a defiant national rebuke to Great Yarmouth's contemporary shortcomings. Britannia, not Nelson, sits at the top of the column, but the statue isn't the original. 'It's our third,' explains Anthony. 'The cement head of the second Britannia is in the local Time and Tide Museum.'

It's a lot to take in. Anthony has brought numerous sheafs of paper, photographs, facsimiles, articles. Make no mistake, Horatio Nelson was a Norfolk man, born 60 miles from here in Burham Thorpe, he soon cut a dash on the high seas. Given his own command aged twenty, it was the outbreak of the French Revolutionary Wars that unleashed his seafaring genius. The pillar lists the vice-admiral's seminal victories against the French: the Cape St. Vincent, the Nile, Copenhagen, Trafalgar.

A celebrity star and viscount long before he died in battle – Norfolk had mooted raising a monument to his glory early on – it was Nelson's heroic death that focused hearts and minds. 'An event distressing to his country but honourable and welcome to himself' intones the pillar in Latin. Nelson didn't just die; he had an outstanding death. While the good people of Norfolk appealed for cash, down in London, the metropole framed him for eternity in St Paul's Cathedral. Buried inside Sir Christopher Wren's giant church, a marble statue of Nelson sits above leonine and Britannia iconography.

Not so in Great Yarmouth, where Britannia takes the lead. She looks across Nelson's beloved Norfolk and beyond into Britain, framed by a great expanse of sea, the control of which was the Royal Navy's gift to the nation. A Christian Achilles, he died in Christ-like style; his cross was HMS *Victory*'s quarter-deck, where he stood erect and visible, sailing fearlessly towards the enemy, before a sniper's shot took him out, when commenced a three-hour struggle between life and death. Nelson sacrificed his own mortality on the altar of Trafalgar, and the iconography of Norfolk's pillar speaks to that greater goal: Britain's pre-eminence on the high seas.

Anthony presses another piece of paper into my hand. The Victorian photograph features an old seadog with a bedraggled beard and clutch of war medals. 'It's James Sharman. He was the original keeper of the pillar. They wanted someone who had served under Nelson. Apparently, he was below deck with Captain Hardy on HMS *Victory* when Nelson died.' More tales of derring-do and bravery. Back in Norfolk, Sharman, who lived in a purpose-built but long since demolished cottage next to the pillar, featured as Ham Peggotty in Charles Dickens' novel *David Copperfield* and led tours up the monument's 217 steps – a shilling a pop. His headstone is in the cemetery of Great Yarmouth Minster.

Among vibrant birdsong, spring's vulgar green, bluebells and buttercups, and thousands of Norfolk's dead luminaries is the grave to Mary and James Sharman. The sailor man outlived his wife, dying at an astonishing eighty-two. I touch the 'sacred' stone, where one of Nelson's Norfolk naval ratings lies. He served on that original Trafalgar morn when informed by his vice-admiral: 'England expects that every man will do his duty.' Sharman did just that until the day he died.

'Can I climb the pillar's steps?'

Anthony shakes his head. 'The Norfolk Nelson Museum used to have a key, but it has closed down since.' Back at the monument, I vault the iron railings (replicas erected for the bicentenary; they are inhospitably padlocked) and scramble up the base. I slap my hands against the sunken wooden door. Only the seagulls reply. Sharman is sorely missed.

33. Nelson's Column, Trafalgar Square, London, 1843

Horatio Nelson, 1st Viscount Nelson, 1758–1805

Cancel Horatio Nelson? Forget it. 169 feet up there, on that giant pole. Untouchable. Originally it was meant to reach even higher – 203 feet – a storming phallic column dominating the skyline, rivalling the heavens. Immortal Nelson, omnipotent Britannia, Homeric victory. Meanwhile, back down on earth among us mere mortals, St Paul's Cathedral, Nelson's burial place, has recently added an explanatory sentence on its website: 'over time' the vice-admiral's behaviour 'has been assessed more critically, particularly his views in relation to the slave trade'.

No need for such caveats at Nelson's Column. This is not a museum or a church. It is a statement of power, a Roman design to celebrate the hero who fought and died for king, country and commerce. And that included Britain's slave trade in the Caribbean. Nelson's wife, Frances, was a planter's daughter. He promptly ditched her, but not his loyalty to a searingly traditional, imperial view of

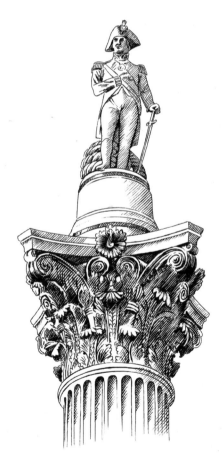

Britain. Born into the family of an arch-conservative Norfolk clergyman, unrelenting Nelson traded his right eye and his right arm for prowess at sea, before our hero gave his life for Britain. An equivocal sentence from St Paul's is as much as his contemporary dissenters – led by *Guardian* commentator Afua Hirsch – are going to get.*

Afua is not alone. Nelson – bumptious, ambitious, and unpopular with his peers – likewise proved an uncomfortable hero for bourgeois Victorians, none too pleased with the admiral's casual abandonment of his wife in favour of the married, flamboyant Emma, Lady Hamilton. But middle-class opprobrium didn't stop his lofty arrival in the middle of London's sumptuously re-designed central landmark, belatedly named Trafalgar Square. By 1843, Nelson was rivalling Trojan. The ancient Roman warrior has his own column in Rome. Once upon a time, Trojan stood on a perpendicular storyboard, but the column emerged from the medieval period with St Peter on the top. At 126 feet, Trojan wasn't beyond the reach of papal sensibilities.

Dominic Sandbrook and Tom Holland, stalwart presenters of *The Rest is History* podcast, are unquestionably infatuated with Nelson. He was their childhood hero; he is bigger and better than Churchill. 'Chillingly heroic', he saved Britain from 'Gallic invasion'. They rightly concur that recent efforts to cancel Nelson were 'fruitless'. Up there, he can weather any storm. As for being pro-slavery – dare we say even a racist – they point to the narrative panels sculpted from French cannon that flank the column. Of the four scenes from Nelson's battles, Trafalgar's panel – which faces Whitehall – depicts a Black sailor, George Ryan, shooting a musket. 'A nice bit of multiculturalism … that may preserve him,' the presenters chortle, well aware that Nelson is going nowhere.

I want to see George Ryan for myself. I am filled with an atavistic urge to straddle one of Sir Edwin Landseer's lions that flank the

---

* https://www.theguardian.com/commentisfree/2017/aug/22/toppling-statues-nelsons-column-should-be-next-slavery

column. Although prohibited, it is a pursuit so enthusiastically embraced by tourists the lions' backs are wearing thin. I have often visited Trafalgar Square in the past; London's giant roundabout is hard to avoid, and the perfect place for a protest. Ironically, Nelson's arrival in its midst was a deliberately anti-radical move. A committee on which sat that other hero from the Napoleonic wars, the Duke of Wellington, concluded that a reaffirmation of Britain's might through the recasting of hero Nelson would dampen Chartist dissent. It merely facilitated their ambitions. Five years after Nelson's arrival, the 1848 Trafalgar Square riots were a sign of the times. Young radicals condemned income tax (how else to fund the navy?) and commended French revolutionary efforts.

When I arrive with pad and pen nearly two centuries later, access to the column is barred. 'Backstage passes only.' Major League Baseball is having a big weekend in London. Billboards strapped across the square promise a 'takeover', big screens flash and speakers blare. One Philadelphia Phillies fan sighs: 'I'd love to see what this place looks like without all the junk.' It's 2024 and protest has given way to profiteering. How much did MLB pay to appropriate our most famous war memorial?

Furkan is forty-seven and from Sheffield. He steers me to his stand. 'I look after the software behind the glambot.' On Trafalgar Square's north terrace, I queue for a red-carpet moment with a baseball and photographic arm. 'Like Hollywood,' he insists, before admitting he finds it all 'a bit offensive. My parents came from Bangladesh. Old India. I grew up in Yorkshire. I know all about Nelson and his navy. I wouldn't be here without the British Empire.'

We reach the front of the queue. 'Give us a spin and look straight down the lens. That's it! Brilliant.' I stare at a ten-second slow-motion gif of me and a friend fake-pitching towards the camera. Behind us, perfectly aligned between two promotional banners, is Nelson's column. Britain's naval hero looks the other way in disgust. Furkan grins. It's a home run.

LEST WE FORGET

34. Collingwood Monument, Tynemouth, Tyne & Wear, 1845

Vice Admiral Cuthbert Collingwood, 1st Baron Collingwood, 1748–1810

'See how that noble fellow, Collingwood, takes his ship into action!' So spoke Lord Nelson of his second-in-command, whose flagship HMS *Royal Sovereign* led one line of Britain's two-pronged attack at the Battle of Trafalgar, off the coast of south-west Spain. Janet Brown, chair of North East War Memorials' Project, is adamant: 'Collingwood was the first to engage the French and he finished them off as well. I always say that he won the Battle of Trafalgar.'

This corrective is just as vociferously expressed on the plaque that accompanies Collingwood's extraordinary Tynemouth statue; the inscription reminds visitors that he 'sustained the Sea Fight for upwards of an hour before the other ships were within gunshot'. Petrified in stone, unambiguously enormous, the naval hero stares across the River Tyne, his expression inscrutable. In death as in life, Collingwood is less accessible than his great friend Lord Nelson.

To research Cuthbert Collingwood (named after the local Northumbrian saint) is to discover how his also-ran status next to Nelson impacted on posthumous ideas of this impressive naval commander. Courtesy of his lofty elevation (visible for miles offshore), giant-stepped base and four flanking cannons, 'Trafalgar's forgotten hero' is hard to miss in Tynemouth.* But for locals with skin in the commemoration game, it is not enough. 'Dear old Cuddie' is not just about the man. Nowhere bar London supplied more sailors in Nelson's navy than the towns of Tyneside and Wearside. Collingwood's military service speaks for generations of northern men predisposed (and pressganged) into martial prowess after centuries of border warfare. But what hope is there of showcas-

---

* The cannon were sourced from HMS *Royal Sovereign*.

ing their hyper-masculinity if local hero Collingwood does little more than elicit a shrug outside his patch? Janet has been fired with corrective zeal ever since the 1980s and the publication of a letter in *The Times* on the preservation of war memorials. 'Would you believe it, there are more than 5,000 memorials in the north east.' This is a tally that speaks to a region where 75 per cent of eligible men volunteered for military service during the Napoleonic Wars, the highest proportion anywhere in England.

Born and bred in Newcastle, Collingwood fares well in this northern Parthenon of the remembered. He received both a large local monument and a burial next to his pal Nelson in St Paul's Cathedral. But beyond Northumbria, his story is little more than a heroic footnote. Collingwood endured no glorious death in battle. He could never compete with Nelson's celebrity (nor did he want to; that he was injured in the back was little known, ditto disfiguring cuts and lacerations on his face and legs). As for mistresses, Collingwood barely had access to his own wife. It is ironic that, today, pity sits with Emma Hamilton and her lovechild in the wake of Nelson's death, when Collingwood, who survived the Battle of Trafalgar, had not been home since 1803 and never saw his family again. Subsequently promoted to commander-in-chief of the Mediterranean, he was consistently refused leave, despite failing health. Small wonder that his ship's dog, Bounce, featured so large in letters home. Who else did he have?

Janet wants Collingwood's former house in the Northumberland town of Morpeth turned into a museum. She has been campaigning for years. 'Once when Collingwood came home, his wife didn't recognise him because he had been away so long and put on so much weight.' She laughs. The throwaway line is a reminder of Island Britain's unique capacity to maintain its men at sea. Starved of a home life, no logistical effort was too great when it came to the physical wellbeing of the nation's maritime fighting machine: live cattle and sheep, gallons of lemon juice, wine and meat before battle. Even Bounce gained weight. Nelson's men were the healthiest alive for good reason. Inseparably intertwined with the rise of the modern British state, naval supremacy was synonymous with national survival, Protestant liberty and empire.

Both Nelson and Collingwood sacrificed a hero's homecoming for that greater patriotic goal. The latter wrote: 'whenever I think how am I to be happy again, my thoughts carry me back to Morpeth'. He died in 1810 at sea, en route home. Nelson will always be the bigger draw, but as Tynemouth's monumental hero – his gaze pulled across the water, his location beckoning imperial glory – it is Collingwood who best captures the commitment of a generation of Northumbrian men who lived and died at sea.

CHAPTER 11

WATERLOO

In 1815, the Battle of Waterloo had everything a dramatic ending needs: a grisly build-up during the protracted Napoleonic wars, a famous anti-hero known the world over and a closely contested bloody battle. But victorious post-1815 Britain quickly discovered commemoration doesn't come cheap. How best to spread the word of Waterloo?

35. Waterloo Bridge, London, 1817

Battle of Waterloo, Plancenoit, the United Kingdom of the Netherlands, 18 June 1815*

It was winter 2005. I was heading south, poorly equipped: one back light, no helmet, no fluorescent Lycra. It had been a long shift on the radio, departing from portentous Bush House, tail up, wiggle-waggle, in the black night air, homeward bound at last. Did he even see me? Probably not. I was flattened, a fighter on a pedal bike, poorly equipped for a modern traffic war on a narrow bridge. 'You alright, love?'

---

* Now in Belgium.

LEST WE FORGET

Conflict in a closely confined space raises the stakes; bunched up with nowhere to go, it's a potentially fatal game. I escaped Waterloo Bridge that night with light concussion. The eponymous Battle of Waterloo 200 years earlier claimed nearly 50,000 lives. Confined by two low ridges in a narrow valley, the experience was deadly for both sides.

Ultimately, the French were decisively defeated by the Allies, although in Britain certain details were quickly dropped. The battle's great hero and commander, Arthur Wellesley, Duke of Wellington, retrospectively paid scant heed to Prussia's late and decisive contribution led by Field Marshal Gebhard von Blücher, with Dutch and Belgian efforts likewise played down. Indicative of his flair for catchy commemoration, it was the duke's insistence on the easily pronounceable Waterloo for the battle's epitaph (after Wellington's own headquarters) that amplified the victory's impact at home.*

'Can a word be a monument?'

Martin, a tour guide in Wellington's victory pad – Apsley House – poses a genuine question. 'Waterloo', an otherwise innocuous village in Belgium 4 miles from the battlefield, quickly became shorthand for Great British success. It was important to spread the word and rebranding was an easy way of doing it on the cheap. The christening of triumphal city planning in London and Edinburgh (we'll find Florence Nightingale standing at London's Waterloo Place, and Wellington gesticulating down Edinburgh's), the naming and renaming of pubs, hotels, streets, glass houses, factories … Waterloo spread like pollen on the wind. The watchword for progress, improvement and superiority, Great Britain responded to the naming-game with alacrity.

Waterloo Bridge, where I had a near miss, was just one example of this cost-effective rebrand. Originally the Strand Toll Bridge (with construction well underway by 1815), it was hastily renamed

---

* The battle was also known as the Battle of Mont Saint-Jean in France (after the proximate hamlet Mont-Saint-Jean) and La Belle Alliance in Prussia.

Waterloo in time for a grand opening on the second anniversary of the battle in 1817. That day, on 'the noblest bridge in the world', Allied flags were hard to spot among the predominantly British crowd. Another bridge in north-west Wales followed suit, but it was London's Waterloo crossing, complemented with an adjoining railway station in 1848, that bonded the name with ideas of engineering and excellence. Rebuilt in the 1930s, hit by a German bomb in 1941 and completed by women in World War II, Waterloo Bridge was reopened in 1945.

These days, my cycle route home has changed. I no longer cross Waterloo Bridge. I am glad of this; seven years ago, Sir Giles Gilbert Scott's 1930s design was studded with concrete blocks and brutish metal barriers. The fallout from Britain's recent foreign wars – Afghanistan and Iraq – has seen terror tactics weaponised in new terrifying domestic forms. Driving a grey Hyundai, Khalid Masood ploughed into passers-by on neighbouring Westminster Bridge in March 2017. Four people were killed, with a subsequent vehicle-knife attack on London Bridge killing seven more. Masood was a British national, the terror group behind the attacks was Isis.*

Bridges are a new battleground, with 'hostile vehicle mitigation' a new form of defence but, in London, only Westminster Bridge has benefited from permanent bollards. Nearly a decade on, unsightly temporary defence measures remain on Waterloo Bridge. Once more, the name is left doing most of the work.

---

* Islamic State of Iraq and Syria.

36. Holy Trinity Church, Kingswood, South Gloucestershire, 1821

Battle of Waterloo, Plancenoit, the United Kingdom of the Netherlands, 18 June 1815

In the immediate aftermath of Waterloo, the dead and wounded clogged the battlefield, a sight one officer described as 'too terrible to behold'. In an era of great men and glorious victories, the humble rank and file were not individually commemorated. They had given their lives for Britain's pre-eminent place in the world, the reward for which was to be picked over in death. Survivors stripped the fallen of their weapons, uniforms and valuables. Dead soldiers were more likely to find their 'Waterloo Teeth' advertised in dental catalogues than their name on a memorial. Individual commemoration was saved almost exclusively for senior officers; the best the privates could hope for was a safe passage to the afterlife.

Back in contemporary Britain, amid the straggle of the high street, Kingswood's Holy Trinity Church offers unexpected respite. Even for the spiritually ambivalent, the imposing structure and Bath stone demand respect, likewise the sprawling graveyard that speaks to centuries of loss. 'Do you want to see the war memorial?' asks Jenny, the genial church administrator, ushering me to the exterior's north-west corner, where a lugubrious Jesus is nailed to his cross.

But I have not come for that war memorial, rather the building to which it belongs. Once dubbed the 'million-pound church', it was here in unlikely Kingswood, 3 miles east of Bristol city centre, that the first church was built in the aftermath of the Battle of Waterloo. The messaging was clear: according to 'the favour of divine providence', the victory was blessed by God; Britons were the chosen people. As the prince regent informed Parliament, moving forward it was 'the religious and moral habits' of the people that guaranteed 'the most sure and firm foundation of national prosperity'.

Hallelujah! More than £1 million was allocated for the erection of 600 'Waterloo churches'. What better way to roll out Britain's God-given superiority? Wary of expensive and time-consuming commemoration, building Anglican churches was the British government's sole contribution towards the commemoration of Waterloo in bricks and mortar. A frontrunner, Holy Trinity was 'consecrated on the eleventh day of September' 1821. Today, golden dating across the back wall is the solitary surviving marker that ties the church back to the Duke of Wellington's Waterloo.

It is big for a parish church – or, as Jenny concedes, 'boxy', without pillars to break up the large, rectangular space. The beginning of Holy Week is always fraught and Janet, an elderly volunteer, is dusting the long pews. Beyond a later decorated altar, there is no disguising the utilitarian nature of this holy place. It was designed to accommodate as many worshippers as possible. 'We do tend to rattle around in here now on a Sunday.' Jenny pauses. 'But that means those who come really want to be here.'

Janet has stopped dusting to contest the location of the children's last supper for Easter Sunday's service. It is a complex business. She shrugs: 'What do I know? I'm just a humble pastor.' Soon, she is waxing lyrical on the arrival of John Wesley, England's original preacherman in the late 1700s. Attracting mass crowds, and with non-conformist chapels mushrooming by the beginning of the nineteenth century, Kingswood had become a 'hotbed of dissent' and was duly earmarked for the very first Waterloo church. Holy Trinity was at the vanguard of an Anglican fightback, intent on muscling out opposition and capitalising on an expanding population.

I stand back, trying to imagine the church in a different time, without the drum kit and sofas, amidst a pre-Victorian congregation stamping feet, blowing hands and entering on foot to stare at their new grand(ish) house of worship. This is a buy-one-get-one-free memorial, a multipurpose building that doubled as a church and a monument to war in an age when lauding victory trumped remembering the dead. Had any of the congregation lost someone at

Waterloo? Was anybody sporting new dentures? I admire old plans of the church grounds and touch the wall where once there was a painted angel. This is what the Waterloo victory looked like back in early nineteenth-century Kingswood; a safe, curated space, focused on the future, heralding man's fleeting progress before a far more fatal war came along, one etched in names and ranks on plaques outside, next to Jesus.

The twentieth-century World Wars saw no equivalent church building project. Was it all the killing that decimated the faithful? Janet keeps dusting. God willing, the flock will muster for Easter.

37. The National Monument of Scotland, Calton Hill, Edinburgh, 1822–29

Battle of Waterloo, Plancenoit, the United Kingdom of the Netherlands, 18 June 1815

The 200th anniversary of the Battle of Waterloo saw the *Guardian* insist that 'Scottish heroism at Waterloo should not be forgotten'. Reinforcing the romantic ideal of Scotland's bravery, an opinion piece by journalist Jonathan Jones, published just after the Scottish independence referendum, focused on the sacrificial role Scotland had played in forging nineteenth-century British patriotism.

To underscore its contribution at Waterloo, the article featured Lady Butler's 'Scotland Forever', the eye-popping 1881 painting of glorious, scarlet-clad Scots Greys. (Of the Royal Scots Greys alone, a quarter were killed.*) Two hundred years after the battle, it was a painting by a British artist that best symbolised Scottish sacrifice, not the gargantuan National Monument of Scotland. Proof, if any were needed, that monumental impact is not size-dependent.

---

* Lady Butler's painting is in Leeds Art Gallery, donated by Colonel Harding of Black Prince fame (see Monument 13). 'Scotland Forever' is the only painting by a female artist in the room where it's hung.

Still standing on Edinburgh's Calton Hill, the construction of Scotland's most infamous white elephant started just seven years after Waterloo to remember the nation's fallen (at least that was the stated intention). The beginnings were auspicious. After a century of Anglo-dominated Britishness, what better way to underscore Scotland's prowess than by out-commemorating their English neighbours? Post-1815, London got a renamed bridge, but Edinburgh, Britain's self-designated Athens of the North, plumped for an identikit Parthenon. Calton Hill would become the new Acropolis – the ideal central summit for taking in Edinburgh's enlightened vistas of towns old and new, offset by the Forth's great watery sweep heading out to sea. In 1822, an army of horses began hauling vast blocks of Craigleigh stone up its central grassy slope. Only the best for Scotland's capital and its glory-in-arms.

On Calton Hill, the National Monument of Scotland remains unmissable. Today, it is almost the exclusive preserve of Edinburgh's youth, who huddle and plot on its mega-base, armed with Insta profiles, cans of Irn-Bru and stacked trainers. I join them; it is a long way up without a winch or step. Hello Edinburgh. Hello unfinished

ambition. Hello humiliation – national and personal (I had to climb back down). This brutish rump, with twelve doric columns, is a monument to national hubris. Scotland was indeed thinking big. Or rather, the 7th Earl of Elgin was.

A direct descendant of Robert the Bruce, Elgin is best known for hijacking his own diplomatic mission in Constantinople 'to improve the arts in Great Britain' by hacking off what are commonly known as the Elgin Marbles and hauling his exquisite loot back to Britain. The entire debacle came at huge cost.

> Dull is the eye that will not weep to see
> Thy walls defaced, thy mouldering shrines removed

Disquiet led by poet Lord Byron recast Elgin as a plunderer; divorce from his very rich first wife compounded the Earl's problems. Ultimately, he was forced to sell the Marbles for a loss to the British nation in 1816, one year after the Battle of Waterloo.

At this point, the *Dictionary of National Biography* suggests 'hereafter Elgin retired into private life'. Not a bit of it. Paul Cartledge, emeritus professor of Greek Culture at Cambridge University, knows all about Elgin. (He has campaigned for the return of the Marbles for four decades.) Paul puts the twenty-three-year British–French conflict into its wider cultural context: 'War with France was central to Britain getting, for example, the Rosetta stone, whereas the Napoleonic army also plundered ancient artworks. But this struggle, in which Elgin's acquisition of the Marbles was central, had largely disappeared by the 1820s.'

Instead, on the other side of Europe, the Greek War of Independence saw Greece reborn from under Ottoman control, at the same time as Elgin attempted to rebuild his sullied reputation with Edinburgh's facsimile Parthenon. The vulgar endeavours on Calton Hill (involving Charles Robert Cockrell, the architect who helped strip the Parthenon's Ancient Greek friezes and metopes for British glory), confirm what Paul has long suspected: 'that Elgin was always in it for self-aggrandisement'. A Parthenon to outshine the Parthenon would have been a salve for the earl's bruised ego. But the project, always divisive, was never finished; its Neoclassical style derided as too English and its raison d'être long forgotten. So much for an inscription to the fallen of Waterloo. Instead, the epitaph 'Edinburgh's Disgrace' stuck – an unfinished behemoth that underlined Ancient Greek mastery and Scotland's folly.

Thanks to Elgin, Scots today have a giant climbing frame for abled-bodied teenagers. It is in England where the culture war continues. More than 200 years on, the Parthenon (aka Elgin) Marbles remain in the British Museum. Ancient Greek antiquities a long way from home. How do you write the epitaph to that?

CHAPTER 12

WELLINGTON

The extraordinary general who triumphed at Waterloo, Arthur Wellesley, the 1st Duke of Wellington, was an incontrovertible war hero who freed Imperial Britain from the scourge of Napoleonic France. He did not die in battle and so lacked the romantic connotations of Norfolk-born Horatio Nelson, but even the Iron Duke's subsequent reincarnation as a reactionary politician and prime minister did not prevent him becoming an avatar for a victory that redefined Britain's public spaces.

38. Statue of Achilles, Queen Elizabeth Gate, Hyde Park, London, 1822

Arthur Wellesley, 1st Duke of Wellington, 1769–1852

Lord Byron has gone green. It is bothering Oliver Webb-Carter, who edits a history magazine but secretly prefers poets to generals, especially progressive Grecophiles. Byron's mottled patina is a sign of neglect, cut off as he is on a central reservation, severed from the glories of London's Hyde Park by Park Lane traffic.

Staring at him from the vantage point of Achilles' plinth feels cruel; the latter's giant ripped body a reminder that warlords really do get the best send-off (and Wellington did not even die for this). The first monument erected in honour of the victorious duke, Hyde Park's Achilles is colossal proof that Byron, with a pen for a sword, had no chance of stemming Waterloo-adulation. The poet did his best, visiting France a year after the battle and lamenting: 'I detest the cause and the victors – and the victory.' He doubled down in 'Childe Harold's Pilgrimage', castigating the battle as the 'grave of France, the deadly Waterloo', demanding to know 'but is the world more free?' No! came the resounding reply. Post-1815, Europe was led by autocrats, while reactionary Britain squabbled in victory's fading light.

How best to capture the glory of the hour? A Waterloo bridge here, a Waterloo pub there. Names are cheap, but peppering the country with victory-style graffiti lacked the 'wow' factor. Surely the duke deserved better. And it duly came with Achilles in 1822. This polished god, sculpted by Richard Westmacott, an idea ripped from Ancient Rome via Ancient Greece, was orchestrated by a Ladies Committee grateful for the peace.* The fall-out was intense. Column inches narked that Britain's largest bronze statue since antiquity, complete with sword and shield, was not large enough (there were bigger, better bodies in France and Italy). Others worried it was the wrong god, insisting that facially the colossus was Alexander the Great, not Achilles (or Wellington).

But the Ladies Committee got what they wanted. Wellington had stopped the European killing spree and deserved reincarnation as a naked god, fashioned from the *spolia* of war. Westmacott duly magicked an incredible hulk from twelve French cannons captured 'in the battles of Salamanca, Vittoria, Toulouse and Waterloo'.

Buff in black bronze, London's polite society feigned shock; it was men who insisted on a strategic fig leaf. Off the battlefield, the

---

* Achilles in Hyde Park is a slightly modified replica of one of the two Quirinale horse tamers in Rome. The identification with Achilles (in vogue in the nineteenth century) is connected to the idea that the pair of sculptures were raised in honour of Achilles and executed by Phidias, master-sculptor of fifth-century BC Greece.

Duke's reputation as the 'sexual swordsman of Europe' went before him. The only lady he didn't pleasure was Kitty, his drab, depressed wife. The recipient of universal hero-worship post-Waterloo, it is perhaps unsurprising that Wellington's marriage was a hollow affair. 'Would you have believed that anybody could have been such a damned fool?' he huffed. 'I was not the least in love with her.'

Poor Kitty. Married to a man who enjoyed sexual liaisons as a 'form of physical relaxation, not a serious matter', she had to make do with a view of thrusting Achilles from her dining table. 'Neat!' is how one American tourist, Meg, summed up Achilles' proximity to Apsley House at London's Hyde Park Corner, the home Wellington bought from his brother with newfound post-1815 riches. Today, it remains the family seat and, shared with English Heritage, is still the depository for the duke's innumerable war spoils.

Meg gives the 18-foot Achilles a once-over. She sighs. 'The fig leaf is small.' As criticism goes, Achilles has weathered worse; twice the strategic leaf was hacked off, and angry crowds tried to topple their god of war in protest at Wellington's politics. In his second career as a politician, the reactionary duke proved a harder sell. He did not want to extend the franchise. To hell with the Reform Bill. The demos railed against the god. Perhaps Byron was right after all. Oliver is sure the poet will have the final word.

'I've heard that the Byron Society are raising money to move him from his island, into Hyde Park.'

39. Wellington Arch, Hyde Park Corner, London, 1846

Arthur Wellesley, 1st Duke of Wellington, 1769–1852

Visually and audibly, there was a lot going on: the scarlet-clad Beefeaters' final white-gloved salute, the pall-bearers and their agonising coffin-shuffle, a gleaming hearse slipping away, then 'God Save the King', all with military precision. Momentarily, it was confusing, the day redolent with conflicting emotions, even anxiety, and the transfer from gun-carriage to car at Hyde Park Corner always a potential sticking-point.

In the end, the execution was smooth. Remarkably so. Commentators murmured approval in honeyed tones: 'Britain does ceremonial better than anyone else in the world.' Perhaps. But beyond the splendid pop of regal colour, had anyone noticed the architectural centrepiece through which Elizabeth II's funeral choreography was commandeered, that understated little archway where 138 sailors, like well-drilled penguins, led their late queen?

It is small (not quite squat, the design too clever for that) and white, and when you look closely, oddly bare. Like a Christmas tree awaiting decoration, Wellington Arch is naked save for the mounted quadriga tactfully racing towards Windsor – a much later (royal-inspired) addition.

Britain came away the winner in 1815, but Paris's Arc de Triomphe is the most impressive arch. Were it not for the Waterloo association, it wouldn't even be clear which London arch this book should feature – unfinished Marble Arch or unfinished Wellington Arch? The French have no equivalent deliberation. Napoleon in death, as in life, was unrivalled; both the peerless emperor and the French army's very own revolutionary soldier. In his wake, the return of Bourbon France quickly gave way to nostalgia for past Napoleonic glories. The Arc de Triomphe was duly finished in 1836, a gilded miracle that commemorates the marvels of the emperor and his grande armée. (The Battle of Waterloo does not feature).

Paris's Arc is a single-purpose monument to France's single-purpose emperor. Not so Wellington Arch. George IV, the Augustus Gloop of British history, was the Duke of Wellington's biggest fan, but the original raison d'être behind both London arches, and a screen for Hyde Park, belonged to the greedy king, *not* the successful general. George coveted elaborate entrances for his new-look house, Buckingham Palace, and adjacent Green Park. Wellington's victory served as a handmaiden to these royal ambitions, convenient proof that Britain's capital was a deserving recipient for the monarch's architectural fantasies.

This is the context for Wellington Arch's confused identity. Today, if you retreat from the delights of Achilles's statue in the south-west corner of Hyde Park, the exit is through a grand engraved gateway – Hyde Park Screen – approved by George IV. Beyond that, trapped on its own giant traffic island, is Wellington Arch. Initially named Green Park Arch, it remains unfinished business. By the late 1820s, the king's revamped palace had guzzled all the money; the arch's architect, Decimus Burton, downsized what he could before matters were taken out of his hands. Plans for victorious ornamentation celebrating Waterloo were binned, including figures of guardsmen, horsemen, and a four-horse chariot.

The indignity of this bare arch was compounded by the completion of the Arc de Triomphe. In 1836, the 'imperishable monument' commenced by Napoleon himself, was, according to *The Times*, an ostentatious reminder of Gallic insolence. Surely Victorian Britain could likewise afford monumental military swagger? The wheels were set in motion with the commission of a Wellington Memorial. A committee was appointed, a sculptor selected, (Matthew Cotes Wyatt) and a thumping great man on a horse concocted in a Paddington studio. Make no mistake, this was the Duke of Wellington in the saddle of his favourite horse, Copenhagen. Even better, there was an obvious place to put him – on top of the naked Green Park Arch, opposite the duke's Apsley House. Hey presto – in 1846, the Christmas tree acquired its very own angel, and a new name, Wellington Arch. The name stuck, but the union would not last.

40. Duke of Wellington Statue, Round Hill, Aldershot, 1885

Arthur Wellesley, 1st Duke of Wellington, 1769–1852

'God, it's enormous.'

Keith Bean nods. 'Sure is. I love it.' He pushes his woolly hat back and smiles. 'Who am I? I'm someone who works as a mechanic and I am obsessed with Aldershot and its history.' Good as his word, Keith has whizzed his white BMW across town to talk up his patch and its crowning glory, the Duke of Wellington.

Standing triumphantly above the gorse and scrub, Wellington is unmissable, a rude apparition straddling an outsized horse with an arse that points to London, the city that rejected him. In the graceful words of English Heritage, the duke once hoisted up on London's Wellington Arch was the 'greatest artistic fiasco of the nineteenth century'. According to *Punch*, this 'awful apparition' offended the metropole's adjudicators of good taste. Decimus Burton, designer of the arch, left money in his will to have the 'colossal equestrian statue' removed, but as long as the duke lived, that was not an option.

The 30-foot equestrian goliath survived Wellington's death, but had no comeback against traffic congestion – an existential threat to the living and the dead. Ultimately, it was the demands of a road-expansion scheme in the 1870s that saw the entire arch dismantled and shunted slightly south. Rebuilt without the duke on top, it was no longer in sync with the Hyde Park Screen but had finally wriggled free of that 'eyesore'.

'Wellington is better with us,' Keith insists. 'Aldershot is a military town. It's halfway between the capital and the south coast, so if the marauding French had invaded, we could have fended them off.' He doesn't think the duke ever actually stayed here, but insists that is 'irrelevant'. Aldershot has many other assets, including a Nazi exemption. 'It was never bombed during World War II by direct orders of Hitler because the idea was that the German army would advance to Aldershot, where they'd already have a ready-made garrison town.' And a military statue.

Keith swashbuckles his way through two continental enemies and swathes of apocryphal history. All the while, the epic proportions of Wellington remain outstanding. He is, we both agree, so wrong on so many levels. Or, rather, his size is, in relation to the horse. Might the duke's back be too long for his body? Keith shrugs. To critique this behemoth's artistic merits is to entirely miss the point. Here in Aldershot, Wellington is a someone. How many statues in London can say that?

Like the duke's later political career, the rejected statue had a bumpy ride after its ignominious removal from Hyde Park, including a short period of homelessness in Green Park. What to do with Waterloo's hero? Edward VII, then Prince of Wales, suggested Aldershot, also the new location for a major military encampment. There, insisted the prince, 'it would be highly valued by the army and would serve as an example to all time'. So far so good. The bronze duke and Copenhagen were severed into seven bits and a royal party selected his new home in Aldershot, 'not far from the Queen's Pavilion and the Church, on a natural mound'.

Crowds celebrated Wellington's resurrection on Round Hill in 1885; Aldershot had inherited a military hero. The adulation didn't last. Despite his size, the duke was soon hidden, mottled and half-forgotten, behind rhododendron and pine. Symbolic of a triumphant age, gargantuan Wellington fell out of step with a military town that fought two devastating World Wars. The Aldershot Military Cemetery is home to a staggering 17,000 graves. Small wonder the icon of Waterloo was temporarily lost from view.

But survival is key, as Wellington well knew. Today, the duke and his trusty steed are freshly buffed and bronzed, and there is a prominent heritage road sign – this way to the reinvigorated duke! Undergrowth has been hacked back and a small chain keeps the obedient at bay.

Wellington's statue is the beneficiary of a resurgent Englishness and regionalism reshaping Aldershot. Keith is part of that change; his parents were in the army, he deals in cars and local history. As Aldershot's military utility shrinks (in line with the British Army), its commemorative muscle grows. For every new apartment and office block pressed out of one-time barracks, there are fresh layers of memorialisation. Keith wants to take me on a whistle-stop tour – 'Come on Tessa, the airborne soldier! On the green where the Gurkha has a stand-off with the Parachutist!'

But I don't want to leave the duke. Like him, I've travelled all the way from London …

41. Statue of the Duke of Wellington, Royal Exchange Square, Glasgow, 1844

Arthur Wellesley, 1st Duke of Wellington, 1769–1852

I found a statue of Wellington in the grounds of Norwich Cathedral (the otherwise obliging canon is non-plussed; apparently it was a council decision to move him there) and a giant obelisk dominates in Somerset. I tried to persuade Jacob Rees-Mogg to accompany me to the top, but he was fighting to save his parliamentary seat. And then there is Scotland. If you're a statue purist, it is here where you will really relish Wellington, exquisitely cast, not once but twice, before his death.

Gavin Doig shrugs. A Scot living a stone's throw from Glasgow's city centre with its large Wellington appendage, he isn't interested. Nor does he care that the duke never visited Scotland. Because in Glasgow, in front of the Gallery of Modern Art's doric columns, the identity of the duke's statue has mutated. The forty-year, near-constant presence of a traffic cone on top of Wellington's head has become an international landmark. Gavin shares a wry smile. 'To be honest,' he says, 'I'm surprised you found anyone who is anti-cone these days.'

LEST WE FORGET

Maria is an eighty-year-old amateur historian from Milngavie and proved very useful on the value of Glasgow's George's Square and its great Victorian men. But Gavin is right: her comments on Wellington and the cone's obstruction of the duke's eyeline (she believes he was sussing out future battle terrain) feel irrelevant. Carlo Marochetti, the nineteenth-century Italian sculptor, did a fine job, but the artistic merits of his work have long been superseded.* The iconography of 'the cone' is now the artistry, the cone's rider and steed mere background props.

Gavin was part of the push-back against the city council, when, in 2013, it proposed to raise Wellington's plinth to prevent further vandalism. Apparently, successive traffic cones projected a 'depress-

---

* Marochetti also sculpted Richard, Coeur de Lion, in Old Palace Yard, Westminster, Monument 7.

ing' image of Glasgow. Yet another faceless intervention to halt a harmless prank (there had been previous efforts by the police and council) unleashed an almighty furore.

Gavin was well prepared. 'Earlier, I had put in a Freedom of Information request to ask how much money the council spent taking the cone down. They couldn't give me a figure – apparently the street lighting department did it. And yet now they were saying they wanted to raise the plinth to save the £10k they spent taking the cone down.'

More than a decade on and Gavin still enjoys a degree of righteous satisfaction. His subsequent petition against the proposal sky-rocketed. 'Not one of the thousands of signatures mentioned the Duke of Wellington.' The council promptly rescinded their decision to raise the plinth. Gavin has taken time out of his working day to meet me at the statue. 'Pro-cono work,' he assures me as we arrange ourselves for a photograph. Wellington's accessories – a red cone and an improvised blue plastic scarf (Rangers FC had a fixture the night before) – steal the show.

Gavin breaks it down intellectually: the petition was about challenging authorised heritage discourse, where the elite dictate cultural mores so that a statue of a dead white guy is art, and the cone on his head disrespectful. 'But now the cone has been there so long, parents who saw it as children bring their own kids along to see it.' On cue, a Brazilian family muscle into the picture.

Gavin reckons he doesn't know who puts the cone on Wellington (it changes depending on the city's mood: a Ukrainian knitted cone in solidarity against Russia, a Saltire for the independence referendum, EU stars to counter Brexit). Other locals tell me it's a secret that only they can know. But these days, we're all in on the joke. The cone is iconic, welcoming you at Glasgow Airport in poster-form and on the side of city buses. In 2023, Banksy held a record-breaking solo exhibition inside the art gallery, all because of the cone on the outside.

Gavin insists that 'Glasgow is not anti-British, just anti-Establishment', a city where the Iron Duke plays second fiddle to a traffic cone.

42. Duke of Wellington statue, Princes Street, Edinburgh, 1852

Arthur Wellesley, 1st Duke of Wellington, 1769–1852

It was a source of wonder as a child that the neoclassical Georgian sweep defining so much of present-day Edinburgh was referred to as the 'New Town'. To understand this adage, and much more about Scotland's capital, look no further than Robert Louis Stevenson's *Dr Jekyll and Mr Hyde*, in which Jekyll's descent is mirrored by a two-faced city. Although set in London (possibly for the Scottish author's preservation), this book is early nineteenth-century Edinburgh writ large. A world of 'freshly painted shutters' and 'well-polished brasses' pitched against doors 'equipped with neither bell nor knocker', bearing the 'marks of prolonged and sordid negligence', recesses for slouching tramps. Towards the end of the eighteenth century, faced with an overcrowded and unsanitary Old Town, came the construction of Edinburgh's New Town to the north. By the early 1900s, to enjoy Edinburgh's dark corners, affluent New Town resident Stevenson had to cross the divide.

This schizophrenic Scottish capital was deemed necessary to prevent a London-bound upper-class exodus. In New Britannia, there was no room for complacency, and much of Edinburgh's forthcoming statuary (including monuments on Calton Hill) requires interpretation in this pan-British context. If the most glorious monument of them all was reserved for a Scot – Sir Walter Scott, the man whose pen reframed his country for the future – British equilibrium was found in Scott's hero, the Duke of Wellington. An exquisite Copenhagen rears up at incomers emerging from Edinburgh's Waverly Station; there is no finer representation of the Iron Duke and his mighty steed.

Does it matter that the duke never came to Scotland? 'Of course not,' scoffs a strident tour guide. 'He is pointing at Waterloo Place. He's amazing ... does my job for me.' Who better to point up this very British New Town with a new Waterloo Place than an (Anglo-Irish) British duke?

Establishment Edinburgh, led predominantly by the Tories, nodded their heads, the octogenarian Duke was suitably impressed, and John Steele's statue duly unveiled in front of Scotland's surviving Waterloo veterans in 1852.* Today, Establishment Edinburgh feels much the same. I talk to a former professor on the telephone. 'Wellington was very proud of his Scottish regiments,' he purrs. 'You must know about the Charge of the Scots Greys.' He offers me a touching exchange between a frail duke and Queen Victoria. 'What do I do about the sparrow problem in the palace?' enquired the young monarch. 'Sparrowhawks' the taciturn duke's reply.

'Wonderful stuff,' insists the professor and proceeds to elucidate on the relevance of Wellington's prime Edinburgh location. 'He stands in front of the National Records of Scotland, the first public building in the New Town. Designed by Robert Adams, it's fabulous. We needed someone very special, someone very pro-Scottish, in front of Register House. Its dome had not been put on because they had run out of money – too busy paying for all the duke's wars!'

He laughs. 'Now tell me, why is Wellington propped up by the horse's tail? Legs in the air? Eh?! What's the significance? You should know that.' But I don't. The records office staff say it signifies death in battle, but both warlord and steed survived.

'Tourists love him,' they insist and point to an information panel that explains Robert Adam's screen wall was moved back to accommodate the giant military man and his horse. Perched on the eastern edge of Princes Street, these days the pair take up an incongruous amount of space. Moving them has been mooted.

Lawyer Michael Gray, a lynchpin pro-cone campaigner behind Glasgow's Wellington, considers Edinburgh's bronze Wellington 'an inconvenience I have to walk around. We have little Greyfriars

---

* Steele also sculpted the Sir Walter Scott statue in Princes Street's Scott Monument.

Bobby statue and people like to touch his nose, and the Enlightenment's David Hume, people like to touch his toe. But Wellington is more anonymous. I think statues should be talked about, grumbled about even, but if a statue just gets in the way or is frustrating …'

Michael has little truck with this British version of Scotland. If Glasgow's Wellington is saved by the cone, Edinburgh's Wellington has no equivalent redeeming feature. Apparently, being a great statue on a plinth is no longer enough. 'The New Town was a British triumph, a symbol of monarchy, union, and military victory. It was clearly of its time. But that's not the political mood now. We can't rebuild the New Town, but we could move a statue …'

These days, Edinburgh has lost none of its schizophrenic appeal. Young forces are afoot who consider Wellington passé, unhelpful even, while the old brigade take solace in the past. Perhaps there is a fateful symbolism behind Copenhagen's raised legs after all. How long can his bronze tail bear the weight of this new, indignant Scotland?

CHAPTER 13

THE CRIMEAN WAR

In the middle of the nineteenth century, the Crimean War delivered a sea change in commemoration. Waged to protect access to Britain's imperial interests in the East against Russia, this was the first European conflict to receive extensive, on-the-ground coverage in the British press. Unprecedented media attention proved transformative in a war that, beyond the Charge of the Light Brigade, is today almost exclusively remembered through the heroics of two women.

43. Crimean War Memorial, Bath Abbey Cemetery, Bath, 1856

Crimean War, Crimean Peninsula, 1853–1856

As memorials go, this obelisk looks unremarkable. It is tall but, at 20 feet, not outlandishly so, and made of white pennant stone that has weathered poorly. The craftsman, Samuel Rogers, was local (other works of his can be found in surrounding Widcombe) and the location is conventional: the memorial stands in Bath Abbey Cemetery, flanked by a yew tree and headstones of the long dead. A dog-walker stops to chat. Nowadays, this feels like her private park, but back then she assures me 'the good and the great drove their carriages up this way'. As for the obelisk, 'more than 15,000 people turned up for its unveiling'.

It was 29 May 1856 – Peace Day, a national celebration marking the end of the Crimean war. Bath's procession stood out. Crowds cheered, North Somerset Yeomanry played the 'Dead March' and minute guns were discharged from Beechen Cliff. The city had good reason to be proud. Their memorial was pioneering: look closely and the faded inscription features the names of thirteen men, from major general to humble private, including William Shell, 'seaman and first who fell in the war'. This was a significant departure in a country accustomed to remembering war through giant reincarnations of Nelson and Wellington.

Today, it is commonly assumed that the mass killings which defined World War I drove a rethink in war commemoration, when in fact the first tentative efforts to memorialise rank-and-file soldiers began more than half a century earlier. Inspired by a widening franchise and the power of pen and picture, war reporting became established practice in the Crimea, the British Army's only European war between 1816 and 1914. Over tea and marmalade, under Bath's high Georgian ceilings, news of unnecessary death and the heroics of ordinary men found a new, engaged, upper-middle-class audience.

A costly military engagement, triggered by Russia's overreach in the Near East with the invasion of (what is now) Romania, pitched Britain, France and the Ottoman Empire against the Russian bear. Britain's subsequent attack on Crimea's Sevastopol came after Russia's defeat in Silistria; this too was a play for power, one that led to the fall of Lord Aberdeen's government, unexpected given the public's initial support for the invasion. Even the sizeable death toll – 25,000 British soldiers – might not have turned opinion but for the graphic way in which Britain's uncensored press reported the horrific losses, compounded by unforgivable insanitary conditions. Alma, Balaklava, Inkerman, Sevastopol: foreign lands quickly became household names and ordinary soldiers heroes.

THE CRIMEAN WAR

The Times journalist Sir William Howard 'Balaclava' Russell was the headline act, his wartime missives delivering the famous 'thin red line' epithet. Illustrators backed up his words, capitalising on new technologies and publishing increasingly graphic pictures that underscored eye-witness accounts. The *Illustrated London News* doubled its circulation accordingly. Elsewhere, a vibrant local press focused on stories of gallantry, loss and incompetence. The *Bath Chronicle* celebrated the hospital train which passed through their city; the paper named every local casualty and campaigned vigorously for better military conditions and supplies. In two short years, the free press changed the way Britain thought about war, fought war and commemorated war. Bath's unusual obelisk, with its thirteen individual names, speaks to that change.

Today, sitting in the quiet hush of Bath Abbey Cemetery, conflict feels a million miles away – and yet once more war rages in Crimea and beyond. The Russian meat-grinder has form, with new frontlines in Kharkhiv, Donetsk, Kherson, Kursk. Household names? Not quite. There are no British boots on the ground – it is exclusively Ukrainians fighting to uphold the West's cherished freedoms. Democratic support for their defence against Russian belligerence depends on press coverage at the same time that international journalism has shrunk beyond recognition and local papers knee-capped. Statistically, in the last five years, it was safer serving in Britain's military than to be a journalist covering the Ukraine war.

It's a Saturday morning and Karola has found the time to talk. Pierre Zakrzewski was her brother. He matters and so does his legacy. A fifty-five-year-old, London-based, French-Irish cameraman with years of experience in conflict zones, including Afghanistan and Iraq, Pierre knew what he was doing. And in the spring of 2022, filming for Fox News behind an ill-defined frontline in Ukraine, he had never felt less safe. This was a very different sort of war from the asymmetrical conflicts he'd previously covered. In Ukraine, just miles from Kyiv, with his little team – presenter Benjamin Hall and fixer Oleksandra Kuvchinova – he was trying to make sense of Europe's first full-scale invasion of a sovereign country since World War II.

'He had a safehouse to go to,' his sister explains. 'He said it was bearable. He was determined to tell the story of what Putin was doing. "I have to stay," he said.' Reliable, seasoned, safety-first Pierre – whose first and only line of defence was his press accreditation, a man who shot with a camera not with a gun – was determined to keep doing what he had always done: to make sure the most dangerous parts of the planet are not forgotten from the safety of our armchairs.

'We are not sure exactly what happened. We think a drone was involved but nothing is confirmed yet. Pierre was filming when they were hit. We have seen some of the footage. It was broadcast in a documentary on the first year anniversary of the attack.'

Karola is calm. She is fiercely proud of her big brother, who died on 14 March 2022 under Russian fire alongside twenty-four-year-old Oleksandra.[*] But questions remain unanswered. 'They were supposed to be untouchable. They were press. But boom. Suddenly against Russia they have a target on their back. You're supposed to be safe to do your job as press.'

I look at a picture of Karola's brother: his Irish twinkle, his bushy moustache, his zest for life. 'I am sorry,' I say. The words are horribly inadequate. In France, a war crimes tribunal is underway, in which Pierre's family are civil partners. 'We just want to get a bit more information.' Information, legacy, memory; Pierre's life was and is important. Karola wants to keep Ukraine in the headlines. And she wants to ensure her brother is not forgotten.

In a war zone, a free press is rarely free. At least fifteen journalists and media workers have been killed covering Ukraine's current fight

---

[*] Reporter Benjamin Hall, whose right leg has been amputated, was the only one in the vehicle to survive.

against Russia.* And yet, despite a proud legacy dating back to Crimea, war reporters have no monument in Britain. Last year, a campaign called On The Record was finally launched to change that; a memorial to Pierre, his fallen colleagues and their shared mission, the pursuit of truth in the fog of war.†

44. Florence Nightingale statue, Waterloo Place, London, 1915

Florence Nightingale, 1820–1910

The curator smiles. 'There's a problem with the statue. Florence is holding the wrong lamp. Hers wasn't a genie lamp.' She points to a more accurate Turkish paper lantern in the Florence Nightingale Museum's exhibition. Such trifles are unlikely to have bothered the 'lady of the lamp'; her beef would have been appearing in statue form at all. Florence Nightingale, the world's most famous nurse, left explicit instructions that 'no memorial whatever should mark the place where lies my Mortal Soul'.

The British Medical Association echoed their great lady's sentiment: 'We honour the memory of Miss Nightingale – on this side of idolatry – as much as any, but we do not think that the addition of a statue to the many grotesque and begrimed specimens that disfigure London is the best way of honouring her memory.'

But neither Florence Nightingale nor the BMA could control the momentum to mark her death. It's fitting, perhaps, that when the heroine of Crimea eventually appeared in 1915 (in the form of London's first named non-royal female statue), Britain was again at

---

* And at the time of writing, the Committee to Protect Journalists is working to establish whether the deaths of two others are related to their media work. https://cpj.org/invasion-of-ukraine/

† www.ontherecordmemorial.co.uk launched their campaign for the first memorial dedicated to journalists reporting from the frontline in May 2024.

war. Unveiled at 6 a.m. on a cold February morning, more than a century later I found Florence bathed in spring sunshine, her fixed expression gazing down from an aqua-blue sky. Two Spanish nurses stood by her pink granite plinth and asked for a picture with their hero. 'We learned about her at university. She turned nursing into a profession.' A previously lo-fi pursuit that often compounded soldiers' ill health, under Florence's exacting professionalism nurses started saving lives.

Her finest hour came in the Crimean War. Miles from home, sick men were dying like flies. *The Times* got straight to the point: 'Not only are there insufficient surgeons, not only are there no dressers and nurses, there is not even linen to make bandages. There is no preparation for the commonest of surgical operations. The French are greatly our superiors.'

In 1854, Florence headed out to Scutari, Britain's military base on the Bosphorus, with her own exclusive army: fourteen Protestant nuns, ten Roman Catholic nuns and fourteen professional nurses. Exacting standards were paramount and recruitment restricted accordingly: 'In future, fat drunken dames of 14 stone and over must be barred. The provision of bedsteads is not strong enough.' (Today, her eponymous museum in the grounds of London's St Thomas's Hospital cautions: 'Here you will discover a woman of many talents – and flaws.')

Nightingale's rigorous approach saved lives, with far-reaching consequences for nursing well into the twentieth century, which she dominated as a leading feminine icon. By the 1980s, my own generation of impatient feminists found one-note Florence messaging tired (did no other professional woman merit a presence on our national currency?). We dreamed of becoming doctors, not nurses. To embrace Florence felt like a cop-out.

Scroll forward forty years and Nightingale has been recast again. Daisy Wright is fifteen and studying GCSE history. 'I respect Florence,' she insists. 'She's a statistician.' These days, the curriculum has pushed beyond conventional Nightingale tropes and found a rigorous analyst, a Victorian woman whose narrative leans into current STEM ambitions for contemporary schoolgirls. 'Like, she literally invented the pie chart!' Or, in the words of Professor Sir David Spiegelhalter, Nightingale 'essentially ran a one-woman think-tank for evidence-based policy'. The first female member of the Statistical Society of London,* Florence's ground-breaking data visualisation laid bare the brutal realities of soldiering and sickness. On her return from the Crimea, she was blunt: without change, the government might as well 'take 1,100 men out upon Salisbury Plain and shoot them'.

By 1915, the horrors unfolding in France would have been even worse but for the basic sanitation standards ushered in under Nightingale. Unlike troops on the Eastern Front, British soldiers escaped the devastation of typhus and cholera thanks to her meticulous graphs that spelled out the dangers of poor sanitation and over-crowding. The same concepts were belatedly recast during the Pandemic. Hands. Face. Space.

The 1915 arrival of Nightingale's statue, in Victorian smock and cap, demanded a reshuffle in London's Waterloo Place. The main Guards Crimean War Monument (once berated as an 'eyesore') was pushed back some thirty yards, and her great friend and facilitator, the war secretary Sidney Herbert, moved from the War Office to parallel his star turn.† Today, there is a gentle symmetry to this triumvirate, with Florence looking wistfully forwards, beyond the busy road, to yet more statues of great men. Given her sex and the era, Nightingale's achievements are little short of a miracle. Perhaps the genie lamp is artistic licence for her magic touch.

---

* Now known as the Royal Statistical Society.

† First erected in 1859, it is often said this was the first public war memorial dedicated to all ranks. However, Bath's Crimean War Memorial cites rank and file and was erected three years earlier.

45. Mary Seacole statue, St Thomas's Hospital Garden, London, 2016

Mary Seacole, 1805–1881

In 1994, a BBC radio documentary on the British-Jamaican nurse, Mary Seacole, opened with the 'screams and cannon fire of the Crimean war', a tableau into which a 'small but determined woman' was introduced, someone who offered 'comfort, nursing and an outspoken voice on the ordinary soldier's behalf'. The male narrator imagined listeners presumed he was talking about Florence Nightingale, before insisting that 'there was another heroine of the Crimea and one whose story has been all but eclipsed over time by the Lady with the Lamp'.

His bald statement speaks to a wearying paradigm long baked into British history: apparently the public can only manage one female hero amidst the bustling cast of officer-gentlemen who adorn our history books and streets. That Florence Nightingale became the convenient catch-all for invisible legions of women attached to war suited the military establishment. Nor is it a coincidence that blame for this blanket-coverage is ascribed to Nightingale herself, not the patriarchy she mastered. Mary Seacole – on the one hand just another woman – challenged that invisible female space with an additional identity; she was a Jamaican-born woman of colour ('I am a creole and have good Scotch blood coursing through my veins'). 'Intersectional' Mary was not invisible. Rather, she was inconvenient, both to the Victorian ruling class and the retelling of their great times. Perhaps inevitably, it required a Jamaican-inspired initiative in the 1980s to trigger today's resurgent interest in a woman who self-identified as a 'doctress, nurse and "mother"'.

It was harder for Mary. A passionate champion of the British Empire, she arrived in London in 1854 wanting to work in the Crimean disaster zone. But her numerous approaches all met with rejection: at the War Office, the Quarter Master General's Office, the home of Sidney Herbert, at the Crimean Fund and yes, so too, rejection from Nightingale's recruiters. 'Now,' she writes, 'I am not for a single instant going to blame the authorities who would not listen to the offer of a motherly woman to go to the Crimea and nurse her sons there.' Yet that is precisely where blame lay. Tearful and alone in a cold London street, she finally asked: 'Was it possible that American prejudices against colour had some root here?'

Stonewalled despite impressive nursing credentials with British soldiers, Mary was stating what we now know to be true: the British Empire and the hierarchy that governed it was inherently racist. Mary was rejected because 'my blood flowed beneath a somewhat duskier skin than theirs'. It is this bar Mary had to climb over, not just in life, but also in death.

MARY SEACOLE

LEST WE FORGET

Undeterred by rejection, off she went to the Crimea, self-funded – a businesswoman with wares to sell and a nursing trade to ply. She established the British Hotel near the frontline, providing succour for sick and recovering soldiers. Returning to Britain after the war, Mary was a star, with a royal fundraising gala held in her honour and a bestselling autobiography.* But this famous Black nurse had no hold over history; it was more than a hundred years before the present started catching up with the past. Only now does a bold new statue stand in her name and for her legacy. Bordering St Thomas's Hospital, a colossus eye-balling Big Ben, sizing up the Thames, bypassing the stone-wall of the world behind her, Mary has been reborn for a new generation.† With a knapsack of herbal remedies on her back, she is no longer 'a small woman' but rather a giant among men, a warrior who didn't take 'no' for an answer.

Red roses are scattered at her feet the day I visit. A group of tourists, commandeered by a London guide, look on. 'Isn't she the best? She's exceptional.' Lena, wrapped in a pink fur, is excited. A couple kiss for the camera with Mary as their backdrop. Someone has chalked 'International Women's Day' beside Mary's big boot. A man draws Lena into the Florence-versus-Mary debate. The tour guide tactfully suggests Mary was more motherly, before remembering that neither were mothers.‡ Would either have achieved greatness had they been?

It was at London's St Thomas's Hospital that the Nightingale Training School for Nurses first opened in 1860. It would be another century and a half before Mary finally arrived in the garden, Britain's

---

* *Wonderful Adventures of Mrs Seacole in Many Lands* was first published in 1857.

† Sculptor Martin Jennings erected a vertical bronze disc behind the figure of Mary, cast from an image of the earth near the site of her British Hotel in the Crimea, which – according to Jennings – performs both practical and symbolic functions.

‡ Sick soldiers referred to Mary as 'Mother Seacole'.

first named statue to a Black woman. Today she has bagged the top spot – a fearless flagship monument, standing at the coalface of Britain's NHS with its talented, international workforce. She speaks to this new era of identity politics. It is no coincidence that the momentum for her statue came just a few years before the Black Lives Matter campaign erupted. Once upon a time, Mary's story was buried for its difference. Now she is reborn in a very different London, one that sees itself in her.

CHAPTER 14

THE BOER WAR

In 1978, the disgraced former US president, Richard Nixon, argued that 'a great nation is certainly pretty able, usually, to fight a big war where everybody participates but it is terribly difficult for a big nation to fight a small war. The British found that out in the Boer War. We found that out in Vietnam.'* Imperial Britain eventually won the Second Boer War in 1902, but the human cost was huge. For the first time, commemoration of rank-and-file soldiers was widespread, with the militarisation of numerous public spaces. But the conflict's legacy remains complicated and, despite the erection of some 900 memorials, the war is sidelined in Britain's story.†

---

* Nixon was speaking at the Oxford Union as part of his rehabilitation tour.

† Sir James Gildea's *For Remembrance and in Honour of Those Who Lost Their Lives in the South African War, 1899–1902: Lest We Forget* identifies 900 Boer War-commemorating memorials including 520 in England, 150 in Scotland, and a number in Wales, Northern Ireland and the Channel Islands, as well as 230 in the wider British Empire.

THE BOER WAR

46. Boer War Memorial, Coombe Hill, Wendover, Buckinghamshire, 1904

Second Boer War, South Africa, 1899–1902

'I don't know what it stands for. It said South Africa on it.'

'Apparently it was struck by lightning and totally rebuilt.'

Bundling between the deciduous trees along the Ridgeway are two dozen walkers, members of a prominent Hindu community fundraising for an ambitious new India Gardens project in London. Of all ages, and kitted out in Lycra with walking sticks and backpacks, they are on a mission. Today, Coombe Hill. Tomorrow, Ben Nevis.

To the experienced climber, Coombe Hill doesn't cut the mustard. It is a modest mound pressed out from the flatlands of Buckinghamshire. But context is everything. Coombe Hill is the Chilterns' highest point, a rare 850-foot peak just half an hour from London, and a convenient perch from which to eye the prime minister's country pad, Chequers.

Like many impressive summits, there is a jewel in Coombe Hill's crown: it is home to one of Britain's outstanding war memorials. A beacon between the trees, the sixty-four-foot monument, capped with a golden finial, owns the landscape; its immediate rebuild after a 1939 lightning strike is testimony to the power of this local talisman. London's climbers may not know the history of the memorial, but they can't fail to see it. They clamber over it, sit on it, snap photos from it, and exclaim at the green and pleasant land unfolded beneath them. Exceptional Buckinghamshire is the Sunday takeaway from Coombe Hill, a timeless sentiment that chimes with the Edwardian memorial committee's ambitions when the summit was selected to remember Buckinghamshire's Boer War sacrifice.

As one professor tells me, 'The big thing about the South Africa war was how the British galvanised a high voluntary service effort.' That's one perspective. What began in 1899 as a 'little imperial war'

– intended to capitalise on the discovery of Transvaal gold and eliminate the independent Boer Republics – quickly deteriorated into ugly guerilla warfare. The British Army were outfought and outgunned by Afrikaner settlers deemed too 'backward' to manage the Gold Rush.* Scorched-earth policies were applied. Horror ensued. And confusion. How had a few Afrikaners humiliated the Great British Empire? Arthur Conan Doyle, reporting on the war, lamented that 'Napoleon and all his veterans have never treated us so roughly as these hard-bitten farmers with their ancient theology and their inconveniently modern rifles'.

'Black Week' – a period of three devastating losses for the British Army in December 1899 – triggered an unprecedented response back home. Men, moved by ideas of imperial adventure and uniformed glory, responded to the call-to-arms. Etonian officers were soon commanding volunteer bands of middle-class yeomanry and working lads, toughing it out in the African heat. Decades later, survivors recalled the horror.

'What me and my comrades went through, I can tell you, was starvation for months and months. We was all alive with lice.'

'A large number of men went sick, I included. I think I had typhoid fever … it really was a cruel time.'

Some 22,000 British soldiers, many of them volunteers, died in southern Africa, the majority felled by disease. The empire limped home to a victory, but at what cost? Civil society had lent into the army like never before and thousands of men were dead. For what? A brutal war involving highly questionable tactics (on which more later). Families and communities needed something to show for their loss. Myopic triumphalism would not do.

What came after 1902 wasn't just the most widespread commemorative movement Britain had seen (there is a Boer War memorial somewhere near you), but also the most inclusive. Coombe Hill led

---

* Afrikaners descended from predominantly Dutch settlers who first arrived at the Cape of Good Hope in 1652.

the way. An outstanding obelisk of Aberdeen granite, the monument's iconography borrowed from standard commemorative tropes and honoured not just the victory but also the sacrifice, naming all of Buckinghamshire's fallen men.

Victorian Britain had witnessed the democratisation of death; funeral processions, horse-drawn with black plumes and cap doffing, were part of daily life. Increasingly people expected to reach a great age and to mark their departure with great ceremony. Small wonder, then, that great care was taken to remember the premature deaths of Buckinghamshire's majestic youth. Every one of the original 148 names and ranks cited was signed off by the War Office.* The Establishment needed to be seen to engage with the loss of each individual soldier. This was a shared sacrifice: local grandee, Major General Lord Chesham, advised the memorial committee. On the obelisk, his only son, Lieutenant Charles Cavendish, is named, and so too local stable hands and farriers whose response to the call cost their lives.

Unveiled in November 1904, extra trains were laid on at Wendover to accommodate the hundreds who came to pay respects. Something special had begun. The following year, protestors on the hilltop demanded year-round public access and, by the 1920s, the National Trust was overseeing the summit. Fused together, the memorial and its location proved greater than the sum of their parts. People have been walking up Coombe Hill ever since; the monument, freshly renovated in 2010, welcomes 100,000 walkers every year.

'What war? Did you say the Boer War?' Mike shrugs. Beneath his cap, he isn't interested. The view is what he's come for. 'See down there! That's the new HS2 that they're digging.' An endorphin hit is

---

* In 2015, a second replacement plaque was fitted, now with 159 names, including eleven recently discovered. For a meticulous record of the memorial and those commemorated on it, visit: https://www.roll-of-honour.com/Buckinghamshire/CoombeHillBoerWar.html

triggered upon arrival at the summit (if the sun is shining, there's even an ice cream van in the car park). From Coombe Hill, Buckinghamshire rarely disappoints; long ago, a forgotten war turned it into a memorable destination.

47. Second Boer War Memorial, Duncombe Place (opposite York Minster), York, 1905

Second Boer War, South Africa, 1899–1902

It was tacked on as an afterthought. I had not come to York, or indeed the Minster, to look at a Boer War memorial. I did not know of it. Of course, that in itself is a naïve statement. In all Britain's big cities, there is a memorial to the war in South Africa. The death toll was later dwarfed by World War I, but in Edwardian England the Boer War and its fall-out was unmatched in living memory. Wide-scale commemoration served two purposes: it acknowledged private grief and platformed public pride (the war machine needed to encourage new recruits). Today, the performative manifestations of Edwardian remembering meet a very different response: York is equivocal about the Grade II Boer War Memorial that stands opposite the minster's entrance in Duncombe Place.

Many of Britain's historic centres of worship are re-interrogating monuments erected during the country's imperial zenith. St Paul's Cathedral is a case in point with its 50 Voices project. York Minster has not engaged in an equivalent list, nor does the Boer War Memorial come directly under its jurisdiction. But there is rumoured disquiet, including unsubstantiated claims on a guided tour that cast the memorial in a negative light. Interest piqued, I ask to see the monument. After all, the Boer War and its imperial backdrop have notorious associations. A statue of Britain's mining magnate Cecil Rhodes, whose backing of the disastrous Jameson Raid against gold-rich Transvaal helped prompt the Second Boer War, has been torn down at the University of Cape Town (accusations of racism the primary driver) and his bust decapitated in its City Park. Back in England, the imperialist's likeness still stands in Oxford University's Oriel College, through no lack of effort on the students' part.

In Britain, the conflict, like Rhodes, has long proved uncomfortable. Historians unanimously agree this was 'not a good war' – unjustifiable aims, dubious tactics, a grievously high death toll and success so hard won that jingoistic euphoria after the relief of Mafeking gifted the English language a new verb: to 'maffick'.

Straight after the war, commemoration was not without controversy. Manchester's Last Shot broke new ground. A standard depiction of the officer class was substituted for an ordinary soldier carrying a bayonet through the city's centre, supported by a wounded comrade handing him a bullet. The arresting scene proved too graphic for certain early twentieth-century sensibilities.* A hundred years later and attentions have moved elsewhere. Newcastle's South African War Memorial, in the city's Haymarket district, has been at the eye of a fresh storm. The Black Lives Matter campaign insisted the astonishing 80-foot monument be reassessed; locals had long dubbed its bronze Winged Victory 'the shitty angel'.

Council documents cite claims the war was 'a colonialist enterprise' which 'does not reflect well on the history of Britain'. But the monument honours 370 dead soldiers from local regiments who fought for king and country. If we follow this logic, in 100 years' time memorials to Britain's recent fallen in Iraq and Afghanistan will be subject to equivalent interrogation. Given the speed at which the cultural zeitgeist moves, it won't even take that long.

In Newcastle, the nub of the issue appears to be Winged Victory's outsized grandstanding over an equivocal war, rather than the dead soldiers it represents. Two new interpretation boards are pending:

---

* The sculptor, William Hamo Thornycroft, an important member of the New Sculpture movement in the 1890s, was also responsible for King Alfred in Winchester, Monument 5, and Oliver Cromwell in Westminster, Monument 23.

one providing historical context, the other local opinion. The shitty angel has survived – for the moment at least.

But what about York's Boer War Memorial that stands on hallowed ground outside Christian Europe's finest gothic cathedral? Cross the road and enter Duncombe Place; there, shaded among the trees, is a dilapidated retro-gothic monument that begs sympathy, not ire. Wildflowers grow between finials, a fat pigeon nests in the lantern form and no one has replaced a missing statue taken out by lightning. Like an abandoned turret that time forgot, I found the memorial filled with demob-happy teenagers, perched on the octagonal steps, enjoying tobacco and cola and the prospect of a long, free summer.

THE BOER WAR

'Dunno, Miss. Is it for the Cold War?'
'Or that fight at Stamford Bridge?'
'I didn't do history GCSE.'

It wouldn't have mattered if they did. The Boer War is not on the curriculum and York has far finer treasures. But, in 1905, the city could not forget this war. The plaque recalls a staggering 1,459 local dead.

The many names are hard to discern, but not the military statuary ringing the summit, each representing a different force. Standing at the back between an infantryman and a cavalryman is, unmistakably, a nurse. Likewise, listed among the dead are women from the Army Nursing Service Reserve. In lessons learned during the Crimean war, the Boer War was the first to deploy large numbers of nurses, but York's monument is the only one I have come across in Britain that acknowledges their number among the fallen. I message the minster on return to London. Rather than cancel or contest it, York's Boer War Memorial is crying out for tender loving care.

48. Statue of Horatio Herbert Kitchener, Khartoum Road, Chatham, Kent, 1960

Field Marshal Horatio Herbert Kitchener, 1850–1916

How can I select an 'English angel' as one of my definitive 100 monuments to war if she has not been memorialised in Britain? While I ponder that conundrum, here is historian Nick Hewitt on Field Marshal Horatio Herbert Kitchener: 'He was a celebrity before there were celebrities. He lent his image to the biggest military recruitment campaign Britain had ever seen. And he died doing his duty mid-World War I, travelling out to Russia to keep them in the war.'

Nick curates a museum in Orkney and lives near the islands' Kitchener Memorial that overlooks the North Sea coast. It was where Kitchener drowned on 5 June 1916 when the armoured cruiser,

HMS *Hampshire*, hit a German mine and sank. This remote monument (and many others) underline Britain's preferred version of Kitchener, the moustached hero behind Britain's vast volunteer army in the early years of the Great War. But the Kitchener I visited in Chatham – on a mighty steed, replete with plumed hat and imperial pose – was not sculpted to commemorate the death of a World War I hero. This statue began life in India, before moving to Sudan, as a deliberate celebration of the British Empire's most lethal operator.

It was in 1898 as 'the machine of the Sudan' that Kitchener achieved public renown. In blazing black boots, sporting that trademark moustache and riding a white charger, the major general and his kilted Highlanders thundered into Omdurman with rifles and machine guns and mowed down 11,000 sand-dwelling, spear-carrying dervishes in patterned smocks. The death of Britain's General Charles Gordon of Khartoum had been avenged and Sudan was subjugated. The new Lord Kitchener of Khartoum returned home a household name among fans of empire. Two years later in 1900, and knee-deep in a Boer war they were not winning, it was to this ruthless man that Britain's military top brass turned.

In command in South Africa from 1900, Kitchener is widely credited with bringing the Boer War to an end. Exhibiting characteristic brutality (some have tried to pin this on a father with masochistic tendencies), he doubled down on a scorched-earth policy to flush out the obdurate Dutch famers and cripple the Afrikaner communities helping them. Towns were erased, crops destroyed and livestock killed. Hundreds of thousands of women and children were herded into concentration camps, where disease was rife. Thousands perished.

'Yes, that's what we call them – concentration camps – without any sense of irony or controversy.' Lienkie Diedericks is an Afrikaans-speaking PhD graduate working in London. 'We learned about "Butcher Kitchener" in year 8 and 9 at school. He was considered a war criminal and Emily an "English angel".' The angel Lienkie refers to is Emily Hobhouse, a Cornish vicar's daughter and leading opponent of the war in South Africa, where she travelled in 1900 to highlight the desperate situation in the camps. 'She was vocal about conditions in both the Black and white camps.'

Emily Hobhouse was before her time; a liberal thinker, a suffragist and a middle-aged woman who made her name calling out British foreign policy and forcing an Establishment rethink. Kitchener was so rattled by 'that bloody woman' he had Emily deported from South Africa in 1901. But her voice had already been heard. Liberal leader Sir Henry Campbell-Bannerman addressed the Commons: 'When is a war not a war? When it is carried out by methods of barbarism in South Africa.' A War Office enquiry was duly held. Emily was not invited onto the subsequent committee, although it arrived at many of her conclusions.

Cornwall-based museum curator Tehmina Goskar has worked hard to drive interest in Emily, who was born in the village of St Ive, near Liskeard, and spoke truth to power long before it was fashionable. Online, there are the remnants of a campaign that Tehmina led to address the region's all-male statuary. 'In the end we hit the buffers. How do you get names like Emily's to be household? She was a massive pacifist during the World War I and famous for intervening in the Boer War in South Africa. The newspaper reports are eye-opening. Under the male gaze she is demonised, that is what you do to women who are too powerful. Or you dismiss them as insignificant.'

Emily's absence in Cornwall, and Britain more broadly, is sorely predictable. Meanwhile, in Chatham, Kitchener enjoys all the props of military grandeur, riding high beneath the former Kitchener Barracks, effortlessly facing down his critics.[*] The statue was a regift from Sudan where Kitchener was unceremoniously dumped, post-independence. Finally, ingloriously, the statue arrived in Britain and was unveiled by MP Christopher Soames in 1960. Back then,

---

[*] Kitchener Barracks is now a swanky new housing development bearing the same name.

the 'winds of change' had not reached Chatham, the Kent home of Britain's historic naval dockyard, where Kitchener attended the Royal School of Military Engineering. These days, locals grumble, but just as memorialisation requires Establishment support, so too does (most) statue removal. As for recycling Kitchener into a statue of Hobhouse, Tehmina laughs. Surely, we are all allowed our dreams?

Today, to see a monument that reflects Emily's legacy requires a trip to South Africa. Her ashes were placed in a niche at the foot of the National Women's Monument in Bloemfontein. White pavings lead up to a central plinth, the sculptures speaking to a mother's pain, all too often the silent collateral in war. Emily's words were read at the 1913 inauguration: 'To the brave South African women, who, sharing the danger that beset their land and dying for it, affirmed for all times and for all peoples the power of women to sacrifice life and more than life for the common weal.'

PART FOUR
MECHANISED KILLING

CHAPTER 15

UNKNOWN WARRIORS, EMPTY TOMBS

In August 1914, a divided Europe cracked in two, the Entente versus the Central Powers, and dragged much of the world with them. The Great War's mechanised killing destroyed four imperial powers, planted Bolshevism in Russia and paved the way for a second global conflict. Closer to home, Britain retained its empire and crown, but the slaughter of so many young men transformed war commemoration. How to remember and honour imperial Britain's fallen soldiers when more than half a million had no known grave and the vast majority were buried where they fell?

49. The Cenotaph, Whitehall, London, 1920

World War I, 1914–1918

'You know it's something important if the royal family is there.'

In one sentence, Jacqui Thompson articulates the value of Britain's most famous family. When it came to the commemoration of senior aircraftman Gary Thompson, Jacqui's late husband blown up in 2008 by a Taliban anti-tank mine in Afghanistan, it was Prince Harry (then a working royal) who honoured his fallen comrades and unveiled the Bastion Wall in the National Memorial Arboretum.

'That was a very emotional day for me. I didn't want Harry to see me cry so I didn't speak to him, but I was glad he was there.'

That long-established, integral connection between commemoration, soldiering and royalty acquired renewed prominence during World War I.* Unremarkable George V was remarkable for his unstinting attendance at army march pasts, military inspections and medal parades. His was the people's army and he was the people's monarch – in France, falling off his horse near the frontline; back in Britain, out and about among his soldiers. This modern, visible version of monarchy, born amidst carnage and despair, gifted the nation a point of order around which hopes for peace could coalesce and grow. Over the last century, that same commemorative umbilical cord between royalty and the military has been doggedly maintained and reiterated.

Walk through the National Memorial Arboretum in Staffordshire today and, among the hundreds of emotive structures, the same names reappear again and again: unveiled by HRH the Princess Royal, or HRH Sophie the Duchess of Wessex, or HRH the Duke of Kent. Walk down Whitehall, stand before the extraordinary, eerily perfect Cenotaph and who springs to mind? The Glorious Dead? Or Glorious Royalty? Stooping in the face of age and infirmity, the monarch lays a scarlet wreath and honours the fallen, then and now.

The Cenotaph was shrouded in Union Jack flags when the funeral procession briefly paused for the unknown warrior's coffin to be adorned by a weary king, on the eleventh hour of the eleventh day in November 1920. George V then pressed a small button and two enormous flags ceremoniously fell away from the world's most famous 'empty tomb' – Whitehall's Cenotaph – and a two-minute silence was observed.

A makeshift wooden cenotaph had been the central feature of a London Peace Day parade the previous July and quickly gave way to

---

* Queen Victoria had taken a particular interest in the Boer War, a conflict that killed her grandson, Prince Christian Victor of Schleswig-Holstein.

this permanent edifice of perfection carved from Portland stone. Within eighteen months of the war's end, celebration became commemoration. Remembrance usurped victory. Early twentieth-century war, with its mindless, mechanised killing, meant something very different from what had come before. And the centrepiece of that expression was, and has remained, architect Edwin Lutyens' Cenotaph.

Much has been written about the design of this universal monument to war. Soon to be replicated in catalogues, stamped out in a variety of forms across Britain and beyond, Lutyens' eye for classical form and abstract perfection articulated a silent, universal grief which few could criticise. The avoidance of religious or national symbolism gifted generations a monument that speaks to everyone. The subsequent proliferation of war memorials suggests that the Cenotaph was just the start point – a totem to Establishment recognition that helped legitimise localised, personalised and religious iterations of loss and honour.

For its time, this architectural structure was exceptionally inclusive – an umbrella statement for more than a million dead men across Britain and the empire. With his meticulous notebooks and mathematical equations, Lutyens precisely calculated the Cenotaph. The classical science between the lines that converge upwards to compensate for the errors of the eye has long been a point of marvel. Even today, after a hundred years of wear, the strikingly tall pylon is graciously present, an unobstructive support for the universal sarcophagus.

Testament to its success, this edifice born of a Peace Day to commemorate the dead had become the stage from which 1920s strikers aired their grievances – and, more recently, prey to 'hate marchers', 'counter protestors' and graffiti artists. As I write, two people have been arrested for spray-painting, in support of Gaza, '180,000 killed' at its base. The ultimate symbol of our hard-fought freedom, the nation's war monument is increasingly hostage to its own iconic status. In November 2023, the Metropolitan Police successfully cleared the area of far-right 'Cenotaph defenders' in time for our elderly King Charles to lay his wreath on Armistice Day. As Jacqui so brilliantly put it, 'You know it's something important if the royal family is there.'

50. The Tomb of the Unknown Warrior, Westminster Abbey, 1920
World War I, 1914–1918

Justin Saddington's face lights up. The curator at the National Army Museum admits it was 'the most amazing project I've worked on'.

The story behind the Tomb of the Unknown Warrior unfolds like a true crime drama. It was the dead of night, and Saint-Pol-sur-Ternoise was cloaked in the eerie black of a cold French November, when the head of the British Army in France, Brigadier General Louis John Wyatt, set about his invidious task of selecting a body. Or was it a privilege? After all, by 1920, bodies were commonplace, but this one was to be exceptional, the solitary military cadaver that made it back to British soil. An everyman symbol of the glorious dead.

'There is no statement of how the process was done,' says Justin. 'Wyatt just happened to be the brigadier at the time. He had to choose a body from several unidentified exhumed ones selected from different points on the Western Front. The whole thing was shrouded in mystery. No one is quite sure what happened to the bodies that weren't selected.' Justin lists several options as to where (the probable three) remaining unknown warriors may have ended up.

This unlikely back-story of gravediggers and dark nights is a far cry from the shiny acceptability of Westminster's Tomb of the Unknown Warrior. The black Belgian marble slab, inscribed with its famous epitaph 'Beneath this stone rests the body of a British Warrior unknown by name or rank' and encircled with a forest of paper-poppies in the abbey's nave, gives no hint of the macabre process behind the unnamed soldier's selection.

UNKNOWN WARRIORS, EMPTY TOMBS

It's highly unlikely, but not inconceivable, that he wasn't even a soldier, hence the warrior title. At the beginning of World War I, the Royal Navy was Britain's senior service (a naval unit operated on the Western Front) and the Royal Air Force wasn't an independent service until April 1918. The tomb needed to represent every dead comrade. Most important was its ability to speak to all grieving parties: the broken mother of a lost private, the air officer without a crew, the bereaved princess mourning her officer brother.

Five years after the war's end, Lady Elizabeth Bowes-Lyon paused beyond Westminster Abbey's west door to lay her wedding bouquet on the grave of the Unknown Warrior. Her elder brother, Fergus, had been killed in 1915 at the Battle of Loos. His leg was blown off and his chest riddled with bullets. The royal wedding of his baby sister was one of the first public appearances that Countess Cecilia, his grieving mother, had made since her son's death. Having deposited the flowers, Elizabeth continued empty-handed down the aisle towards her bridegroom, Britain's future George VI.

The question of what to do with the dead from imperial Britain's enormous, predominantly civilian army was highly charged. In the same year Fergus died, 1915, Britain banned the exhumation and repatriation of fallen soldiers. In previous wars – Waterloo, Crimea, South Africa – the majority of the dead were buried in pits near the battlefield. Only the sons of the wealthy were brought home. But like no other conflict, World War I had mobilised the ordinary man and, from 1916, conscripted him. It was vital that mass support was maintained. Illegal attempts by notable families to reclaim officer-sons were met with a stiff reminder of the 'difficulties of treating impartially the claims advanced by persons of different social standings'. After the war, cemeteries were erected on the other side of the Channel, but it was an imprecise science. Amid the chaos, in November 1918, more than 200,000 British men were still missing.

Back in Britain, a two-minute silence and mushrooming local shrines and scrolls highlighted the ghastly void where a body might have been.

LEST WE FORGET

'Have you news of my boy Jack?'
Not this tide.
'When d'you think that he'll come back?'*

In July 2024, I meet Jacqui Thompson. As previously mentioned, sixteen years earlier her husband, senior aircraftman Gary, was killed in Kandahar, Afghanistan. Jacqui fixes me with her grey-blue eyes: 'Because they brought Gary's body home, I can't imagine what it would've been like if he hadn't come back.'

Jacqui then proceeds to relive a day etched out in a kaleidoscope of competing colours. 'I will never feel anything like that again.' There were the logistics required to get her large family into Wiltshire's RAF Lyneham. 'They treated us so well. Military precision.' She looks up and smiles. 'I thought "I am not going to cry," I was determined not to miss any of it.' Re-entering Britain on a C-17 troop carrier, with the ceremony overseen by the Queen's Colour Squadron, and fellow service personnel bearing Gary's flag-draped coffin into a hearse, Jacqui 'felt like I would shatter into a million pieces'. And then homewards to Nottingham, for a funeral with the vicar who married them. A pot of ashes still sits alongside all his 'bits and bobs' in a cabinet made of oak. 'How can I part with him?'

It is over small details that we shed a tear. God bless Jacqui and her Gary. I assure her that she has helped me reach back to 1920, when the groundswell of opinion was unstoppable and the press ran with the idea of anonymity. After the war, the families of those lost longed to 'shatter into a million pieces', but for the lack of a body. And so the germ of an idea first conceived in 1916 by the Reverend David Railton, an army chaplain stationed on the Western Front, was revived and enacted: imperial Britain's very own unknown warrior. He departed on 8 November from Saint-Pol-sur-Ternoise, onwards to Boulogne, across to Dover, and by train to Victoria, where he rested overnight. Millions lined the coffin's autumnal route

---

* Rudyard Kipling, *My Boy Jack*, 1915.

through London to Westminster Abbey, pausing briefly at the Cenotaph, where the king added a wreath of red roses and bay leaves. His Majesty's hand-written card read: 'Unknown and yet well known; as dying and behold they live.'

My boy Jack. And yours too.

51. The Belfast Cenotaph, Donegall Square West, Belfast, 1929

World War I, 1914–1918

Unlike the rest of the United Kingdom, World War I plays a far bigger part in Northern Ireland's national story than World War II. Fearful of destabilising relations in the newly created north and worried about nationalists acquiring guns, no conscription was introduced in the province in World War II. For this fraught corner of the British Isles, it is World War I, particularly the Battle of the Somme, that is held up as a symbol of national pride among the Unionist community.

To understand more, I approach Nicholas Tate, a BBC Ulster journalist. Before we meet, he sends photographs of Somme memorials pinned to the brickwork of residential streets near his Belfast home. Alongside traditional silhouetted soldier-and-poppy iconography are the hallowed words: 'Lest We Forget'. Beneath giant banners, a uniformed group of girls march past, bearing Ulster and Union flags. These community-driven commemorations are not confined to the Somme anniversary in July; they spread throughout the year. The eastern quarter of Belfast does not take its identity for granted. As Nicholas explains, the deaths of men of the 36th Ulster Division at the Somme (some 5,500 in the first two days) are considered a 'blood sacrifice' – the community's ultimate commitment to a continued British union.

When I arrive in Belfast, we upscale from Somme murals to the city's Cenotaph: a monument of epic proportions built in 1929, girdled by a colonnade of Greek order columns, complete with cornice and balustrade. This is a memorial fit for an imperial city, which is what Belfast once was, its docks the enormous jaws of empire that serviced the world's shipping lanes, alongside industrial Glasgow and Liverpool. In this British context, and with the prospect of a third Irish Home Rule bill looming, politics in north-east Ireland before August 1914 took on a paramilitary edge. Ahead of the first fatal shot being fired in Sarajevo, ethno-religious tensions crystallised with the formation of the Ulster Volunteer Force, armed (ironically) by Germany. Under the canny stewardship of Unionist Edward Carson, Protestant Ulstermen refused to be handed over to a Dublin parliament without a fight. The Cenotaph sits within the grounds of Belfast City Hall, where on 28 September 1912 the Ulster Covenant was signed by nearly half a million Unionist men and women: a solemn, binding oath to resist Irish Home Rule.

Within two years, a greater call came: to take the fight to Germany across the English Channel. The same Ulstermen turned their military training and discipline to the service of Britain and her empire. They were mown down in their thousands. After World War I, and in the wake of a bloody Irish struggle, the partition of 1921 recognised the unique British status of Northern Ireland, a separate entity from an independent Republic of Ireland. Ever since, the Unionist community have weaponised their forefathers' World War I loyalty and sacrifice.

But Northern Ireland is a tale of two halves. Protestant Ulstermen died in French trenches alongside their Catholic Irish neighbours. I meet Social Democratic and Labour Party leader Claire Hanna in London. If her political dreams came true, she would represent South Belfast in Dublin not London but, one of a few moderates in Northern Irish politics, Claire works for all her constituents and that currently involves sitting in Westminster's House of Commons. Born into a Catholic Irish family, it was only recently that Claire discovered she has a personal stake in Remembrance Day. 'My father's cousin joined the Royal Irish Rifles and died in France aged nineteen in August 1916. I had no idea.'

Previously renowned in the family as the cheeky sixteen-year-old telegram boy who snuck into a ceremonial Unionist photograph celebrating the signing of the Covenant, Dennis Hanna's tragic end at the Battle of the Somme was not something Claire's politically charged family shouted about. The 1916 Easter Rising in Dublin raised the stakes for Irish independence; dying for the British Empire was to have backed the wrong cause. Claire presumes 'the fate of Dennis has been excised' because 'having a dead British soldier in the family' would have been embarrassing.

More than a century on, Dennis's previously unacknowledged death is better understood. Claire travelled to France to find his grave and while, unlike her Unionist colleagues, she believes 'Dennis and many thousands like him were sacrificed in a needless and unjust war', for her the real sadness is that he was written out of his own family's history because of politics.

These days, Nationalists join Unionists to lay a wreath at the Belfast Cenotaph on Armistice Day.

52. The Bristol Cenotaph, Colston Avenue, Bristol, 1932
World War I, 1914–1918

In 2022, the 'Colston Four' were acquitted of the toppling of slave trader Edward Colston's statue in Bristol's city centre and tipping it into the harbour. Two years after that fevered summer of 2020, the city caught the world's imagination once more. George Ferguson, its former mayor, concedes that the four defendants' single act of defiance 'did more for Bristol than anything we politicians tried to do in terms of recognition'.* The court heard the felling of Colston placed Bristol 'on the right side of history' and how the 1895 statue was 'so indecent and potentially abusive that it constituted a crime'.

---

* George Ferguson was Bristol's first mayor. He was independent and served between 2012 and 2016.

LEST WE FORGET

Today, Colston, rescued from the water, lies on the other side of Bristol's harbour, shackled and humiliated in a museum pen, an object of vilification, even pity. Opinion in the city was split regarding the statue's demise, but its ignominious end undeniably offers Bristol's remaining statuary a new beginning. Prior to Colston's fall from grace, his graven image had dominated Bristol's recent civic and political conversations. And when council inertia proved too much, it was his removal that hogged the headlines. Beyond questions regarding the empty plinth, few have interrogated the broader space that Colston's statue left behind in (ahem) Colston Avenue, and the view his removal has opened up.

Walk past grandiose statesman Edmund Burke, step across the bus lane and, minus the bulk of Colston, today your eye is drawn forwards, towards a patient, sombre structure of Bath stone, neither flash nor controversial. It is Bristol's Cenotaph, into which is baked a story almost as liberating as Colston's upheaval. It has stood for nearly a century but, like so much history involving women, it got used to being in second place.

Former mayor George is standing on the base, his scarlet trousers match the scatter of bright poppy rings. The Cenotaph's rectangular structure dwarfs him, but it is relatively small. War commemoration has a pecking order. 'It's about half the size of London's Cenotaph and I believe is the only one to refer to the fallen as "sons and daughters".' He points at the bronze plaque. Bristol's monument to World War I honours both men and women.* And it is the only cenotaph with a woman behind its design. Surely not a coincidence?

The details concerning architect Eveline Blacker's role are somewhat opaque. At a time when less than 0.1 per cent of architects were women, she cut her teeth with Bristol's best, George Oatley, before establishing her own firm alongside Harry Heathman.

---

* Approximately 4,500 service personnel from Bristol died in World War I. The vast majority were men, but women also served overseas in the First Aid Nursing Yeomanry, Women's Army Auxiliary Corps, Voluntary Aid Detachment, etc.

Heathman & Blacker were successful in the interwar period; winning a competition to design the local cenotaph just one of their landmark achievements. Predictably, Messrs Heathman and Blacker were presumed to be gentlemen. It took a female historian, Dr Sarah Whittingham, to uncover Eveline's story some sixty years later.

This gendered narrative makes Bristol's otherwise conventional cenotaph exceptional. The design takes much of its inspiration from Whitehall's, but while London's memorial tries to be all things to all people, its Glorious Dead are unquestionably male. Not so in Bristol. Beyond a great bronze sword pinned to its stone flank, this is as feminine as a cenotaph gets.

'Bristol's Sons and Daughters … died that Mankind might learn to live in peace.' The wrangling over the cenotaph's location went on so long that, by the time of its unveiling, public opinion had shifted. In 1932, any glorification of war had been dwarfed by an increasingly fragile peace. The inscription reflects that sentiment. If the cenotaph could not stop another war, it had a remarkable ripple effect on the surrounding architecture. George, a former architect himself, interprets the surrounding office blocks; the dimensions, the materials, the shapes are inspired by this cenotaph. Its influence quietly radiated out across the traffic island to create a new mid-century, post-art-deco style in Bristol.

Much of the city did not want the cenotaph erected here. Historic divisions between Anglicans and non-conformists, merchant venturers and dissenters tussled over the new Colston Avenue and the superior College Green opposite Bristol Cathedral.* Colston Avenue won out; the Green was considered too full of statuary already. So the cenotaph, with its peaceful, inclusive message, was erected on Bristol's recently paved River Frome, opposite the effigy of Colston, in the shadow of his reputation.

'It is odd, really,' sighs George. 'This cenotaph represents everything that Colston didn't with his dirty money.' Together, we

---

* Then known as Tramways, it has always been a significant traffic junction.

walk over to the latter's empty plinth and marvel at its narrative panels that remain intact. 'Philanthropist' Colston pats a small child on the head. George wants this plinth as space for contemporary installations, akin to the fourth plinth in Trafalgar Square. I worry they might obstruct the Cenotaph's quiet pre-eminence, so long in coming.

CHAPTER 16

PILLARS OF THE COMMUNITY

After World War I, Britain witnessed its largest-ever public art movement, as the population sought ways of expressing their grief for the deaths of over 880,000 people.* In a nod to a new era of suffrage and the sacrifice of the common man, soldiers were often listed not by rank, but alphabetically for the first time. Individual regiments and private organisations likewise sought to immortalise their dead. Schools, churches and village squares changed forever; today, those visible reminders of the cost of war still provide the backdrop to our daily lives.†

---

* This figure contrasts with the 1 million-plus fallen men and women, including those from the empire, who are represented in national memorials, such as the Cenotaph and the Tomb of the Unknown Warrior.

† The erection of memorials was a government-inspired initiative, with local authorities permitted to levy a small rate towards costs and maintenance, a power they still hold today. Locals decided on the memorials and how much money to raise.

LEST WE FORGET

53. Colchester War Memorial, High Street, Colchester, Essex, 1923
World War I, 1914–1918

'I moved to Colchester in 2009. Merville Barracks was home to our 16 Air Assault Brigade. I've been here ever since.' Former sergeant Ashleigh Percival-Borley is a pocket-sized blonde with a buzz cut and is leading the way through Castle Park in the heart of England's oldest town and newest city.* 'It's lovely, isn't it? I bring my daughter here.' She stops and looks at me. 'I am a contradiction. How do you deploy for six months and be a mother?' It's not a contradiction Ash has to wrestle with any more. After thirteen years of military service, she left the army in 2021.

'As a soldier, you are not meant to question. But, now I am studying for a history PhD, I think about things differently.' We walk through the park's majestic iron gates – 'A gift of Viscount and Viscountess Cowdray 1922' – and step into the commemorative climax of Colchester's war story. Meticulous town-planning, generous gifting (the Cowdray package included the Norman castle in the park) and exquisite sculpture has stood this ancient Roman town in good stead. The World War I memorial is more than 28 feet high; summer clouds chase Winged Victory, her sword pointing down in Christian reflection. Beneath her, Ash circles Peace ('Oh course she's a woman!') and doubles back to find England's manhood in the figure of St George, underfoot an impaled dragon, surely the defeated Central Powers?

This memorial is where Ash chooses to remember. She has paraded here often; the big band, the regiments all in a row, the march-past up to the town hall. 'I am inspired by the stories of soldiers. I feel connected to them.' A small plaque reads: 'The names of the 1,265

---

* In 2022 Colchester was one of eight newly designated cities to commemorate Elizabeth II's Platinum Jubilee.

men of Colchester here commemorated are inscribed on vellum and displayed inside the principal entrance at the town hall.' Too many names to feature, even on a monument this large. Ash frowns. 'There is an existential universality to having served in war. I wanted to be on the frontline. It is the epitome of human experience. The best and worst of it.'

The brutal mechanics of World War I changed conflict forever. Men fell like dominos. Those that came back were changed, disfigured, traumatised. Ash is also changed. 'I was a combat medical technician. For a time, I was in the ambulance response team in Camp Bastion, Afghanistan. When dead soldiers were flown in, we called them angels. Then you didn't rush to the hospital. You kept driving and turned left for the morgue.' She pauses. We are sitting on a bench near the memorial that stands for death in war. 'I remember a quadruple amputee, an engineer with injuries unsustainable for life. The poncho slipped that was covering him. He had gingerish hair and blue eyes.' She stops. 'And I remember thinking it was odd to see a human being in a poncho with no feet at the bottom. It must have been a massive anti-tank IED.'

There is something deeply moving about this young woman, a veteran at thirty-five, wrestling with her military past (the high days and the horror) and her civilian identity. A divorcee and a gay mother, this ex-soldier was a minority within a minority. These days, Ash is sure of one thing. 'I knew I had to join the army. I wanted to give something back to the generations who gave so much.' The memorial speaks directly to her. 'They strove for peace, they served for freedom. They died to live.'

According to Ash, 'A true soldier will not tell you if they have killed someone. It is not what being a soldier is about.' Ash served on the frontline in Afghanistan 'patrolling with a rifle, thirty rounds of ammunition in my magazine, being shot at'. She joined the army when she was nineteen, older than many men in World War I who, likewise in the early days, volunteered. Rolls of honour appeared in the local press, extolling which lads had signed up and from where.

All too soon, special marks and crosses identified the fallen. Rolls of honour acquired a new and darker meaning: dead boys who never came home. Instead, in every town a memorial emerged, of which Colchester's is a fine example.* Patriotism, pride and belonging. A memorial to the past and a rallying cry to the future. We stand back once more to admire the statue's monumental contribution to the city. 'I miss the army,' Ash admits. Young and vital, her appearance is hard to reconcile with 'veteran' status. I touch her arm, relieved this soldier has come home.

54. The Response 1914 (Northumberland Fusiliers Memorial), grounds of the Church of St Thomas the Martyr, Barras Bridge, Newcastle-upon-Tyne, 1923

The Northumberland Fusiliers, World War I, 1914–1918

'I think it's one of the most incredible war memorials in the world. It perfectly captures what was happening on Tyneside in the early part of World War I.' I am sitting in central Newcastle in a neat public garden fringed with bedding plants. Opposite and unmissable is Sir William Goscombe John's The Response. Dan Jackson stares ahead, his gaze rolling from left to right, as he nimbly translates what he sees. 'It is brilliant. It depicts a column of Northumberland Fusiliers not marching to France but along the Great North Road to their first training camp.' Dan effortlessly picks out two drummer boys beneath a melodramatic angel blowing her horn, and identifies old sweats, grizzled NCOs and workmen rushing to join up. 'There are flat caps, and mufflers. Some are holding tools. They've come straight from the shipyard, the armament factories, the coal mines.'

---

* Colchester is home to more than fifty other memorials connected to the 1914–1918 war.

The exhilaration is palpable. It is 1914 and thousands of Northumbrian men have responded to the call, this is the 'Rush to Arms' personified.* These are Dan's people. Born and bred in northeast England and author of the luminous book, *The Northumbrians*, these days Dan fights with his pen. Goscombe John's epic monument confronts him with an age-defining era that he has spent years trying to make sense of. 'It is said that nowhere responded to the call to arms more enthusiastically than Tyneside. Getting under the skin of why that might have been the case is interesting because the economy of the north east was pretty buoyant just before the war.'

Across the road, Lord Armstrong glistens in the sun. A Victorian mega-industrialist who had no qualms about making munitions to service *any* war, he stands as a reminder to Northumbria's muscular armament industry, facilitated by extensive mining and shipbuild-

---

* At the beginning of World War I, the Northumbrian Fusiliers was the second-largest infantry regiment in Britain. The London Regiment was the largest.

ing. This production trinity heralded the high-water mark of an industrial success story. The region was thriving, so why the mass exodus to war? Here, Dan burrows deep into the local psyche, identifying a masculinity born from centuries of border warfare with neighbouring Scotland, a martial mentality subsequently reshaped into a pronounced British patriotism, focused eastwards across the North Sea. With its industrial tail up, on the eve of war the north east drew on its military heritage and men responded in droves. The eponymous Response stands as testimony to the draw of war. Back then, the region had something worth fighting for. You can almost hear the brouhaha, the drums, the fond farewells.

Dan picks out a touching scene that bookends the rear of the monument. A husband bids goodbye to his 'bairn and wife', a tender moment underscoring the statue's otherwise outstanding manliness, its bravado and its sacrifice. With so many men, so much noise, the individual stories reveal themselves slowly. Look carefully and another sweetheart in her skirts embraces her brave fella. In this tableau of war, the future is unknown, the horror unforeseen.

On the first day of the Somme, 1,644 Northumbrian Fusiliers died, most of them before noon; this sobering statistic is the dark shadow that haunted the region's fulsome response to war. The monument was subsequently paid for by local shipping magnate and Newcastle MP Sir George Renwick. Occasionally possessing too much money in grief could prove an Achilles heel – where and when to stop commemorating, searching, mourning? But here, in Newcastle, it was gratitude that inspired the city's finest memorial. All five of Renwick's sons returned from war alive. The Response was his thank you, a moment in time caught before the essence of Northumbria was blown to pieces.

Dan loves what Goscombe John has created in the heart of his city, but he's conflicted about the emotional messaging behind the piece. On the one hand, its bronze monumentalism preserves forever the final hurrah of Northumbria's industrial-military past: its men and its metal. Things would never be the same again. Some 60,000 young lads did not return home, and many of those who did were maimed, traumatised and unemployed.*

'Post-war saw retrenchment. Coal, shipbuilding, armaments ... Industry craters up here in a way it doesn't in the south, with its booming suburban growth.' Steadfast in his commitment to Newcastle, Dan can read and write about Northumbria's great industrial era, but he has not lived it, a period that, by the late twentieth century, was already a distant memory. As for World War I, Dan is not even sure it was a conflict worth fighting for. 'I know about the arguments to keep the channel ports open, to keep the shipping lanes out of German hands, but ...' He stops. 'All those dead men, and a crap peace that led to another war.'

We look back at the monument and wonder at the heady combination of hope and hell, the proud north east on the cusp of catastrophe; workmen and military men sharing the same naïve faith that might and right were on their side. Dan stands to go. I thank him for his time and ask what his next book will be about. He smiles. 'The history of Newcastle United.'

55. The Crypt Chapel, Harrow School, Harrow, London, 1918

World War I, 1914–1918

Father James Power has a certain bonhomie, a comfortable confidence that comes with thirty-five years of service as the chaplain of Harrow School. He strides ahead in a cream linen jacket and dog collar, gesticulating right, then left. 'That's the main building, half Jacobean, half reconstructed Victorian. On the left, we have the

---

* In *The Northumbrians*, Dan observes that the North-East War Memorials Project estimates 60,000 names are recorded on World War I memorials in the region, putting the scale of death on a par with Scotland's, often cited as the highest in Britain.

school chapel. Indeed, yes, high Victorian gothic. It's a Gilbert Scott.'

Boys in straw boaters float past, two old Harrovians clap backs and exchange pleasantries. One, Oliver Webb-Carter, is my host. I comment on their smart-casual attire and purposeful gait. The chaplain laughs. 'Yes, it's a bit like a cult! It's powerful, you know. And they are listened to.' Privilege is what we are talking about, high up on Harrow Hill, overlooking London's giant sprawl. This prestigious boarding school has been educating impressive, world-famous men for centuries: King Hussain of Jordan, Robert Peel, Stanley Baldwin, Winston Churchill, Jawaharlal Nehru … On goes the list. But in World War I, that privilege was inverted. Father James puts his fist to his chest. 'Six hundred and forty-four alumni were killed. That is the number agreed upon. It catches one every time.' In a school of around 500 pupils, the decimation of so many freshly educated young lives hit hard.

Reared on a muscular Christianity, privileged youth in Edwardian England expected to live intensely and die old. Imbibing gallant notions of valour – bent heads on the rugby field, pitched as if in battle – patriotism took on a whole new meaning. Before 1914, conflict on a mass scale had not been seen for a century, and it was easy to glamorise ideas of glorious war. Public school boys were the first to join the fray in August 1914, and, the backbone of the officer class, they died in disproportionate numbers. Reading broadsheets became a grave ordeal. Harrow started issuing their own monthly *Harrovian War Supplement*, which began with a list of 'killed'. Today, their leather spines line the shelves of another high-Victorian building – the school's Vaughan Library. Beside them sit six fat volumes: *Harrow Memorials of the Great War*. Every fallen man has a double page featuring his war service, personal history and photograph. Hundreds of sombre, handsome lads with moon faces and proud uniforms.

'Let's go to the crypt chapel next.' Father James takes us underground, into the inner sanctuary of Gilbert Scott's religious goliath, where the pale buttressed walls of a one-time vestry were converted first into a chapel to remember dead Harrovians, and then a sanctuary of remembrance. Reams of names spool up and down, left to right. The chaplain notes: 'Thirty-five dead in July 1916, the start of the Somme, so many boys.' Thirty-four wooden panels filled with black and red calligraphy – a great hole in the heart of privilege. A former pupil, Conservative prime minister Stanley Baldwin would later concede 'there is nothing in the first twenty years after the war that can make good to this country the loss of so many men of that age'. How many fellow Harrovians was he thinking of?

Ex-Harrovian Oliver stands against the crypt's whitewashed wall. He invited me here; for him, the impact as a teenager was lasting. 'Our English teacher brought us down to the crypt so we could better understand the war poets.' Unlike his father, after much soul-searching, Oliver didn't join the army. It was a difficult decision, but at least his generation had a choice. 'I remember a school friend lost a brother early in the Iraq War. It was a consolation of sorts that he had wanted to be in the military.'

The day is bright and the crypt's closed space oppressive. Hundreds of English names – James, George, Basil, Edward, Frederick, Cyril, Harold, William, Percival – are hard to process. It's difficult not to ponder the long tail of a war that killed so many well-educated, wealthy young men. Theirs was 'a dust whom England bore, shaped, made aware'.* The loss was huge, the debt immense. Stanley Baldwin believed he 'was in command only because better men lay underground'.

---

* A line from Rupert Brooke's 1914 poem 'The Soldier'. Brooke went to Rugby School.

56. The Alex Fitch Room, War Memorial Building, Harrow School, London, 1926

Second Lieutenant Alex Fitch, R.G.A, 1899–1918

I am racing through *Harrow Memorials of the Great War*, leafing too quickly across many pages of individual trauma. But Father James has singled out Alex Fitch, as his mother would have wanted, and surely planned. According to Alex's Crypt entry, this nineteen-year-old died in September 1918, just two months before war's end. In Volume VI, I find Second Lieutenant Alex Fitch's page and all the salient details that match his truncated life.

Treasured 'only son'. Head of House. Selected for the shooting VIII. A rower. An archer. Alex managed a year at Cambridge before he was called up, but this renaissance boy belonged to Harrow, where he spent four formative years between 1913 and 1917. His face is broad and handsome, his cocked arm languid, his free hand holds a cigarette. The photograph brims with abundant youth, and the testimonial with emotion.

'He was nobly doing his duty at the time,' writes Major J. W. Tompkins, 'and by his presence inspiring men to serve his second gun in trying conditions … I loved your boy and I trusted him with very responsible duties … His personality was so great he held his men in the hollow of his hand.'

I close the book and follow Father James. 'There is more to come. We have the War Memorial Building.' As early as May 1917, Harrow made a decision about a brand-new build; the foundation stone was laid by the Archbishop of Canterbury in 1921 and the two-storey monument opened by prime minister Stanley Baldwin in 1926. We climb the steps and pass under an arch. 'Harrovians like big things.' There was a big hole to fill – the Crypt Chapel just the start. Inside the forecourt, it is silent, the space deliberately hallowed, formal. A sarcophagus foregrounds the loss; it honours 'Harrow's sons'.

'Sons'. Father James walks among the inscriptions, he the paternal guide to so many boys, Harrow the halfway home to countless sons. We enter the building and mount the stairs, past busts of old boys Palmerston and Byron, beyond the recent plaque that commemorates the Battle of Britain. 'Yes, the building also honours World War II. Here is the room …'

The smell is distinct, strikingly so. Old, polished, important wood sweating gently in the afternoon sun. Elizabethan panels, Tudor fireplace, Cromwellian refectory table … Under foot, Georgian teak groans.* And there he is, the same boy recast in oils, presiding silently over his wooden mausoleum: Second Lieutenant Alex Fitch, the nonchalant pose, the harmless cigarette. Despite the sunlight, his face is lit with an electric bulb in a brass mount. It is never turned off.

'This room was not what his mother wanted.' Father James looks across at Alex. 'But the school rejected ideas for a swimming pool or gym. It was meant to be a space for boys to meet parents. Nowadays, it's used for committee meetings, bagpipe lessons, that sort of thing.'

The cul-de-sac of a mother's pain leaps from the wooden walls. Jamie Ingham Clark is Alex's great-nephew and the great-grandson of Lady Fitch. 'Her only son, Alex was doted on. She could not accept he had been killed. Everything was kept the same, as if he might walk through the door tomorrow. At home, his room was cleaned every day.'

An American woman of considerable private means married to a British barrister, Alex's mother tried to make sense of her loss through wood and light. For Jamie, the room is tragic, but brilliant, too. 'There is always hope if the light is on. The picture illuminates him, makes him the centre of attention.'

I walk down the stairs with Father James, a photo of Alex's picture pocketed on my phone. Later, I will share it with Helen, a mother

---

* The room, designed to last, was to contain nothing that 'moth or rust doth corrupt' (a biblical line from Matthew 6:19).

whose son, Aaron Lewis, was killed in Afghanistan ninety years after Alex's death.*

'What a terribly sad but lovely story. I can fully understand how his mother channelled all her energy into making that room happen … It is very hard to get your head around the fact your son is not here anymore. In the early days, it is like you are going mad. You are searching for them because you cannot comprehend they are not here … I found it very scary.'

And there it is, in Helen's text, and in Alex Fitch's room, as bright now as it was then, the undimmed constant behind every frontline: a mother's love.

57. Balmoral Estate Workers War Memorial, opposite the entrance to Balmoral Castle, Crathie, Grampian, 1922

World War I, 1914–1918

'My great uncle Alex was an assistant gardener.' Later, Ian Aitken-Kemp will send me a photograph. Alex has a large round bonnet, boots, breeches and waistcoat. He is standing with a hand on his hip and has the implacable gaze of a young male. Behind him sits a large Victorian glasshouse and, on his left, two colleagues, likewise in bonnets. The flowers are abundant. It is high summer at Balmoral.

Highland estates are feudal and the hierarchy works best when it is not disrupted. The assistant gardener, the head gardener, the groom, the gamekeeper, the farrier, the stalker, the head stalker, on upwards to the factor, and ultimately the laird. Along the black course of Grampian's River Dee, amidst purple grouse moors and pine forests, that laird was (and still is) the king.

Gardener Alex McNerney was married to Annie, the telephonist in the big house; the couple's lives were entwined in the estate, the

---

* See Monument 99 for Aaron Lewis's story.

king and queen the distant peak of their humble existence, one otherwise dictated by the seasons and the royal calendar. The latter changed radically with the outbreak of war in 1914. George and Mary did not return to Balmoral for six years. Estate life continued, albeit with the workforce much depleted. By early September 1914, Alex had joined the Gordon Highlanders. It is a very different man pictured in a sporran and military jacket; his wide-eyed wife and two babies speak to new responsibilities, but king and country came first.

Back at Balmoral, the gardens made do with a new recruit, Charles Rose, just sixteen at the outbreak of war. Patricia Purves is his great niece. 'Years later, I remembered the aunts, his sisters. But they never mentioned their brother Charles.' Patricia found his picture in her late father's effects. Short dark hair, military uniform, baby face. So that was where her father's name came from. Charles, like Alex before him, was an assistant gardener at Balmoral. He joined the Highland Light Infantry in July 1916, the same month that Alex died in France. Details about his death are scant; Alex succumbed to his wounds somewhere near Rouen. He was twenty-six and had survived trench warfare for two whole years. Back at Balmoral, his wife would have to fend for herself and their two children. At least she had a job in the big house.

Ian wishes he had asked his late grandfather – Alex's brother – more questions. He moved away from the area long ago, but something has stuck. A sense of belonging? Perhaps. Ian isn't sure. He is not a royalist (quite the opposite), but is certain that his predecessors were treated well by the royal family. 'A lot of them worked on the estate. There are stories of George and Mary popping in for tea. One relative was allowed to extend his working life to get a fifty years' service medal.' Just little things, but they matter. It was a community, and it still is.

When she retired in 2017, Patricia returned to live in this eastern corner of Scotland. It was there, on the edge of the Balmoral estate, that she found her great uncle Charles. Or, rather, his name. He had died age nineteen after contracting meningitis in the Persian Gulf in

LEST WE FORGET

1917. 'I am sad it happened so far away. But I am glad he didn't die in action.' Another boy from Balmoral's gardens who didn't make it home. Two of Charles's three sisters never married; Patricia muses that, after 1918, there must have been a shortage of men in the villages.

A total of twenty-eight local lads, the flower of Grampian's youth, never returned. No one area of estate life was exempt from the unspoken cost of war. On 3 September 1922, two years after he walked behind the coffin of the Unknown Warrior in Whitehall, George V unveiled the Balmoral Estate Workers War Memorial. He stood shoulder to shoulder with local men and women. They all knew the warriors this community had lost. When it comes to pain, there is no hierarchy.

Today, the simple Celtic cross stands just outside the entrance of the estate, hewn from the same granite as the king's baroque castle, the names etched in red, the decorations ancient swastikas.* Alex is there, and Charles too. And, every year, the children of the local primary school in Crathie march out to remember them: the boys who served and died for their king and country.

---

* The swastika was a symbol of widespread ancient usage associated with the sun. The design had no sinister associations when the memorial was erected.

CHAPTER 17

EMPIRE'S HEROES

A spat about the necessity of a Muslim war memorial arose from the last Conservative budget in 2024. The then chancellor of the exchequer, Jeremy Hunt, sought to diffuse tensions over the war in Gaza with a £1 million pledge to build a memorial to the Muslims who served in two World Wars. Nigel Farage, currently leader of Reform UK, hit back, insisting that 'over 100 years ago, we had men of more brain and foresight than our chancellor'. His logic focused on the Commonwealth War Graves Commission cemeteries, where 'the principle was equality in death' with headstones 'for those of all faiths and none'.* However, the vast majority of CWGC graves are located overseas.

Neither man was apparently aware that both Hindus and Muslims were memorialised in Britain during World War I.

---

* Originally named the Imperial War Graves Commission, this organisation was established in 1917 and is responsible for commemorating all the Commonwealth dead equally and individually.

58. Chattri Memorial, South Downs, near Brighton, East Sussex, 1921

World War I, 1914–1918

Walk through the South Downs National Park and the Chattri Memorial's pristine marble dome appears suddenly, a flash of brilliant white among the greens. It glows like a luminous wild mushroom, marking out something special.

When I visit in late June, traces of a remembrance weekend remain. The scaffolding for a temporary stage still stands in front of the granite terrace where Assa Singh once sat. His son, Jaimal, recalls it was here, in the sanctuary of the Chattri, that for the first and only time in his life he witnessed his father shed a tear. 'He was an old man and he held a picture of Manta Singh, his own father, who was cremated at this spot.'

Manta was from a village in Punjab, one of a million men recruited from the sub-continent to serve the British Empire in 1914. While lads in Britain were still being enlisted and trained, Manta had already left his small family miles behind and arrived in France, where the Indian Expeditionary Force provided a third of the manpower on the British frontline in the early months of the war.

Jaimal, Manta's eighty-nine-year-old grandson, recounts his story: 'The war had just started. My grandfather's regiment was fighting on the border of France and Belgium. His senior officer, Captain George Henderson, was wounded and my grandfather wanted to bring him back to safety. He found a wheelbarrow in no man's land and rescued George.'

The image is arresting; a 6-foot Sikh soldier wheeling his British military senior to safety. Nowadays, a common refrain against empire is that Indians were fighting for another man's country. But Manta was a soldier, and soldiers fight for each other. When pushing the wheelbarrow and his captain to safety, Manta was shot in the leg. Nothing fatal, or so it seemed. He carried on fighting in the November mud and blood.

There were no antibiotics and the leg became infected; Manta got sicker and sicker. Eventually he was transferred to Brighton on England's south coast, where a rash of hospitals for the wounded had sprung up. The Oriental-inspired Royal Pavilion was converted to look after wounded Indian men from the frontline. A workhouse was likewise adapted; this became Kitchener's Hospital, where Manta was sent. Care was taken to accommodate the needs of the 12,000 Sikh, Muslim and Hindu soldiers. There was no genuine equality (white female nurses were not allowed to care for Indian men), but spices, ghee and religious books were sourced. In Brighton, Britain's first halal butchers set up shop; to accommodate the inclement weather, Sikhs were given waterproof turban covers. But Manta was too sick to worry about any of that. He died in February 1915.

LEST WE FORGET

Back in Punjab, Manta's wife had to make do, one of the many thousands of Indian women whose husband never returned from his foreign war. Her young sons, aged four and six, grew up believing that their father had died somewhere in France. They knew nothing of Brighton or of the care extended to their father in both life and death. 'At the time, cremation was not permitted in England,' explains Jaimal. 'The rules were bent and a farmer gave land. Fifty-three Hindu and Sikh soldiers were cremated on the South Downs, including my grandfather. There was no coffin; they were just taken on a horse and cart. It was makeshift but their ashes were scattered. It was done properly.'

The Chattri was built straight after the war and unveiled by Edward, the Prince of Wales, in 1921. Three granite slabs cover the cremation site, its white marble 'umbrella' symbolising protection offered after death. Beneath the shelter of the Chattri Memorial, the vista stretches south across the Downs, beyond Brighton and the Royal Pavilion, to the English Channel. Skylarks sing and the air is light and clean.

Manta's son, Assa, visited the Chattri for the first time in 1981. Like his father before him, Assa had also fought for the British Empire (but during World War II) and in his father's regiment too – the 15th Ludhiana Sikhs, where he served alongside an officer called Robert Henderson, the son of George Henderson. The two men shared a deep connection. In old age, Assa moved to England to be with Jaimal, who had emigrated here twenty years earlier. The two army veterans, Robert and Assa, resumed contact. Through Robert, Assa discovered that Manta was cremated at the Chattri. He found his name inscribed on the wall – Subedar Manta Singh – and shed a tear for the father he had never known.

If you walk out to the Chattri Memorial on the second Sunday in June, you will be embraced by an extraordinary community who remember those who fought for another country's freedom.* Among

---

* The Chattri Memorial Group is run by Davinder Dhillon, who in 2017 won the prime minister's Points of Light award for his outstanding voluntary service.

them, perhaps you will be lucky enough to spot an old man in a turban called Jaimal Singh, sitting beside his friend in a Panama hat, Ian Henderson – the grandson of Captain George Henderson, the officer saved by Manta Singh all those years ago.

59. Muslim Burial Ground Peace Garden, Monument Road, Woking, Surrey, 1917

World War I, 1914–1918

Let us stay a moment with the Indian soldiers recruited to fight on the Western Front early in World War I. 'We are being mown down like bullocks in the field,' said one letter home, a rural reference to a different world, one up-ended by the Indian Army's arrival in Marseille, France, in 1914. Soon gas ripped lungs, bullets tore out eyes and shallow trenches gave men nowhere to hide.

Zafar Iqbal pulls on the handbrake and we stare across at an unlikely golden finial heralding something special among the trees. It's beautiful. Deliberately so. 'Yes, it is. Pictures were taken and they were sent back to India in World War I to show that Britain knew how to look after the Muslim fallen.' With war raging against the

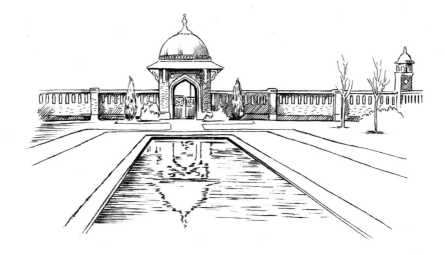

LEST WE FORGET

Ottoman Empire, Britain's dependence on a large Muslim contingent in the Indian army had to be handled with extreme care. Injured Hindus and Sikhs arriving and dying in England were cremated near Brighton, while deceased Muslims came to Woking, home to both the Shah Jahan, Britain's first purpose-built mosque, and Brookwood Cemetery, the largest military and civilian graveyard in England.

To honour the Muslim fallen, in 1917 a sacred burial site was completed. It nestled among pine trees on Woking's Horsell Common, with a beautiful chattri dome and neat brick walls. A total of twenty-seven Muslim men were laid to rest here, nineteen from World War I. But, by the later twentieth century, with inward migration from the former colonies and Britain and British identity in flux, England was a less hospitable place.

'It felt pretty bad, yeah.' Zafar admits that, in the late 1960s, when he first arrived in Woking from Pakistan, it was tough being a Muslim. The febrile atmosphere saw charged language, a million mini-Enoch Powells, imagined rivers of blood, and a vandalised Muslim burial ground. Zafar shrugs. 'It's fine now to be a Muslim here.' And back then, he was just a child, playing football and hide-and-seek on Horsell Common. The desecrated burial ground was the least of his worries. The Commonwealth War Graves Commission stepped in and the soldiers were reinterred, with white headstones engraved in Arabic, facing Mecca, in nearby Brookwood Cemetery. They are still there today, surrounded by fellow Allied service personnel, gurgling wood pigeons and a manicured lawn that glints in the evening sun.

Meanwhile, the original burial site fell into a further state of disrepair. The finial disappeared, the Portland stone chipped off and graffiti spoilt the brickwork. For Zafar, by now a civil servant, the matter was personal. 'To me as a Muslim, it was very important to understand that these people gave their lives as part of the British Empire. Our shared histories are important.' He spotted his opportunity with the imminent 100th anniversary of World War I; this quiet, unassuming man set about contacting organisations, sourcing funding, writing to lord lieutenants and tracing Muslim ancestors. The blossoming of an abandoned burial ground into a mesmeric Peace Garden, complete with pond, proved so touching the BBC made a documentary about it and Prince Edward attended the opening. The return of the golden finial on top of the domed entrance was just one dramatic high. In 2015, Zafar travelled to Pakistan to find the relatives of a particular soldier, Sikandar Khan of the 82nd Punjabis. 'I discovered he was an only child, so his death really was the ultimate sacrifice for his family.'

Together, we sit in front of the new Indian granite memorial. Its meticulously inscribed white stone insets were researched and scripted by Zafar. His finger gently rests on the message above the names:

In memory and honour of all Muslim soldiers who gave their lives for Britain in both World Wars.

CHAPTER 18

BROKEN SOLDIERS

'The Fallen' is the much-used wartime euphemism for dead soldiers, where the sacrifice is quantifiable and the tally finite. But what if the fall was incomplete, the body broken and the brain bruised? In World War I, men peering over the parapets of trenches saw a vast increase in facial injuries; hot flying metal was a new form of hell. Heavy artillery, machine-gun fire and poisonous gas all led to injury on an unprecedent scale. In their 'convalescence blues', the war wounded returned to Britain. But when did their war end? Where is their memorial?

60. Machine Gun Corps Memorial, Hyde Park Corner, London, 1925

World War I, 1914–1918

Light rain did not deter respectable numbers gathering for a much-anticipated unveiling in London's Grosvenor Place on 10 May 1925. The event was led by the Duke of Connaught and Strathearn and four recipients of the Victoria Cross. *The Times* believed the memorial would 'tell future generations how heavy a toll was taken of the officers and other ranks who fought in the machine gun companies'.

Stand next to exquisite David (naked and beautiful), run a finger over the bronze Vickers machine-guns that flank his perfect form and wince at the prophetic messaging: 'Saul hath slain his thousands/But David his tens of thousands.'* A century after its erection, curatorial literature discreetly acknowledges this memorial is 'perplexing'.† The Machine Gun Corps were renowned for excessive fatalities, with one quarter of their men dying; proof of 'gallantry' in 'all ranks', according to the Duke of Connaught. 'The Suicide Club' was the Corps' invidious epithet.

English Heritage has written a neat sidebar in its memorials guidebook, proporting to have solved this mystery. The statue's sculptor, Derwent Wood, joined the Royal Army Medical Corps in World War I and went on to establish the Masks for Facial Disfigurement Department, creating prosthetics to 'restore the lost features of mangled youth'. Derwent Wood is one of several fêted 'facemakers', artists who saved the day (and men's shame) with their 'innovative masks'. English Heritage believes the sculptor's naked David 'was alluding to the weapon's destructive impact on the body' and, presumably, human vulnerability. Wood is featured in the pamphlet, alongside one of his masks. But there is no image of a disfigured man. Out of sight, on the rear of the plinth, there is an acknowledgement that beyond the confirmed 13,791 dead, an additional 48,258 men from the Corps were injured or missing.

'I guess Wood believed he was creating a Greek god in David, and that echoes with the idea he was god-like and could recreate men's faces through artwork.' Ellie Grigsby is midway through a history doctorate and has spent years researching the impact of disfiguring injuries sustained in World War I. According to Ellie, David and his

---

* Originally the memorial stood on a traffic island south of the Royal Artillery Memorial. It was removed in 1945 and re-erected in 1962, facing down the Wellington Arch in Hyde Park Corner.

† English Heritage look after this statue which features in their *Guidebook: Wellington Arch, Marble Arch & Six Great War Memorials*.

gorgeous male form are part of a greater problem: a societal fixation with the heroes' narrative which sees the Glorious Dead reborn in David and modern doctor-gods, who recreated the male form with tin and paint and pioneering surgery. There is a gaping hole in this war story: who were the men behind the masks, on the operating tables, hovering in the post-war shadows? And where were they on 10 May 1925?

I long to scale the plinth and touch David's perfect bum, warmed in the summer sun. Unacceptable. A bit like the statue. Later that evening, Ellie emails me a research document. Meet Harry Gatonby. It was March 1918 and he was fighting in Abbeville, northern France, when a bullet entered his mouth, exiting from the back of his neck. Harry's jaw was shattered, his bottom teeth obliterated. No dentures were fitted, gastric problems ensued, his sight was affected and there was a constant stabbing pain in his face (known today as trigeminal neuralgia). Mental breakdowns were frequent.

Between 1918 and 1926, Harry's pension payments were decreased from 100 per cent to 30 per cent and he was not getting any better. In fact, he got worse. The pain in his face was so bad that he solicited the help of a Scottish surgeon. In 1938, Dr Notts removed all the brain nerves on the left side of Harry's face. Harry started having blackouts, and there were aggressive, upsetting episodes when he targeted his wife, Phyllis. Dr Notts had neurologically rewired Harry, but this was not the man Phyllis had married.

Seven years after his operation, Harry's body was discovered in the driver's seat of his car. Blood and brain matter covered the interior of the vehicle. In 1945, suicide was illegal; 'death due to a gunshot wound, probably self-inflicted' the coroner's thoughtful verdict. Harry's story is messy, protracted and tragic. World War I killed him, but he belongs to a very different type of 'suicide club'. Where is the gallantry in Harry's story? Which part of perfect David speaks to Harry's war? Where is Harry's statue?

61. 'Gueules Cassées': The Men With Broken Faces memorial, Queen Mary's Hospital, Sidcup, London, 2019

World War I, 1914–1918

I am drinking oat-milk coffee with PhD student Ellie Grigsby in Queen Mary's Hospital in Sidcup, south-east London. First opened as the Queen's Hospital in 1917, it was a landmark rehabilitation centre for facially disfigured soldiers. Ellie is beautiful, startlingly so: strawberry blonde hair; smooth, tanned skin; a green velvet headband. I joke that her face is perfectly Instagrammable. We laugh, compare notes on make-up and exchange social media handles. Ellie is the tantalising reverse of the men she's researching. 'I had their pictures on my wall. I felt that if I couldn't look at them, who could?'

Archival work is time-consuming and unpredictable. 'I was poring through boxes of documents, turning over inter-operative pictures,

whole faces peeled off, burns pictures. Pictures that are very hard to look at.' A century after World War I, Ellie was at the coalface of a horror story only ever studied from the perspective of pioneering doctors. We both know the exceptional historian, Lindsey Fitzharris, whose book *The Facemaker*, featuring wartime surgeon Sir Harold Gillies, shot both the biographer and her subject to fame. Gillies took his work seriously; his job was stressful and his addiction to tobacco understandable.

'Gillies's patient, Henry Ralph Lumley, was one of the men I had on my wall,' says Ellie. Second lieutenant Henry had newly enrolled in the Royal Flying Corps and his portrait is one of boyish anticipation: a debonair chap sporting parted black hair and a pipe clenched between smiling teeth. In 1916, finally awarded his wings, pilot Henry was flying over Wiltshire when his plane crashed and he was severely burned: a casualty of war and he had not even left England.

Henry shored up in the care of Sister Agnes, an experienced nurse. Ellie shows me her handwritten note: 'his face is burnt beyond recognition. One eye removed, the other practically blind. Legs burnt, arms burnt, thumbs and some fingers amputated.' This is the same Henry that Ellie had on her wall. Agnes concluded that 'he has very little to live for poor boy, but we are doing our best'.

Weak, depressed and apparently addicted to morphine, desperate Henry ended up on Gillies's operating table in the Queen's Hospital. The pioneering surgeon, against his better judgement, cut skin from the pilot's chest and tried to stick it on his face. Henry's surgical wounds turned gangrenous and the chest graft didn't take. Gillies learned valuable medical lessons, but they cost Henry his life. The second lieutenant died in March 1918.

Ellie shakes her head. 'I uncovered so many stories. I had all these bits of paper, real lives untold. I was often teary thinking about these men. Many never took their masks off, except to eat and sleep.' Somewhere between the pictures on her wall and the boxes of distressing photographs, Ellie morphed into more than a PhD student: 'I became an activist. I found these men, thousands and thousands of them [the official statistic of 60,500 is unrepresentative] who existed in a no man's land. They weren't the glorious dead. Who were they? Who remembers them?'

We go outside to one of the appointed blue benches erected 'for wounded soldiers recovering from their operations to sit in peace'.

'Don't believe that plaque,' insists Ellie. 'It was like social apartheid. They were kept separate to stop people feeling uncomfortable.' She knows all about plaques. Back in Queen Mary's internal courtyard is Ellie's own addition to wartime statuary: a bust of an anonymous man on a granite plinth in a tin hat, his face half covered by his hand. 'There is no memorial in the world where the face is part hidden. Many people never saw the disfigurements. They were hidden. I hope this bust makes the person looking feel uncomfortable.'

Ellie circles the artwork her research inspired. It is discreet, asking as many questions as it answers. How hard was it to erect a memorial? 'Very. People looked through me – I was young and female. And I didn't get the inscription I wanted on the plinth. I wanted to quote a nurse who wrote of "the skin left hanging in shreds, and the jawbones crushed to a pulp". The Trust thought it would offend contemporary cancer patients.'

The citation opted for, from a hospital orderly, has a certain masculine acceptability: '... hideous is the only word for those smashed faces ... to talk to a lad who six months ago was probably a wholesome and pleasing specimen of youth and now a gargoyle, and a broken one at that, is something of an ordeal.'

Is it possible to commemorate pain without inflicting pain? Ellie was eventually persuaded by a psychologist to remove the photographs of disfigured soldiers from her wall. 'She said I was suffering vicarious trauma. It took me three days to put the men in an envelope. I thought *I'm no better than the people who rejected them*.' Her face crumples.

It required Ellie Grigsby, a young doctoral student, for Harry and Henry and thousands like them to finally come out of the shadows.

The enigmatic bust inside St Mary's Hospital sits as a timeless reminder to 'the men with broken faces' and their hidden trauma.

62. Victory Over Blindness, Piccadilly Station, Manchester, 2018

World War I, 1914–1918

I am careening out of Piccadilly station's main entrance – a train derailment has pushed me off course – and they stop me in my tracks: seven blind men. How dare I rush to Wellington in Glasgow when they stand so sorry and still? Heads bowed, eyes bound, arms forward, one holding out for the other. Reminiscent of John Singer Sargent's landmark 1919 painting 'Gassed', sculptor Johanna Domke-Guyot forces us to confront these casualties of war.* They stand at eye level. And, crucially, you can feel them, touch them, hug them. No plinth bars the way – just you and seven blind men amid the rush of modern life.

Erected in 2018 to commemorate the 100th anniversary of the end of World War I, Victory Over Blindness is an affecting statue, and Sir Arthur Pearson an effective man. The self-made publishing tycoon lost his sight in 1913 aged forty-seven and went on to establish the Blinded Soldiers and Sailors Care Committee during the war (later renamed St Dunstan's and now known as Blind Veterans UK). In its current guise, the charity helps all British veterans with sight loss, irrespective of how or when they go blind; it was the force behind the statue outside Manchester Piccadilly. Several visually impaired veterans were at the 2018 unveiling of this memorial to their predecessors. The photographs are touching, the real-time frailty of old age standing alongside the damaged youth of yesterday.

---

* Singer Sargent was commissioned by the British War Memorials Committee to document the conflict. He visited the Western Front in July 1918 and his painting captures the immediate aftermath of a mustard gas attack.

The statues are walking forwards, the veterans are standing straight; all of them are conquering blindness. They are victory over blindness.

Able-bodied and distracted, I bid them farewell and rush on to my train connection and back to Ellie Grigsby's notes. A private in World War I, Alexander Mcleod was shot in the face; a bullet smashed through his temple and obliterated one eye. But he was not registered blind until he was eighty-three, when sight in the second eye began to deteriorate. Wrongly diagnosed as a cataract, Alexander developed chorioretinitis – inflammation and lesions of the retina. Groping in the black, Alexander was soon totally blind, a condition the Ministry of Pensions attributed to traumatic stress disorder a full six decades after World War I. Here was another victim of war that the first actuarial survey of 300 blind soldiers, conducted by St Dunstan's in 1922, totally overlooked.

In his eighties, it was difficult for Alexander to adjust. He could not live alone and his daughter, who worked shifts, struggled to cope. She spooned tea into his mouth, heard him stumble and fall in the dark, and fed him cornflakes because he could not feed himself and she had no time.

LEST WE FORGET

I wonder where Alexander fits into Victory Over Blindness. He was not a proud erect pensioner, but a broken old man. Sarcoma, a rare cancer, necessitated the removal of his penis when he was seventy-nine. War wounds and a missing eye were just the start of it. In the 1980s, blind and invisible, where was Alexander's charity? Where was his dignity? Refused a constant care allowance, the burden sat with his long-suffering daughter, picking up the pieces sixty years on.

I like the statue outside Manchester Piccadilly, with its seven blind men, but its epitaph is misleading. Victory Over Blindness was not universal. Unveiled amidst a nostalgic wave of World War I centenary commemorations, the statue's name glosses over the dark corners of military disability that live on, long after everyone else has forgotten.

CHAPTER 19

FEMALE HEROES

World War I saw unprecedented female mobilisation, both on the home front – where more than a million additional women entered the workforce – and in uniformed nursing and military organisations, which were frequently deployed overseas. Female wartime service, which cost over 1,000 lives, found its repository in one female hero: nurse Edith Cavell. Alongside the Unknown Warrior, hers was the only other body exhumed and returned to Britain, where she was given a state funeral in Westminster Abbey before being buried in her local Norwich Cathedral.

63. East Window, St Mary's Church, Swardeston, Norfolk, 1917

Nurse Edith Cavell, 1865–1915

'If you look, there is an indentation in the ground. Do you see? This is where she would have walked every Sunday as a girl.' Nick Miller sweeps his arm up from the startling green of the grass towards a painted gate, beyond which sits a red-brick former vicarage, the one-time home of Reverend Cavell, his wife and four children. I close my eyes and envisage three sisters – clutching prayer books, petticoats in hand, younger brother in tow – walking behind their Victorian mother and father.

It is an easy scene to imagine. And a soothing one. I visit the Cavells' Norfolk village on a beautiful May day; there is bewitching sunlight, overwhelming birdsong and a quite lovely little church. We are standing in the grounds of Swardeston's St Mary's, a simple medieval structure that was the spiritual and childhood home of World War I nurse Edith Cavell. Nick has been active at St Mary's for nearly thirty years. Perhaps it is his faith, or maybe his background in social care, but Edith's story has touched him deeply; 'I knew nothing of her before I came here.' Now he is the keeper of her extensive local archive. We step into the lime-washed interior and Nick tells me of a Sunday school inspired by Reverend Cavell, the money for which was raised by his industrious eldest daughter. Edith wrote to the Bishop of Norwich requesting episcopal help, crafted cards to sell, and taught village children in the new building.

FEMALE HEROES

This was Edith Cavell's start in life, one she cherished. Years later, writing to cousin Eddy from her prison cell in Brussels, the nurse recalled Norfolk: 'I like to look back on those happy days when we were young and life was fresh and beautiful and the country so desirable and sweet.' It is unusual to meet Edith for the first time at the beginning of her story. All too often, the narrative starts at the end in 1915: two firing squads, enemy guns at dawn and a brutal October execution in occupied Belgium. It was a German doctor who observed that Edith 'went to her death with a bearing which is quite impossible to forget'.

Nor would the enemy be allowed to forget it. Such was the international outrage at this murder of a female nurse that the British Army, weaponising Edith's image, saw a surge in volunteers, the United States drew one step nearer to entering the war, and the German Kaiser insisted that no more women were to be shot without his permission. Edith Cavell's life of service ended on 12 October 1915. It was in death that she quickly became much more than an English nurse in occupied Belgium who helped allied soldiers escape to Holland. Edith was reincarnated as a victim, a hero and a martyr. Four Edith Cavell biographies were published within a year of her death.

Nick sent me a list of all the many monuments, organisations, hospitals and streets bearing her name. They number more than 100 worldwide. In Canada, there is even a mountain. Her posthumous identity has morphed and changed: a symbol of purity hovering above the murder and chaos of war, the idealised feminine nurse, the English patriot who saved Allied soldiers and, more recently, a spy. Driving up to Norfolk, I listened to a version of this latest Cavell reincarnation on BBC Sounds. Stella Rimington, former director general of MI5, pieces together Edith's past in order to suggest she was immersed in an espionage network, sending clandestine information back to Britain. The evidence is scant, but revisionist history is bankable. Cavell the spy has a certain postmodern ring. We all love secrets.

Nick shakes his head. That is not the Edith he has evidence for, nor the one that inspires him. We walk towards the church's chancel and look up at the stunning east window – a religious portal for the rising sun, a crucified Christ and Edith Cavell in Christian service, a red cross on her arm, dressed in nursing blue, hands clasped in prayer.

'This east window came first,' Nick explains, 'before everything else. Erected in 1917.' Edith's commemorative journey began here, in St Mary's, with an exquisite stained-glass window paid for by local friends and family; 15 shillings the donation from her younger sisters, £1 from cousin Eddy.

Before I leave, Nick hands me a pamphlet he authored himself – 'Edith Cavell: A Forgotten Heroine' – with a cross emblazoned on the cover.* 'Of course,' I say. 'Before all her other identities, it was Edith Cavell the Christian.' He smiles and ushers me out, through the Tudor porch. There, in the sunlit churchyard, Edith's Norfolk is just as she remembered it: 'so desirable and sweet', as if God is beaming down, his hand upon our heads.

64. Edith Cavell statue, St Martin's Place, London, 1920
Nurse Edith Cavell, 1865–1915

'If you look at the inscription "Patriotism isn't enough", it fits in with us. We are trying to get our government to stop selling arms to countries, to stop them chasing profits and war.' It's a Wednesday evening in April and the Women in Black are about to start their fortnightly vigil. Liz is bundled into a dark anorak, and co-protestor Sheila wears a woolly hat and carries a stick; readjusting her folding chair into a nook of the large plinth, at eighty-seven she has lived a

---

* It speaks volumes that Edith Cavell, the most remembered of all World War I's female heroes, can today be considered 'forgotten'. More about her life can be found at www.edithcavell.org.uk, including the material in Swardeston's archive.

life of protest. These women won't be moved, not on the subject of war.

At the junction of Charing Cross and Trafalgar Square, they've found their home. Here in the centre of London, Edith Cavell's statue is monumental. Unveiled in a swell of patriotic fervour in 1920, Sir George Frampton's idealised nurse in Carrara marble is dwarfed by the giant pylon that props her up. Back then, the monument was widely derided as a massive 'hideous lump', but today its size and spacious granite surface lend easy refuge to buskers and protestors.

Sheila invites passers-by to complete a sentence which begins with Britain's military budget in 2023: 'If I had £54.2 billion, I would spend it on …'

'Paradise where no conflict exists and all live peacefully with one another.'

'Climate justice.'

'Feeding the world.'

I stick responses onto Cavell's bulk beneath the original expressions of valour emblazoned on her plinth. FORTITUDE. DEVOTION. SACRIFICE. The Women in Black identify with a later inscription: 'Patriotism is not enough. I must have no hatred or bitterness for anyone.' Added four years after the statue's completion, at the behest of the National Council of Women of Great Britain and Ireland, the sentiment was uttered by Cavell prior to her execution.* With the legacy of war increasingly contested after 1918, the omission of this phrase from Frampton's original was considered a travesty. Words matter.

Edith Cavell, once the posthumous poster girl for World War I military recruitment (around her photograph, the slogan read: 'Murdered by the Huns. Enlist in the 99th and help stop such atroc-

---

* These same words, spoken by Edith Cavell to Reverend Stirling Gahan the night before her death, are also engraved on the ledger stone surrounding her grave in Norwich Cathedral.

ities'), now provides the base camp for pacificism. It is a tad ironic. Liz shrugs. Her female group don't pretend that war isn't complicated. They're adamant that there must be an immediate ceasefire in Gaza, but confess to feeling huge sympathy for Ukraine. 'That has been very difficult for us.' But if the start point was always peace, how different would the world be? 'Did you know that Costa Rica doesn't have an army?'

Women Against War became the Women in Black in the early 1990s. The movement morphs from country to country, conflict to conflict. Women in Black are in the Balkans, Italy, the US and the Middle East. Liz points to a long history of women and pacificism, and to the Women's International League for Peace and Freedom. 'These were suffragists who wanted to stop war through negotiation, by approaching heads of state. They went around governments but no one changed their position.' Liz pauses. 'They started their movement the same year that Cavell was killed.'

When we meet in mid-April 2024, the UK foreign secretary Lord Cameron is in the Middle East, cautioning Israel against retaliation for an unprecedented Iranian attack. In Gaza, the conflict is ongoing; more than 33,000 Palestinians are dead. In the West, few have the bandwidth to acknowledge the civil war in Sudan, while the killing in Ukraine has fallen down the news agenda.

Do the Women in Black ever give up hope? 'One doesn't always maintain morale,' admits Liz. 'But doing something is better than doing nothing. We are here. We are a nuisance. The bee with a sting. They can't get rid of us. We keep reminding them war is evil.'

I take a picture of nine mature women in black and their careworn banners and hopes. I lie back on the pavement, framing them against Cavell's enormous structure, including the figurative mother and child cresting the pylon and Edith in her white marble nursing cape. Liz looks at her hero. 'There are so few statues of women in London. It is quite right we should be with Edith. She has four sides, so we can approach every bus, every car, every bicycle.'

What would you spend £54.2 billion on?

65. Five Sisters Window, York Minster, York, 1925
World War I, 1914–1918

The execution of Edith Cavell proved an unexpected boon for the Allies. Germany's decision to murder a nurse in the cold dawn light gifted Britain an ideal recruiting tool for their volunteer army, which they fully exploited. Men were the agents of war and Edith Cavell was one more reason to fight. Framed as an innocent victim, her posthumous mega-fame conveniently overshadowed the actions of almost all other women.

So who were those other women? And where are they remembered? It was Barbara Weatherill, a World War II veteran aged ninety-nine, who first told me about the Five Sisters Window, re-dedicated to all the women of the British Empire who lost their lives in the Great War. Amidst the jaw-dropping splendour of York Minster, it stands out; a staggering feat of early medieval art, five vast grisaille glass panels that shine with a dim and ancient allure. The stories attached to the thirteenth-century window sparkle with intrigue. Oliver Cromwell, Francis Drake,* Charles Dickens … few were left untouched by the Five Sisters' iridescent appeal. It is hard not to marvel at a structure so impossibly old, that continues to inspire, shining its silvery light on the changed expectations of every age.

Barbara was deeply moved. Attending a Minster reunion in honour of World War II's Auxiliary Territorial Service in the late 1990s, as the piper's lament wended its way through the Great West Door, down the aisle and faded into the Chapter House, she gazed up at the Five Sisters' Window with wet cheeks and new resolve. Its re-dedication as a memorial to the women of World War I spoke to Barbara directly.†

---

* The eighteenth-century antiquarian, not to be confused with the sixteenth-century explorer.

† For more on Barbara's World War II, story see Monument 87.

Almost eighty years earlier, the north transept's intricate lead-lined glass panels had likewise transfixed those who beheld them; in 1921, their 'quiet dignity' triggered a vision. The recipient of that vision was Helen Little, a colonel's wife who had spent much of the Great War in Cairo where she was haunted by the human fall-out from the Gallipoli disaster.

Cairo was Britain's military headquarters in Egypt and, by 1915, its temporary hospitals heaved with broken bodies, rampant disease and desperate overcrowding. The main enemies were gangrene and dysentery, and the makeshift medical defence manned by women, miles from home, on hospital ships and on shore. Vast numbers of dying men presented a horror scene against which neither a white uniform, nor a Red Cross, guaranteed survival.

Louisa Annie Bicknell was thirty-five and an experienced nurse; back in Australia she had run her own private hospital, but war was a different game. Washing, feeding and moving sick men proved difficult, dangerous work. The scratch was just a small one on the back of her hand, but within six days Louisa had died, sepsis her killer. Another female casualty of war.

Handmaidens in hellfire, Louisa's story and many like it were repeated across every conflict zone: on the western front against shrapnel that 'tears through flesh and cuts off limbs'; in the east – Serbia, Russia, Romania – where typhus killed more indiscriminately than German bullets; and in Indian hospitals, up against intense heat and cholera. By the end of the war, 1,400 women who served in imperial Britain's name as military auxiliaries and nurses were confirmed dead. These are the fallen that Helen could not shake from her mind's eye on return to England. 'Memorials on all sides were being erected to our brothers, I often thought that our sisters who also made the same sacrifice appeared to have been forgotten.'

Back in York, evensong is sacrosanct in the Minster; the early gothic setting, exquisite acoustics and a grand organ's intensity insist on a moment of contemplation. Helen was at one such evensong, beneath the faded light of the Five Sisters Window, when she had her vision: 'The window moved backwards as if on hinges', revealing 'wondrous flowers' and women and girls, reincarnated, 'gliding' in 'misty grey-blue garments'. They inched nearer and nearer, then suddenly, in a cruel mimic of death, 'the window swung slowly back, blotting out the garden'.

In the vision, the sisters that could no longer be seen were the dead women who had answered the call of war. Helen stood, pulled from her trance, crying out 'The Sisters' Window for the Sisters!' And with the same power of certainty, she started raising the necessary funds for the temporary removal and restoration of the ancient window. The project was a magnum opus, with the glistening result re-inserted into the northern transept, including an inspirational re-dedication, which took place in 1925 – a unique occasion when the Duchess of York (later to become the Queen Mother) began her life-journey of succour and commemoration.

Today, on the oak panelling adjacent to the window, Edith Cavell is a first among equals, just one woman among the 1,400 named who answered the call of imperial Britain and paid for it with her life. Australia's Louisa Annie Bicknell also takes her place in a story that asks fresh questions in the twenty-first century. Those named are predominantly white women who had the means required to travel and serve and die for empire. What of the other sisters of empire touched by a war not of their choosing? Where is their service remembered?

Nearly 800 years on, the Five Sisters window remains as important as when early medieval Cistercian monks created its timeless alchemy, gifting us centuries of eternal transparency. Today, a hundred years after World War I's re-dedication, the half-filled commemorative panels are quietly biding their time.

CHAPTER 20

WHEN TWO BECOMES ONE

Alongside local art, the scale of loss in World War I found its echo in specific, often enormous, commemorative structures. Individual military services built to honour their own, but ultimately, irrespective of their size, these monuments to heroism and sacrifice did not prevent a second World War. German revenge took a little more than twenty years to burst into another conflagration.

After 1945, getting on with the peace and rebuilding bombed Britain took precedence over spending on commemoration. Big and small, monuments nationwide had to make space for a second military narrative as they gradually became the foundation stones to a century of warring.

66. Chatham Naval Memorial, Chatham, Kent, 1924, modified 1952

Royal Naval Service, World War I, 1914–1918; World War II, 1939–1945

'It's like a big, tall effort at dignity.' These are novelist Graham Swift's words for the sense of achievement upon arrival at Chatham's Naval Memorial. Swift's careful, crafted prose, from his poignant novel *Last*

WHEN TWO BECOMES ONE

Orders, carries me up the hill. Before I can even see it, I too feel 'as though the tower of the memorial is pulling' me forwards.* I walk in early summer; the air is musky with the scent of cow parsley, a dog-rose dances among a million greens, a young man in an England shirt slopes on ahead. And when I reach the top of this Medway hill, it really does look like the obelisk is floating, washed 'white and tall' in sunshine, a light sabre with a bobble on top, piercing through the scrub.

The structure is fenced in; for a moment, I worried I was locked out. 'Nah.' A lad stands up from lying horizontal with his girl. 'The gate is open for sure.' He nods his head towards the entrance. And inside it is huge, just like former lance corporal Matt Lyons said it would be. Matt is an ex-Royal Marine. He came here as a reservist on parade. Standing in a line, among all those 'green lids' as he calls the commando berets, that is when he knew he had to make the grade. 'The commando training was 30 weeks. Phase one is basic soldiering skills – the blue beret cap badge, physical tests, speed marching, things like that. Then it's the cap comforter stage, those little hats. And onto 30 weeks with tactics, skills, drills and the physical tests – the 30-miler, the Tarzan assault course …'

Matt was training right on the edge of life and then parading among the dead. He grew up on the Medway, his great-grandad served in World War I with Chatham Division, Royal Marines. 'No, he is not named on the memorial.' Ernest Flaherty survived. Matt sends me his service papers: Marine Ernest was with HMS *Vengeance* off the African coast, on HMS *Jupiter* icebreaking Russia-bound, then on HMS *Havelock* guarding the Channel. Matt loves this stuff. It's why he signed up. 'Think of Marines as naval soldiers. Remember Nelson's vessels side by side, the boys swinging across the ropes to get to the enemy, or on the rigging. And it progresses to World War II and we are on the back foot and Churchill says "We've got to let the

---

* *Last Orders* was published in 1996, when it controversially won the Booker Prize.

Germans know we are in the fight." So he develops the Royal Marines Commandos.'

Matt says I can find this information on the internet, but it's better when he tells it, a living trail between him and Nelson's superheroes via his grandfather in one World War and Churchill in another.

'How was Afghanistan?'

'Testy,' he says, 'Kinetic.'

He tells me he lost one of his operatives, Paul Warren, on tour.

'I'm sorry.'

It feels massive. That one life. At the memorial, I walk along the wall erected to honour the 10,098 dead naval personnel of World War II. The panels rack up like cards on a deck, name after name: signalmen and carpenters and cooks and stokers and sick berth attendants and midshipmen and telegraphists ... On it goes. Graham Swift's character Ray reckons 'you can't tell nothing by looking at the lists', because there are no odds given. 'You can't see no larger mathematics.' All I see is death.

The obelisk, with its lions and steps and sad soliloquy honouring Chatham's ranks and ratings with 'no other grave than the sea', is the centrifugal force. That is where the death listings begin, with 8,517 named from World War I.[*] And, after a 20-year break they pick up again with panel 33 and a fresh architect for the monument's post-World War II walls.[†] Britain had three naval manning stations – Chatham, Portsmouth and Plymouth (a trio of historic deep ports) – so, after World War I, three giant uniform naval memorials were erected. Only Chatham's sits on a hill. You can see one town merge into

---

[*] British service deaths were three times higher in World War I, where the majority of fatalities were in the army. However, World War II casualties in the Royal Navy and the Royal Air Force were greater.

[†] The Commonwealth War Graves Commission looks after all three naval memorials. The 1920s architect was Sir Robert Lorimer and the additional structures designed by Sir Edward Maufe in the early 1950s.

another down below and, beyond the Medway, imagine where the sea might be.

I ask Matt to send me some pictures so I can visualise him on parade up here and out fighting in Afghanistan. The images are very different. For memorial day, he is clean-shaven and spick-and-span under a white pith helmet. He explains that 'it is the one day we allow ourselves to mourn, to remember who we lost. It is a tough day. "The Last Post" normally gets me shedding a few tears.' In the photograph from Sangin in Helmand Province, Matt is an Action Man doll in camouflage, standing next to other Action Men. He tells me that Paul Warren is the one on bended knee. I stare at the young lad in the picture and try to imagine 10,000 more.

'He looks like Tom Cruise.'

'He would have loved that,' says Matt.

67. Royal Artillery War Memorial, Hyde Park Corner, London, 1925

Royal Artillery, World War I, 1914–1918; World War II, 1939–1945

Grace Taylor had a good war. Military service lifted her out of servitude, recognised her acumen, gave her meaningful work. Latterly, she has been acknowledged as one of the few remaining veterans from World War II. 'I do belong to the Royal Artillery Association now, but after the war, me and Bob didn't think to join anything or go to armistice days. We were just glad the war was over.'

Although Grace's work as a height-finder and plotter on an operational gun-site is now recognised by the Royal Artillery, during the war she was strictly a non-combatant and belonged to the Auxiliary Territorial Service. Women died on gun-sites from falling shrapnel and enemy fire, but Grace didn't know any personally. She met her husband Bob at a gun-site; he too survived relatively unscathed. Like I say, Grace had a good war. Armistice is important to her now, because it ties her back to that time when she was young, vital and, in her own small way, important.

Aged 100, she is president of her local Royal Artillery Association. 'I am the only one left from World War II.' But living down in Poole in Dorset, Grace is unaware of the Royal Artillery's landmark monument in central London. 'I should like to see a picture, though.'

Built to commemorate the 49,076 dead artillery men in World War I, a large plaque was added on the southern face to recognise the additional 29,924 fallen from World War II. The north-facing side features a dead gunner, covered in a trench coat. This realism proved hugely controversial in 1925, likewise the life-size reproduction of a 9.2-inch howitzer, the field gun used to blast the enemy from close quarters. Critics were sceptical; 'a spitting frog' one caustic comment. It was a lot for genteel London to take on board. But this monument was concerned less with service and gratitude. Instead, it focused on the fall-out from mechanised death. The sculptor, Charles Sargeant Jagger, lived his own hell as an infantry officer in the Artists' Rifles; Jagger the soldier was twice wounded and awarded the Military Cross. His graphic engravings speak volumes; the bronze gunners, erect and fallen, are personal. After completing the monument, he took six months off to recover.

More recently, foreign wars have manifested themselves in charged protests on the streets of London, including antics conducted from the strategically located Royal Artillery memorial. The outgoing Conservative home secretary James Cleverly threatened to imprison the culprits. 'You are effectively clambering over someone else's grave.' Former lieutenant colonel Andy Astbury is matter-of-fact. Hyde Park's Royal Artillery Memorial is first and foremost a monument to the dead — more specifically, the 79,000 dead who served with the Royal Artillery in two World Wars. To help with scale, Andy explains: 'the missing gunners alone in World War I numbered 6,500. That's bigger than the whole of the Royal Artillery today.' However, he does concede the monument is an inviting shape for weary passers-by.

WHEN TWO BECOMES ONE

Its rectangular levels and shelves give the large structure a certain functionality. Andy shares a recent anecdote from a couple of parachutists who arrived early one Armistice morning to find a sleeping reveller on its bulk. 'They crossed the road, bought a coffee, woke him up and said "On yer bike!"' If there is a line (and James Cleverly, himself a Royal Artillery reservist, clearly thought there was), in Andy's book the drunk didn't cross it. 'When people climb to the top, and damage the monument, that's when it becomes a problem.'

The widely shared image of a pro-Palestinian protester with a flag, mid-leap, was the trigger for mooted greater punishment in early 2024. Headlines read: 'Protestors climbing war memorials could face jail and £1,000 fine.' Can you legislate against something like that? Andy is not sure, but for him this monument really matters.

'There has been an Armistice ceremony there every year since 1925.' He should know. After thirty-five years in the Royal Artillery, Andy became a civil servant in charge of ceremonial, dress and sport for its regiments. For years, he organised the open-air commemoration between the Wellington Arch and the Royal Artillery Memorial. 'There is the communality of death in war. Nowadays, technology means we are much more dispersed. The monument is a focal point, a chance for a reunion and to remember.' Andy remembers four men from his troop in Northern Ireland killed by an IRA explosive in December 1979. He pauses. 'No, there is no training for that. I had to keep my soldiers in check. They were all close. It hit them hard.'

In 1925, the Royal Artillery monument was unveiled to honour the dead in World War I. By comparison, later conflicts have been small and asymmetrical. But terror is a killer, and any death in service to the state demands commemoration. I'm not sure where that leaves the pro-Palestinian protester scaling the monument, championing his asymmetrical cause. Every theatre in which World War I gunners operated is listed on the memorial's walls: Dardanelles, Mesopotamia, Persia, Africa, India, Egypt, France, Flanders, Italy, Arabia, Russia. And Palestine. There is no escaping the past, which is why we must take care of our memorials.

LEST WE FORGET

I WhatsApp Grace my photographs of the monument, including the World War II plaque. She is pleased. 'It looks like a lovely, impressive sculpture – although I'm quite blind these days, dear.'

68. Kinloch Rannoch War Memorial, Kinloch Rannoch, Perthshire, 1930

World War I, 1914–1918; World War II, 1939–1945

It was the trig point for this book – a Scottish cairn at the loch's end, a rare piece of public art in Kinloch Rannoch, the Highland village in north Perthshire where I grew up. As children, every November we filed in behind Peter Brown, his red hackle fluttering in the icy wind, his kilt kicking out behind sturdy, stockinged legs. He was a good piper, one of the best in the glen. Anne Gerber smiles. 'Aye, the village misses Peter. This year we had no piper, but it was good to see a few of the younger folk come along. We had a fair turnout.'

These days, eighty-five-year-old Anne is one of Kinloch Rannoch's oldest residents, a last living link to the names marked out on Rannoch's memorial. The exposed cairn faces down towards Glencoe – a reminder of Rannoch's Jacobite roots, its stones collected from the loch side, the construction postponed to accommodate a giant hydroelectric scheme. Finally, in 1930, remote Rannoch joined the legion of villages with their own monuments to grief. Many of the names from the first war are familiar, including MacPhersons and Robertsons (I was at school with a Macpherson and the neighbouring tenant farmer was a Robertson).

When Anne's family arrived in the village in 1938, the cairn was still novel, a public memorial that really meant something, untouched by lichen, uncompromised by a second conflict; a local landmark to the war to end all wars. These days, the well-appointed structure boasts forty-four names, more than twice the population of the local primary school. Twenty-eight lads from the first war sit in the centre, while, on a second, lower plaque, fifteen additional

WHEN TWO BECOMES ONE

names; a postscript to a failed first peace and a flawed humanity.* By the time World War II broke out, two-year-old Anne was living on one of Rannoch's big estates – Dunalastair. Her father had plenty to be getting on with – driving, gardening, that sort of thing – and her mother looked after five children, including Anne. 'My grandfather came to live with us from Paisley. So, in all, we were eight in Drumcastle Cottage. It was a lovely place.'

I know well the granite cottage Anne lived in. By the time I was a child, it was run as a holiday home and I got paid to clean it. The floors were uneven and the doorway old and low, and at the back

---

* An additional World War I casualty, Scots Guard guardsman Robert Innes, who died at the Battle of the Somme in September 1916, was added later on a small separate plaque, taking the total to 44.

was a ramshackle kitchen where once Anne's mother had her scullery. 'There was a girdle on one ring and soup on the other. Mother was a very good cook.' Anne redraws her childhood in the cosy home with its thick walls and reassuring log fire, miles away from war. 'I remember Uncle David coming to stay. By then, I was older. It was 1944.'

Anne was six when, into this Highland idyll, walked David, her mother's baby brother – all 6 foot 2 inches of him. 'I was keen to show David off in school. He had a wonderful American uniform and he was very good looking.' American? 'Yes, David emigrated between the wars. He thought he had escaped military service, but then Pearl Harbor happened. He came over with the American Air Force.'

Anne was wide-eyed. Her dashing uncle wowed them with gifts; a bag of shiny apples and hot chocolate packaged in polystyrene. 'David had quite a lot of leave, because he was going on a dangerous mission.' Anne is talking fast now. She is remembering her uncle and his bewitching otherness. I scroll down the names on the cairn, through the thicket of Black Watch servicemen onto the World War II plaque, and there he is: Staff Sergeant D. Mackenzie, P. H. USA A F. I never noticed an American airman before now.

'You only see what you look for. Yes. David died in '44, sometime after D-Day. A man came to the door with a telegram. Mother was in the scullery at the big black sink. She took the letter and put it in her pocket. She kept on with the washing. She knew the drill. Her other brother had died in 1940.'

Her other brother?

'Yes, Jack. He was in the Navy and was killed early on in a minesweeper. But, you see, I don't remember him because I would have only been three at the time. I remember Mum spent a lot of time on the phone to his fiancée, Morag.'

We look for Jack Mackenzie. He is not next to his brother. Ordinary seaman Jack is a lower rank and a different service; he is five lines down. 'I never thought about that. He should be next to

WHEN TWO BECOMES ONE

his brother.' Anne is briefly indignant. Highland memorials reflect their feudal homes, honouring the men by order of rank, not alphabetically as was commonplace after 1918. The extant laird's cousin, a lieutenant, is near the top. Anne is less indignant; she likes the local order and keeping things as they should be. We move back to David and his hot chocolate. Jack fades to second place. The power of six-year-old Anne's memories makes David distinct; it is almost possible to imagine his American presence in the village.

'Ach, yes. Mother really had to fight to get David's name on the Rannoch memorial. He had no other home. That was my mother – she wouldn't stop 'til she got what she wanted. Apparently, there's a nice grave to him at Omaha Beach in Normandy as well.' Anne smiles; she is back in 1944. 'I'd be sent in to sit with Granddad if he was feeling sad. But he never said anything. Adults didn't back then. And on our bikes beyond the quarry, we'd cycle fast past the wood. My brothers told me there were Nazis in that wood.'

She sits back, heavy with memories. 'Gerber? My surname? Yes, it is unusual. It's German. I married a German when I grew up and left Rannoch. They're talking about conscription over there now because of Putin. That would be terrible. My grandson's German. He wouldn't suit military life at all.'

PART FIVE

AN EXCEPTIONAL WAR

CHAPTER 21

READJUSTING TO PEACE

World War II has become the central plank in our nation's story, the high noon of Britishness when the country defied the odds and held out against the scourge of European fascism. Framed against the quagmire of World War I – and later, contested, smaller wars – these days Britain's role in World War II is routinely celebrated. This was not always the case. After 1945, while mindful of the exceptional military service that had saved them, the vast majority of people wanted to crack on with the peace.

69. World War II Avenue of Remembrance, The Tilt, Cobham, Surrey, 1946

World War II, 1939–1945

I am walking down a line of forty-six cherry saplings. It is April 2024 and they have been pummelled by Storm Catherine. This was not the spring they were expecting and still there is a bitter wind. Most have lost their candy-pink blossoms. Hanging from the bare neck of each baby tree is a large collar with a number, a name, a service and a QR code.

LEST WE FORGET

Meet James Tidy, RAF. His memorial tree is number eighteen. Except you can't meet him. He is dead and, according to information gleaned off the QR code, he has been dead since October 1943. His minesweeper HMS *Hythe* was torpedoed by a U-boat when escorting a convoy across the Mediterranean. North of the Algerian coast, sixty-two men perished, including twenty-nine-year-old James, who was Cobham-born and -bred, and apparently loved cricket. Other QR codes burrow further into the deep and yield photographs of young men in uniform, but not James's. Cobham Conservation and Heritage Trust have made do with a grey male silhouette. At least his tree has blossoms.

'We've got war all wrong.' Philip Jarman shakes his head. 'It's awful, really it is.' Philip should know: he's 101 and, unlike the British men and women who join the military today, Philip, and James Tidy before him, had no choice. 'Well, I would have been conscripted at nineteen so I thought I may as well volunteer at eighteen.' Perhaps inevitably, Philip followed his big brother John into the army, although he suggests that neither was bloody-minded enough to be ideal soldier material. But Philip can't forget the impressive figure his brother cut in 1936. 'I had just started my first term at Canford School and was taking a break from the rugby field when John appeared. He was six years my senior and I remember how magnificent he looked: much taller than me, 6 foot 3 inches and in uniform – polished boots and a Sam Browne.* He was a second lieutenant newly commissioned from Sandhurst. He went into the Indian army.'

Philip pauses. 'I never saw him again.'

A gentle soul who has spent a lifetime trying to forget what happened, Philip reluctantly tells his brother's story. John served in the 2nd Punjab Regiment, posted to Malaysia shortly after the outbreak of war. By Christmas 1941, a small tenacious Japanese

---

* A leather belt with a supporting strap that passes over the right shoulder, worn by military officers.

READJUSTING TO PEACE

force smashed through Britain's south-east Asian empire, mopping up Thailand in a matter of hours and then cutting south through the Malay Peninsula.* Britain's numerically superior army fell back to Singapore, John's regiment included. It was a farce. Philip sighs. 'The great naval guns were facing out to sea, when everybody but the army could have predicted the threat would come from the north.' Touted as Britain's foremost military base in south-east Asia, Singapore capitulated within a week; the British signed the biggest surrender in their history. John was among 13,500 prisoners of war, at least so his family thought.

'It was not until war's end we knew for certain that John was dead.' Philip looks up. 'Does one not always hope?' Emotional displays were kept to a minimum at home, but a persistent lack of clarity over John's death gnawed at his parents. 'It was the only time I clashed with my father. I'd been in Singapore at the end of the war. He wanted to know what I had found out.' Philip imparted horrible news. '"I didn't want you to be the person to have to tell his wife that her favourite son was beheaded by the Japs when taken prisoner!" Father went absolutely white.' Philip's research overturned the War Office's conclusion that John had died in action during the fall of Singapore. 'My brother was tall and European, you see.' He leaves it at that.

But the story does not end there. Philip gets up and pads down the corridor. He is looking for a photograph. The couple are young, hopeful and modest; John is the bridegroom, a sweet-looking man, almost gauche, and his wife is pocket-sized in large spectacles and a simple white dress. 'They married in India, in 1940. Diana was the daughter of John's colonel.'

Within months of John going missing, Diana left for Britain. 'She wanted to serve and that was easier done from England. She was on a passenger vessel, *City of Cairo*, and they were completing their last leg from Durban to the UK when it was a struck by a torpedo.' Diana's lifeboat held approximately fifty survivors. After thirty-five

---

* British Malaya became independent Malaysia in 1963.

235

days at sea, four were still alive, including Diana, the only surviving woman. 'They had been tipping bodies overboard for weeks. A German blockade runner found them off the South African coast. The German doctor asked the remaining English men for permission to operate on Diana. Her throat was closed. She didn't survive the anaesthetic.'

Philip stops. I had come to ask questions about war memorials. Philip doesn't believe in them; he thinks they are 'useless'. But, in the 1960s, he did like to sit under abundant blossoms in Cobham and think about what might have been, had John and Diana survived.

'The cherry trees have been replanted,' I tell him. 'Apparently, the original Women's Institute Avenue was past its prime.'

'That they've redone it is proof they were a jolly good idea in the first place. Much better than any other sort of monument.'

70. Portsmouth Naval Memorial, Southsea Common, Hampshire, 1924, extension unveiled 1953

Sinking of HMS Hood, 24 May 1941, Battle of the Denmark Strait, World War II

I am still sitting on Philip's floor in his well-appointed Hampshire home.* I suggest that perhaps his reticence about memorials stems from the fact his brother died miles away in the Pacific war. He nods. 'There is a memorial at Kranji in north-west Singapore. That is where John is named, but I've only been there once.'

We move to Philip's earlier childhood in Bournemouth; there were the usual japes and a boys' school at Cranford. This is easier terrain, but the war keeps cropping up, including the slew of boys who left Philip's school and never came home. 'Over six years, 180 died. And the school was only 300 strong.'

---

* Philip's late wife, Cora Jarman, was a Wren at Bletchley Park and featured in my first book, *The Bletchley Girls*.

READJUSTING TO PEACE

'I lost my best friend before I even joined the army. He was a couple of years older than me.' Philip smiles, memories of Richard Combes flood back. That bit older, Richard had a car and a certain panache. There is a favourite story concerning a Morris Minor and the two boys driving up to Bournemouth Pavilion. The commissionaire came down the steps, uniformed and sombre. 'The door handle came away in his hand.' Unfazed, Richard leaned across and asked what programme was being shown that afternoon. '"Oh," said Richard, "that's not our cup of tea. Thank you very much. Now, would you mind putting my door handle back on again?"'

Richard made a big impression on Philip. The latter remembers well his friend's eager efforts to embrace the conflict early on. 'He tried to get into the Fleet Air Arm, but was turned down because his landing skills for the aircraft were unacceptable, so he was transferred to the Navy proper.' Ordinary seaman Richard Anthony Combes went to war two years before Philip, who looked forward to his friend's first leave and the news of life at sea.

'About three days before we were due to meet, his father rang up and said, "I am afraid you'll not be meeting Richard this weekend."' In his usual jocular fashion, Philip replied: 'Is he confined to barracks?' Mr Combes's quiet retort was devastating. 'No, he was on HMS *Hood*.'

Philip chases the crumbs on his plate with a finger. 'That shook me so much that, although his parents lived nearby, I couldn't bear to go and see them for six months. He was their only child.' The quiet parlour, the ticking clock, the terrible pain, the accountant and his wife without their precious boy. Philip never went back. 'Oh dear,' he says. 'You have made me dredge it all up.'

The largest battleship of its kind, the *Bismarck's* sinking of HMS *Hood* in May 1941 was felt nationwide. The aft magazine exploded and the ship sank within minutes. From a 1,418-strong crew, there were three survivors. Philip's story of Richard sticks with me all the way home. I put his name into a memorials search. There's a remembrance book and annual service in St John's Church in Boldre, a village in the New Forest, where the ship's captain used to worship, and Richard is named on the famous Portsmouth Naval Memorial. I ring Philip and tell him I am going to find Richard in Portsmouth. 'Okay, dear. Let me know how you get on.'

A month later, I am back on the telephone. 'It wasn't a successful mission. I didn't get to see Richard's name. I couldn't get access to the naval memorial.'

'Why ever not?'

'I visited Portsmouth a week before the 80th anniversary of D-Day and the whole area had been cordoned off for the king's arrival. A stadium was being built for the memorial service.'

'How ridiculous.'

It felt ridiculous. A buoyant-sounding brass band was playing on the shoreline, anticipation in Portsmouth mounting. Two security guards refused me access to the naval goliath that was first opened in 1924. They offered to take a picture of Richard's entry instead. 'It's all a bit celebratory, isn't it?' one added with a shrug. 'Like we've forgotten what war is about.'

I nodded, feeling strangely gutted. I didn't know Richard or his family, but I longed to see his name on the Portsmouth Naval Memorial. Part of the Chatham, Portsmouth and Plymouth naval triumvirate, it honours 24,500 men who died at sea without a grave in both World Wars. The Commonwealth Graves Commission insist that the memorial is 'accessible at all times'.* I can confirm this is not true. A high green metal wall blocked my way. I had to make do with a truncated view of the unmistakable obelisk, crested with a copper ball.

An engraved name isn't much, but it is better than nothing. RIP Combes R. A. L.

---

* https://www.cwgc.org/our-war-graves-your-history/explore-great-britain/south-region/portsmouth-naval-memorial/

READJUSTING TO PEACE

71. The Commando Memorial and Memorial Garden, Spean Bridge, Lochaber, 1952

The Commandos, established June 1940

'It's hell. I'm not getting out in that.' Our little car is rocking in a gale, driving sleet smashing at the window.

'You bloody well are! They did and you are.' Mum and I have driven miles, sometimes on a single-track road, down from Inverness – wipers thwacking the windscreen, a wet fug muzzying the mirrors – on a mission to arrive at the Commando Memorial. The cloud sits low, a sodden grey blanket obliterating legendary views of Ben Nevis. Scottish weather is unpredictable, like war, I think.

In Edinburgh, on my way north, I find a former soldier repairing Nelson's Monument. Echoing many others before (and after) him,

he selects the Commandos as his favourite war memorial. Why? A shrug. 'You'll see for yourself.'

I touch a wet metal boot at head height and look up at the Scottish sculpture. Three Commandos on a plinth, Action Men in battledress, stand tall with the accessories of their war – Tommy gun, Commando knife, binoculars.* When unveiled by the Queen Mother in 1952, this statue was a landmark monument to a unique military force. It still is. Winston Churchill's brainchild, the Commandos, were the prime minister's solution to the dark days of 1940. Beleaguered Britain needed an extreme and unorthodox military force to fight outside conventional lines. This was much more than soldiering. And it came at a cost; 1,700 green berets lost their lives in World War II. Their outstanding memorial, located just miles from the original Commando Basic Training Centre at Achnacarry, on the exposed southern tip of Scotland's Great Glen, speaks to that risk.

'United We Conquer' is the inscription, but Alan Marnes, the son of a World War II Commando, has coined a different motto – or at least his father did. '"Kill or be Killed" – that's what my dad used to say. He was in 30 Commando, who were a tough bunch. Dad specialised in underwater stuff.'

Alan's dad, John Marnes, was just a young lad working as a store assistant down on the Thames when war came calling. In 1943, 30 Commando Information Exploitation Group was formed. They found John and trained him as a diver. 'He was never out of the water. He would swim around the Isle of Wight for fitness.' Today, re-formed as the 'eyes and ears' of 3 Commando Brigade, the MoD website insists that, during World War II, 30 Commando operatives were instrumental in the stealing of top-secret German technology. It is a sanitised summation.

Alan sighs. He is shadow-boxing his father's story. 'Dad wouldn't talk to me about it, the atrocities that he saw. The level of killing

---

* In 1949, Scott Sutherland won a competition, open to all Scottish sculptors, to design the Commando memorial.

READJUSTING TO PEACE

impacted on him.' Alan is trying to piece together a story his father did not want to share. 'My aunt said that he would get a telephone call or a telegram telling him to report to base and he would disappear for a month. Then come back. He wouldn't tell them what he'd been doing.'

Alan has few clues to go on. 'I know he moved about a lot. Germany, Italy, Norway, around Palestine, even Yugoslavia.' He still has his father's Commando knife. 'Like the one on the statue?' No, not quite the same. 'On the leather of Dad's scabbard, he carved notches against the Italian and the German flag. Each notch is a death, a kill.' There are five notches.

And Alan has a photograph, a picture of John standing in front of the mini submarines he worked with. 'They were attack submarines. He used them to go into various places. He attached mines onto large enemy ships and got the hell out.'

John wore a great big diving suit with a copper helmet and weights attached. Alan wants to know more – he has visited the Commando statue several times. 'It's very …' He pauses. '… thought-provoking. Dad was a trainer up there in Scotland. He spent a lot of time in the north.' John trained young men to be as tough as him, before he went back out to the coalface of war on another secret mission. John is Alan's hero.

As for John, he had no time for ideas of valour or heroism. 'He would not accept any medals. None of them. He could not stand the glorification of war.' Did he ever visit the Commando statue? 'Yes, he did. To honour those who didn't live. He appreciated the comradery of war.'

I stare through the rain at the three Commandos on their plinth and I look at the knife in its sheath. I think of John and the weight he carried with him after the war.

'Kill or be killed.' That was John's war.

* * *

LEST WE FORGET

These days, David Matthews is the Scottish representative of the Commando Association. In retirement, he is still working; for him, being a Commando was much more than a job. It had to be.

'We lost thirteen guys I was attached to,' he says. 'Theirs is the plaque, the men of 29 and 95 Commando. A lot of personal memories. I served in Northern Ireland, the Falklands and in Iraq. I knew guys who died in those wars and in Afghanistan. So, yeah, it resonates with me. It reminds me of how lucky I am because I've got a wife and family.'

He stops. It was my question about the Commando memorial garden that got him. 'So it's my honour to … sorry. I'm getting a bit emotional.' He reprimands himself – 'silly bugger' – before continuing. 'It's my honour to go up there and remember those boys. Because as long as you remember them in your heart, they're still alive.'

David, formerly of 29 Commando Regiment, Royal Artillery, trained in multiple roles. An elite fighting machine, he had to be match-fit in jungle, Arctic and desert conditions – whatever war threw at him. 'We went straight from winter training in Norway to being called up in the Falklands. It was freezing. We knew we had to sweep across very quickly and evict the Argies from British territory. Snow, sleet, minus temperatures. And we managed it because we knew how.'

David's son followed him into the Commandos. Both men earned the coveted green beret, still worn by the Royal Marines and those in the Royal Navy, Army and RAF who serve within 3 Commando Brigade and have passed the 13-week All Arms Commando Course. David insists that 'the Commando tests today are exactly the same tests the boys did back in 1940s Scotland'. Then, even the 60-minute hike from the station to Achnacarry training centre was an in-built challenge. Failure to arrive in time saw the men sent back to base. David's service stretched from the jungles of Belize to facing down the enemy in the Falklands, and losing his comrades closer to home in Northern Ireland. For him, the Commando Monuments is where it all began: an odyssey, a birthplace, his ancestral home.

READJUSTING TO PEACE

At Spean Bridge, respect is a given. Even my old mother prised herself out of the car, with two sticks and a dog. But respect alone is not what chokes David. That is the loss, which underlines the respect. Today, World War II has almost passed beyond living history, but the story of the Commandos hasn't. If you visit the Commando Memorial, look beyond the action men on their plinth, not towards Ben Nevis and Aonach Mòr, but to the discreet memorial garden sitting to their rear. A 180-degree pivot is required.

There you will find an assortment of plaques, memorials and photographs, 'placed for Commandos only'. These days, David helps oversee the entries. Grief can result in odd decisions – teddy bears, a windmill, fairies, a mini-bar. Occasionally, a misplaced memento is removed 'with dignity and integrity'. But the majority of predominantly small metal plaques are left in peace.

Marine Chris Maddison/KIA OP TELIC (IRAQ)/30 March 2003/Aged 24 Years

IN LOVING MEMORY OF MARINE PAUL WARREN KILLED IN SANGIN AFGHANISTAN. 21 JUNE 2010/ AGED 23/SADLY MISSED BY ALL HIS FAMILY*

Captain Tom Sawyer RA 29 Cdo, KIA Afghanistan, 14 January 2009, loved and missed always.†

And on it goes, an assortment of personal memorials holding on to something already gone.

There are so many plaques I lose count. Beneath the incessant rain, the names and faces are bleary; rows of young men removed

---

* This is the same Paul that Commando Matt Lyons remembers at Chatham's Naval Memorial every year.

† This memorial is a photo, not a plaque. It hasn't weathered well, but despite the elements, Tom will always look impossibly young and optimistic.

from this earth prematurely. The memorial garden is alive with death. If the causes behind some of Britain's recent wars are less clear-cut, families can take consolation that their offspring died serving the military elite – 'Commandos only'. For ex-Commando David, the garden reminds him 'of the boys, my friends who aren't here anymore. The fittest of the fit. Good guys.' Young lads who signed up to 'fight for the freedom of their fellow man'.

CHAPTER 22

GREAT MEN

Nineteenth-century philosopher Thomas Carlyle insisted that 'society is founded on hero-worship'; he shared his generation's fixation with great men. It is an obsession that has not gone away. Walk through London's historic centre and it bristles with statues of important men, many of them military. Even the Blitz didn't manage to knock out the physical manifestations of this hero-worship. Instead, World War II served to add another raft of war leaders to the venerated.

72. Winston Churchill statue, Parliament Square, London, 1973

Prime Minister Winston Churchill, 1874–1965

When were you first aware of Winston Churchill's giant bulk in Parliament Square?

The war leader's outsized statue is quite brilliant. It captures his silhouette and gait: the greatcoat, the stick, the slight stoop. Sculptor Ivor Roberts-Jones did a fantastic job in the early 1970s, but by the end of the twentieth century, how many of us were framing up Churchill as our go-to London backdrop?

LEST WE FORGET

Sir Anthony Seldon, a recognised authority on both the office of the British prime minister and Churchill's post-war premiership, believes it is unlikely 'many people noticed the statue until people tried to desecrate it and put paint on it'. He may well have a point. My outstanding first memory of Parliament Square's Churchill is of the great man sporting a grass mohican hairstyle, with red paint dribbling from his mouth. It was the year 2000 and anti-capitalist riots had swept the capital. A former Marine, James Matthews, was convicted for 'intentionally or recklessly damaging' the statue. He apologised, explaining: 'I thought that on a day when people all over the world were gathering to express their human rights and the right of freedom of speech, I would express a challenge to an icon of the British establishment.' Matthews was imprisoned for a month.

Two years later and the nation overwhelmingly selected Winston Churchill as their favourite in a BBC 100 Greatest Britons competition. With Churchill's iconic status riding high, more iconoclasm was predictable. Banksy cashed in with his 'Turf War' canvas of Churchill, again sporting a mohican; it was art that claimed to underline 'the anti-establishment wit' of the graffiti artist, asserting a double-edged idea of Churchill as both a great war leader and someone criticised 'for his fervently monarchist and imperialist views.'

The genie was out of the bottle. Churchill's statue has subsequently become the whipping boy for an increasingly divided nation, most notably during the 2020 Black Lives Matter campaign when the plinth was disfigured with a scrawled accusation: Churchill 'is a racist'. In the wake of this, Cambridge University offered a new summer course. 'Winston Churchill: The Greatest Briton?' reminded students that 'the people's Winston is a mass of contradictions'.

It is ironic that the controversy surrounding Churchill's legacy finds its genesis in a statue commissioned under a Labour administration to commemorate a great war leader. According to *The Times*, the focus of sculptor Roberts-Jones was the Churchill who inspired Britons during World War II, the man whose oratory recast the dark

GREAT MEN

days as great days in Britain's history. In line with this martial theme, Churchill wears an army greatcoat not, as originally intended, Order of the Garter robes.

At the unveiling in 1973, Lady Spencer-Churchill stepped forward, shoulder-to-shoulder with Elizabeth II. Watching on were four former prime ministers and one incumbent, and a crowd that spilled out beyond the square, rippling with spontaneous applause. People weren't there to remember Churchill the imperialist, nor Churchill the monarchist. They were there for Churchill the saviour, the war hero who helped Britain hold its nerve.

It is perhaps inevitable that, with the passage of time, this iconising of wartime Churchill has morphed into Establishment notions of Britishness, shored up by the bulwark of his colossal statue facing down Parliament. Dissenters have plenty to rally against.

That Churchill apparently selected his statue's own site when looking at plans for the reconstruction of Parliament Square in the 1950s magnifies ideas of a self-regarding individual. Most Churchill experts, Seldon included, caution against this interpretation, with David Lloyd George's statue a reminder that there was already a precedent for victorious wartime prime ministers in the square. As for Churchill's 12-foot hulk, commissioned several years after his death, the art reflected his reputation, not his ego. According to Richard Langworth, senior fellow of the Churchill Project at Hillsdale College in Michigan, 'when asked about a London statue Churchill replied he would much prefer his name on a park where East End children could play'. Seventy years later and there is still no park.

Countries need heroes. And when mob culture rails against them, it affords society the opportunity to re-evaluate the individual and the period. Churchill the war leader stands undiminished. As for Churchill the man, Langworth believes he would probably have enjoyed the furore and points me to Churchill the writer, who noted in 1931: 'Just as eels are supposed to get used to skinning, so politicians get used to being caricatured ... if we must confess it, they are quite offended and downcast when the cartoons stop ... They fear old age and obsolescence are creeping upon them. They murmur "We are not mauled and maltreated as we used to be. The great days are ended."'

World War II remains the high point in modern Britain's story and, with the culture wars in full swing, Churchill's end is not in sight. As *The Times* pertinently predicted in 1973: 'the heroic statue ... will become an emblem and a spectacle for generations not yet born'.

GREAT MEN

73. 'Monty' statue, opposite the D-Day Story museum, Clarence Esplanade, Southsea, Hampshire, 1997

Field Marshal Viscount Montgomery of Alamein, 1887–1976

It's December 2023 and the third month of the latest war in Gaza. On Whitehall's Raleigh Green, clusters of apologetic liberals shelter under umbrellas in the dismal rain. 'No emblems, no flags' is the strict instruction; this is a peace vigil at which a rabbi, an imam and the Archbishop of Canterbury take to the stage. The speeches are well executed, but the event strap-line 'Together for Humanity' proves futile. The Middle East is another world, miles away from Britain's identity politics, with its 'humanity' vigils and 'hate' marches.

People re-cluster for a better look, many straddle plinths, yesterday's warlords the props for today's plea for peace. I am cheek-to-jowl with Field Marshal Viscount Montgomery, save for his black beret hard to discern from Field Marshal Viscount Alanbrooke (more popular as a viewing point) and Field Marshal Viscount Slim, who sports binoculars and a bush hat. We are protesting for peace in a veritable museum of great white men from World War II. Try as I might, Montgomery of Alamein's unblinking stare refuses eye contact. I admit defeat and go home. Do peace vigils ever work?

Apparently, Monty was a grumpy bugger when it came to sittings for his London statue. 'How long will it take you to finish this sculpture?' he huffed at the reputable Oscar Nemon. The wily artist was having none of it and lied that the queen had sat ten times (it was just seven). 'What a waste of time!' barked Montgomery and succumbed to ten. The trace of irascibility is stamped on his Whitehall face – a military man for military men, erected at the dawn of Thatcherism in 1980. The Queen Mother, in a white-heels-and-handbag combo, a veil shading her face, did the honours.

'You have to win the war before you have peace. That is the problem with the Middle East. What does winning mean over there?' Pat

LEST WE FORGET

Owtram, a 101-year-old Y-station listener, part of the Bletchley Park code-breaking nexus and former Wren, shakes her head. 'In World War II, we knew what winning meant. The defeat of the Nazi war machine.' And with that, she tips into a favourite wartime anecdote.

It was a May morning in Kent, 1944. Pat had spent the night in the Abbot's Cliff direction-finding tower when she stumbled out into a cow-field and was confronted by an extraordinary sight. 'I saw some heads coming over the cliff top. I couldn't believe my eyes. It was Churchill's Homburg hat and Monty's beret. I am sure it was.' Pat was briefly rooted to the spot – without sleep, not in uniform and confronted by Britain's wartime colossi. 'I didn't know whether to wave or salute.' She opted for a wave. 'Morning!' It was reciprocated. 'Hello!'

'They walked on. I think it was all part of the ruse to make the Germans think the D-Day landings were heading for Pas-de-Calais. It was very obvious who they were because of their head gear. Monty always wore that beret.' Pat grins at the memory – the sunlit morning, the big beasts cresting the brow of the hill and the beginning of the end of the war. Bernard Montgomery makes her smile. She touches her thick thatch of hair; 'he always had his beret on'. The general's self-selected prop of war was a superpower that worked on many levels. It rallied troops, it tricked Germans and it made Pat skip a beat early one May morn.

They say familiarity breeds contempt, but I was pleased to bump into Monty again. His statue took me by surprise outside the D-Day Story museum in Southsea a week before the invasion's 80th anniversary. Born in London to a family of Ulster Scots, Montgomery ran Portsmouth Garrison before the war and was in charge of the Allied ground forces that set off from the city on 6 June 1944. This Monty is older than his London counterpart, wears a thick army jacket and his expression is insouciant, with the tiniest hint of a twinkle.

I know immediately the statue is a woman's work. Vivien Mallock has caught the older man who had moved beyond 'hunting on mainland Europe' and clashing swords with Supreme Commander Eisenhower and has softened him into the soldier who existed beyond the caricature. It is a replica of a cast unveiled a stone's throw from Sword Beach in Normandy, and Vivien's detailed touch has been meticulously applied to Monty's famous cocked beret with its two distinct cap badges (which were strictly against the rules).*

Montgomery's care for his men (he was appalled by the losses in World War I) and his unbeatable reputation were symbolised in that beret. Early on, he selected it over a bush hat in north Africa before his victory at El-Alamein. Later, he claimed it was worth three divisions. It was headgear that gave him much more than two inches; whether in the desert's heat and or crossing the Rhine, it gifted him a warlord persona.

I think back to the wet gathering on Raleigh Green: 'No emblems, no flags.' What hope does peace have when the trappings of war turn men into military giants?

74. Alan Turing statue, Sackville Gardens, Manchester, 2001

Alan Turing, 1912–1954

Ruth Bourne sighs. Liberal, Jewish and ninety-eight years of age, she is applying her standard perspicacity to the question of war memorials. 'There are very few good outcomes of war. At the moment, war seems to be a total disaster that doesn't appear to benefit anybody.' When we speak, Putin's Russia is in its third year of pounding Ukraine and, five months on, even the United States is feeling queasy over Israel's response to the Hamas attacks of 7 October 2023.

---

* Inside the D-Day Story museum, outside which Monty's statue stands guard, is one of his famous berets. Made by Kangol in 1945, it features a metal Royal Tank Regiment Badge and an embroidered Field Marshal's emblem.

LEST WE FORGET

But Ruth is not one to be deterred. She continues her verbal tussle with the concept of military commemoration. 'It would have to be to someone who has left some kind of lasting legacy because of conflict. I am thinking of things which were invented that wouldn't have been invented had there not been a war.' That is how she arrived at the commemoration of Alan Turing, the father of computer science. 'I believe nowadays he is even remembered on the £50 note, with what looks like a Bombe machine behind him.'

It is unsurprising Ruth has plumped for Turing, given that her entire adult life has been indirectly connected to his wartime endeavours. Aged eighteen, in 1944, she swapped her school uniform for a Wren uniform and was selected to serve as a Bombe operative in an outstation attached to Station X. 'Of course, I had no idea of the significance of the machine I was using. The only thing we were told was that we were "breaking German codes". I didn't know that my Bombe was in fact helping to crack Enigma codes. I had never heard the word Enigma.'

GREAT MEN

Nor had she heard of Alan Turing, the lead cryptologist at Bletchley Park whose genius included the development of the Bombe, an enormous electromechanical machine that facilitated the rapid decoding of Enigma-encrypted German messages. Ruth's knowledge concerning Britain's much-vaunted Bletchley Park and her small part in its secret nexus came much later, from retrospective learning. 'The security blanket was lifted in the 1970s. That was when I filled myself up with knowledge about Turing's Bombe.'

It snowballed from there. By the 1990s, Ruth was a vital cog in a commemorative venture initiated by the Bletchley Park Trust, travelling from her north London home to show curious onlookers in Buckinghamshire how she once worked night and day, plugging up giant black Bombe machines.

Given her keen engagement with the now well-known Bletchley Park complex, I anticipate that Ruth will select its life-sized statue of Turing, unveiled in 2007, to celebrate his staggering wartime contribution. She knows the statue well and is taken with its artistic integrity, constructed as it is from thousands of pieces of grey Welsh slate. But it isn't Ruth's first choice. Aged nearly a hundred, her perspective is broader than World War II. 'The thing is, our generation experienced a watershed. We've been up the mountain and down the mountain. In that time, the world I knew has changed into another world.' Ruth is alluding not just to Turing's life but also his death. Her sizeable ancient brain is trying to make sense of the country she and Turing fought for, both then and now. It is the same country that arrested Alan Turing for homosexuality in 1952, resulting in a conviction which ultimately led to his suicide. Ruth provides context for those times: 'My father was a doctor. He was a pretty open-minded man, but he would talk about homosexuality as an abomination. At the time, I didn't know what gay was, but you got the gist.'

She says the word again slowly. 'Abomination.' Back then, homosexuality was illegal, but as Ruth and many others testify, Bletchley

LEST WE FORGET

Park operated under its own bohemian rules.* One veteran, the late Pamela Rose, confided: 'Yes, my future husband and I were having sex out of wedlock, but there were many more people doing much worse!' In comparison, 1950s Manchester, where Turing was working in the University's computing laboratory, proved a far less forgiving place.

Today, it all seems so innocuous and unnecessary. Back then, Turing's confession to the police of a consensual sexual relationship with another man led to charges of 'gross indecency', resulting in compulsory hormone treatment, the removal of Turing's security clearance and the end of his cryptographic work for GCHQ.† He was found dead in his home in 1954, a half-eaten apple laced with cyanide next to his body. It is a statue of Turing unveiled in Manchester that speaks to the whole of his life.‡

The cryptologist sits on a bench in Sackville Gardens, flanked on one side by the university buildings in which he once worked and Canal Street on the other – home to Manchester's gay village. For Ruth, who was born in nearby Salford, this is the most honest monument to Turing's life. I travel north to sit beside him, to send him Ruth's good wishes and to take a photograph of the fatal apple in his hand, on my Apple phone.

Later, I will post a picture on social media to Alan Turing, a man who saved countless lives with his genius, and who fought tirelessly for the freedom of others, only to discover at war's end he was not free.

---

* Homosexuality was decriminalised in stages in the UK, starting with the Sexual Offences Act in 1967.

† Government Communications Headquarters.

‡ The sculptor was Glyn Hughes and the statue unveiled on 23 June, Alan Turing's birthday.

75. Freddie Gilroy and the Belsen Stragglers sculpture, North Bay, Scarborough, 2008
Liberation of the Bergen-Belsen Concentration Camp, 1945

A pitman's son from north-east England, Freddie Gilroy was a colliery bricklayer until he signed up for action, entering the war early, serving with the Royal Artillery and surviving right the way through to the fall of Germany. In old age, he'd stop by the local tool repair shop in South Hetton to have chat with his neighbour, Ray Lonsdale.* 'Freddie was a typical ex-pitman – rough about the edges, took no hassle. A quiet man but well respected.' For men in County Durham, male companionship had its limits. Freddie was not one for emotions. Each to their own.

'He didn't talk about the war. Then I moved premises. It was harder for him in old age to reach me in the industrial park. Up the hill, it required more effort. I saw him less often.' There, towards the end of his life, Freddie unburdened himself one morning. Ray doesn't know why. Maybe it was easier to talk to a non-family member. Perhaps he needed to share before he died.

In the story, Freddie is a young man and a seasoned soldier, or so he thought. It's April 1945 and he's in northern Germany, a military policeman with the 11th British Armoured Division, picking his way through the rubble. They are south of Hamburg and the smell is suddenly arresting. Quite revolting, worse than anything else. Freddie is among the first Allied soldiers to arrive at the Bergen-Belsen concentration camp; the smell is rotting human flesh.

'He told me about the horrors he saw,' says Ray. 'People dying, just skin and bones. He tried to share his rations, bits of chocolate and that, but the rich food made it worse. Put their bodies in shock, killed them sometimes. The army prepared a weak gruel instead. Some were too far gone. They couldn't be brought back.'

---

* Formerly a steel fabricator, these days Ray Lonsdale is an acclaimed sculptor.

LEST WE FORGET

The Allies found 20,000 emaciated corpses. Another 13,000 died after liberation. How could Freddie forget that? BBC reporter Richard Dimbleby had 'never seen British soldiers so moved to cold fury as the men who opened the Belsen camp'. Freddie turned twenty-four in Bergen-Belsen; birthdays were never the same again. Back in 1945, curated reports were broadcast on the radio, delivering what the BBC thought people could manage. In one, a woman flung herself at a soldier from the 11th Armoured Division: 'She begged him to give her some milk for the tiny baby … she put the baby in his arms and ran off crying … and when the soldier opened the bundle of rags to look at the child, he found that it had been dead for days. In the shade of the trees lay a great collection of bodies … there were perhaps 150 of them flung down on each other, all naked, all so thin that their yellow skin glistened like stretched rubber on their bones.'*

Freddie was in Bergen-Belsen for five weeks. After the war, he returned to South Hetton, where he never married and kept his feelings to himself for more than half a century. Freddie was well into his eighties when he finally talked to Ray; their conversation about the horrors Freddie witnessed had a profound impact on the young sculptor. 'He died shortly afterwards and I saw a documentary on the TV about the same concentration camp. Things came together and I started working on the sculpture.'

The statue is of the man Ray knew – flat cap, big boots, worn face – only this Freddie is twice-life-size. You can sit under the crook of his arm on a giant bench, look across the North Bay in Scarborough and pretend you are a child again, without any horror in your head.†
Made from individual pieces of Corten weathering steel, thanks to Ray's emotional craftsmanship, Freddie has grown in death. The

---

* Richard Dimbleby's BBC report, 19 April 1945.

† Both sculptor Ray Lonsdale and Maureen Robinson, the woman who bought the sculpture for Scarborough, are keen for the local council to relocate Freddie from the edge of the seafront where salt water is eroding his outsized features.

result is a memorial to the holocaust cast through one soldier's experience. Freddie is staring out to sea, an ordinary man who speaks for all ordinary folk, changed forever by war.

CHAPTER 23

THE GREATEST GENERATION

A marked uptick in interest and commemorative events relating to World War II occurred in the 1980s and has continued unabated ever since. Set against The Troubles in Northern Ireland at home and military prowess in the Falkland Islands overseas,* remembering British exceptionalism under Thatcher's premiership served both an emergent jingoistic appetite and a nostalgic longing for an era increasingly personified by a diminishing group of veterans.

Four decades on, and with very few frontline servicemen still alive, the definition of what it means to be a member of The Greatest Generation has seen several reincarnations.

---

* For more on monuments associated with the conflicts in Northern Ireland and the Falkland Islands, see chapters 28 and 29.

THE GREATEST GENERATION

76. The Overlord Embroidery, The D-Day Story museum, Clarence Esplanade, Southsea, Hampshire, 1974 (the museum opened in 1984)

The D-Day Landings, June 1944

The *Daily Telegraph* indulged in a spot of handwringing prior to the 80th anniversary of the D-Day landings. Its headline insisted that 'nearly half of young adults do not know what D-Day is'. Elsewhere, in the small print, one in ten young people admitted finding commemoration events 'boring' and 'repetitive'.* The article was picked up by right-wing TV channel GB News, with predictable indignation. It's a question of perspective. Flip those statistics and over half of today's young know that D-Day was the Allied invasion of Europe on 6 June 1944, and an unbelievable 90 per cent are not bored by commemoration.

What we can be sure of is, nowadays, more young people know what was at stake on that June morning in 1944 than their peers did twenty years after the liberation of Western Europe. Straight after the war, Britain was pushing on with the peace, there were relatively few commemorative events. Art student Sandra Lawrence's experience is a case in point. Born in 1945, she came of age in the heady 1960s. 'Heavens!' she laughs. 'I didn't know anything about the war. It wasn't considered history so we weren't taught it in school. All I can remember is Henry VIII.' It's ironic that this same young woman would soon become a leading visionary in World War II's nascent commemorative market, producing the blueprint for the Overlord Embroidery, a work so enduring that a D-Day museum was eventually built to house it.

'You mustn't call it a tapestry. That's so important. It is an embroidery of the D-Day landings. I was asked to provide the artwork.' The mistake is a common one; Lord Dulverton of Batsford, the embroidery's patron, had been directly inspired by the Bayeux tapestry (also an

---

* The survey was conducted by the Commonwealth War Graves Commission.

embroidery). From a family of tobacco barons, presumably looking for a legacy of his own, Dulverton sought to flip the 900-year French narrative with his own epic-scale needlework. Now it was Britain's turn to memorialise their invasion and, even better, their rescue of France.

Sandra is a wild card in the story. An art school drop-out ('My parents insisted I did graphic design. I was on the wrong course') and in need of a project, it was a friend with military connections who recommended her. 'I was given a chance. I went down to Cornwall and hung out with a group of wild artists. I took my work back to London and Lord Dulverton said "Forget it. I don't like it."'

Sandra's sample proved too abstract and she scrambled to save the situation. 'I begged for another go. He said I could try my hand at one more panel.' The realistic depiction, cartoon appeal and fresh approach of her second attempt led to an unlikely collaboration between a committee of military top brass – air marshal, general and admiral – and Dulverton and Sandra. Just weeks earlier, she had been the receptionist in a seedy Paddington hotel. 'It took me a while to get into my stride. The admiral would say 'we need a minesweeper' and I had no idea what a minesweeper was. Or which tank was which. Then some chap popped around with copies of a World War II magazine, *Purnell*, full of photographs. That was a godsend.'

Sandra proved a talented foil to the male egos involved. 'Mountbatten got wind of the project and insisted he was included, something to do with the special landing craft. I had to redo panel six. Princess Anne said it was the best likeness of him she'd seen.' The job of her life, Sandra spent four years working up massive 8-foot panels, with traced equivalents so London's Royal School of Needlework had an exemplary base from which to appliqué their magic. The end result in 1974 was 15 metres longer than the Bayeux tapestry and exhibited all over the world, before it found a permanent home back in Britain.* The purpose-built D-Day Story

---

* The thirty-four original colour design paintings by Sandra Lawrence now hang in The Pentagon, Washington, DC.

museum in Southsea was opened by the Queen Mother in 1984, forty years after the Allied invasion of Europe and just two years after the Falklands War. Lord Dulverton had successfully predicted the commemorative zeitgeist.

'Oh! Just look at that detail! It's exquisite! Do you see the screw on the gun? The detail of the stitching. And medals. Their ribbons!' Kay, an elderly woman from Minneapolis, is mesmerised. The handiwork is better than she had even imagined, an epic sweep of history perfectly pricked through the feminine prism of embroidery. It is one week before D-Day's 80th anniversary and, inside the museum, we admire a stitched King George VI and Churchill, and chuckle over the clear distinction between the square-jawed allies and the German soldiers, sometimes faceless, elsewhere resembling heavy-set trolls.

Kay's English friend, Joyce, approves: 'We held out a long time on our own.' For her, it is personal. 'My Dad was a glider, one of the

airborne troops.' We move slowly around the glass-protected, thirty-four-panel epic. Joyce lets out a sudden cry and stands up in her mobility scooter, leaning forwards. 'It's Caen. This is where my uncle Harry died. Here in Caen!' In 1944, Allied bombing destroyed the target they sought to save. Many French in the town died, as did Uncle Harry. He is Joyce's hero. The embroidery is picked out in dystopian browns and yellows. The scene demands silence. It was the last panel Sandra drew, and her favourite.

'I love the colours, and the devastation. The evocative purple sky. It's very beautiful.' The Caen panel is a nuanced oasis amidst an otherwise startling rendition of a successful Allied campaign. Were Germans deliberately drawn to look uglier? Sandra is noncommittal, but clear that while her generation weren't taught about the war, everyone knew about the destruction of Europe. The abject horror of the Nazi regime lent easily to the casting of warring goodies and baddies, a story that Britain has long relished telling.

As for Sandra, her job drawing the world's largest amphibious invasion was the biggest of her career. 'Afterwards, I thought *I've had enough of all this*. I turned to pastels and focused on drawing vegetables and the beauty of nature.'

77. Kemble War Memorial, Church Road, Kemble, Gloucestershire, 1920

The Campaign for Normandy, 1944

Alan McQuillan taps his walking stick on the floor, marking out each individual beach.

'Juno's there. That's Gold. That one there is Sword. And further along is the big American one with all the mess-ups. Yes, Omaha. And that is Utah.'

'And which one were you meant to land on?'

'Gold.'

'And which one did you land on?'

'Juno.'

'Why?'

'Because it was so tight. I can see it now. I can still see it, all the landing craft.'

Alan puts down his stick. He's 101, but there are some things you don't forget. He is back in 1944, a leading aircraftsman in special unit 3210 Servicing Commando, a group of self-contained, elite technicians at the vanguard of Operation Overlord, tasked with the establishment of advance airfields for the Allies' push across Europe.

Alan's military service had begun three years earlier, aged eighteen. 'I wanted to fly, but at the RAF medical I was told I was short-sighted. So I became a technician, an armourer. You know, loading guns and bombs on aeroplanes.' Alan did his stint loading up four-engine Lancasters, winching bombs onto aircraft. '500lb bombs, 1,000lb bombs, 2,000lb bombs. Bouncing bombs. Sometimes the Lancaster had to be altered to get them up. No, I didn't think about the bombs' impact. You didn't. There was very little news.' And then came the call.

'They said volunteers were needed, technicians for special units. They told us: "This could be dangerous."' Alan and another armourer walked towards that danger. They signed up to become part of the RAF Servicing Commandos, units of 150 men trained by the army, the RAF and the British School of Motoring to secure airfields ahead of Allied military assaults.

'The first four units went from England into the African and Italian campaigns. And the next six, including mine, went to Normandy.' Alan stops. He is back in a landing craft, a thicket of vessels choking the Channel. They are waiting to land and Alan is nervous. Seasick and tired too. The journey's a long one. 'We were not told anything. The main road to Gosport was packed. We had to report to an orderly room when we got there. They took all our English money away and gave us francs. All those francs we took for the invasion were made in England.'

LEST WE FORGET

Alan left Portsmouth on 6 June 1944. D-Day. 'We got on our boat just as Eisenhower shared his message that everything had started.' Alan's crossing began at 11 a.m. 'Each unit had four lorries. I remember dozing at the wheel, waiting.' There was almost twenty-four hours of jostling at sea before the lads touched down on the wrong beach. 'We weren't on the list for Juno.' He chortles. Bureaucracy.

By the following day, special unit 3210 Servicing Commando was working from a temporary airfield, B-3, at Sainte-Croix-sur-Mer. Planes were refuelled and repaired, ammunition loaded and injured men flown home. Churchill made a fleeting visit in late July and, by late August, Alan's unit had moved on. The battle for Normandy was won and 22,000 Allied servicemen were dead.

Alan ended his war in the Far East; his brow puckers with memories of VE Day in Calcutta and the vicious Battle for Java. 'I didn't go back to Normandy for forty years. In the 1980s, I took my wife over there. I'm not sure why. Yes, perhaps there was more talk of the war by then.'

Alan discovered B-3 airstrip was one of the few that hadn't been built over. The farmer's daughter recognised him. He likes the French; the connection is deep and enduring. In 2019, he was awarded the Légion d'Honneur, which he keeps alongside a rack of shiny medals. 'They are all service medals.' And he lists them, patiently answering all my questions, until suddenly he stops and shouts. 'I am NOT a hero. I was just doing my job. I am NOT a hero.' Later, I will look him up online. It is June 2024 and he is in Normandy talking to King Charles and giving prime minister Rishi Sunak a piece of his mind. But he is not a hero.

We change subjects back in his modest home in Kemble, Gloucestershire, where he worked as a dairyman after the war. 'You want a monument? Well, there is a little wooden monument on B-3, that first airfield we secured in Sainte-Croix-sur-Mer. It's just down from the big British Normandy Memorial in Ver-sur-Mer.' Alan describes both in detail.

I explain I need a monument in Britain that means something to him. He slowly gets up and puts on his blue RAF special commando beret with its emblems and red poppy. He retrieves his walking stick with a poppy dongle. Together, we walk through the door adorned with a poppy sticker, and push past the back gate, a memorial cross attached, onwards to the car (Alan's knee is playing up). A few yards down the road, on the same street, is an unremarkable World War I memorial, the sort you see in every village across England. It is a damp January day and the modest crusader cross on a two-step plinth is ringed by a blaze of poppies. Alan gets out of the car to have a look.

'That's my wreath.' He points with his stick. 'Gloucestershire's Normandy Veterans' Association wreath. I lay one every year for the men who never came home. They are the heroes.'

78. Memorial to the Women's Transport Service (FANY), St Paul's Church, Wilton Place, Knightsbridge, London, 1948

First Aid Nursing Yeomanry, World War II, 1939–1945

Inside the quiet hush of St Paul's Church, you can't hear the incessant rain or dim roar of Knightsbridge traffic. The building is sufficiently all-consuming to distract from daily trifles. I am assured by the administrator that, in Victorian London, the pews were at capacity – 800 regular worshippers in a church which underwent a facelift in the 1890s. By the time Joyce Wilding entered this hallowed building in 1943, the interior had long since given way to a gothic revamp. 'Yes, High Anglican is exactly what it is. Bells and smells, that's right.' It was here, in Wilton Place, that the adjoining vicarage became the imposing World War II headquarters of the First Aid Nursing Yeomanry (FANY), an exceptional female military service, for whom the church was a place of prayer and spiritual sustenance, and remains as such today.

Christ up high on his golden crucifix, exquisite statuary either side of an ornate altar, priests in their vestments; just like the FANY, the church is relentlessly traditional. It is easy to imagine rows of eager girls pressed into tailored uniforms, hair neatly curled beneath caps, bowed heads in prayer: 'Our Father, who art in heaven.' Nor do you have to imagine it; the FANY still have a commemorative service here every year. Established in 1907 for the administration of succour and assistance on and behind the frontline, the FANY are the world's oldest uniformed 'military' voluntary organisation for women. Today, 150 exceptional members serve in the name of their commandant-in-chief, Anne, the Princess Royal.

Joyce Wilding was, in so many ways, an archetypal recruit; well brought up, privately educated and keen to do her bit despite parental reservations. 'Father was injured very badly during World War I and had something of a breakdown, and mother's brother was killed.' The couple were disinclined to relinquish their only daughter into the jaws of another war. But Joyce and her friend Primrose were from a different generation. Eighteen years old and raring to go, in 1943 they took themselves to London's Knightsbridge for an interview at FANY HQ. Joyce recalls an emphasis on secrecy, a fitting for a fine uniform and interviews with terrifying women. 'We chose the FANY because we thought we'd be driving men around, just like in *Foyle's War*.'*

There is much about Joyce's wartime service that elicits a smile, including her indignation when told the job she'd been assigned was 'a transmitter hut attendant'. '*Good God*, I thought, *is that cleaning a loo?*' The unlikely presence of her screwball horse, Pinto, at Oxfordshire's Thame Park, and home-spun social efforts in the evenings, including Joyce's soprano singing voice, were surely an antidote for the many at Thame Park training to go behind enemy lines. 'We never knew their real names. I remember one was a

---

* Initially working with horses, by World War I the FANY were renowned for their driving skills, an expertise which they carried into World War II.

Norwegian aristocrat.' Joyce was operating in a space where schoolgirl FANYs and SOE – Churchill's Special Operations Executive, established to 'set Europe ablaze' – intersected. Her war was relatively safe. Theirs was not.

She spent hours in a transmission hut, waiting for a command to tune into communications arriving from agents in France. 'No, I didn't understand Morse. I just had to operate machines that looked like microwaves.' Until she was promoted to driver in 1944, this was Joyce's war work. It is unsurprising, therefore, that when I asked her for a war memorial which resonates, she cited the FANY church in Wilton Place; it speaks to Joyce's conventional wartime path. 'After 1918, my mother became a Christian Scientist, which I always found rather embarrassing. There had been so much loss you see.' Joyce, whose later experience of war took a very different form, went on her own spiritual journey. 'I got confirmed into the Anglican church after the war.'

Traditional Joyce in traditional England had much to be grateful for. Today, having just celebrated her 100th birthday, she remains cognisant of that good fortune. 'Well, of course, Primrose and I were just SOE housekeepers. I think that is what they called us.' Joyce, with her pony and pretty voice, was an essential link in a lethal chain. 'We were based at a training station with mainly men. But there were women SOE operatives too. Many FANYs did terribly dangerous work.'

I step outside St Paul's reassuring bulk and walk through the rain to the discreet FANY war memorial with fifty-two names etched into the church's western wall – the women who never came home. Scratch the surface of Joyce's story and the vicarage in Knightsbridge, with its capacious church, becomes part of a disarming façade. For a chosen few, the FANY uniform was a point of no return.

LEST WE FORGET

79. Special Operations Executive (SOE) Agents/ Violette Szabo, Albert Embankment, London, 2009

Special Operations Executive, 1940–1946

The plastic flowers resist the pouring rain. Red poppies and purple violets sit in perpetuity beneath a FANY plaque full of names. I plug one into Google: Lilian Rolfe. Up pops a sepia photograph of a young woman with dual nationality, multiple languages and a codename – 'Claudie'.

In wartime Britain, Lilian was extraordinary to the FANY's ordinary. The schoolgirl vibe that the organisation so brilliantly cultivated was excellent cover for women employed to do clandestine work. Courtesy of FANY autonomy, Lilian was permitted to travel abroad and bear arms. Regular service women were not. It was a privilege that cost her life.

Dropped in Orléans in central France in April 1944, within three months a German sweep of the area caught Lilian with her radio. Next came interrogation and heavy work in a labour camp that left her unable to walk. She was shot dead in Ravensbrück on 5 February 1945, aged thirty-one. In the shadows of commemoration, Lilian's legacy lives on. She is named on the Runnymede Air Forces Memorial in Surrey, and there were posthumous awards, including an MBE and Légion d'Honneur. But, unlike some SOEs, she has not been included in the recent spate of busts. Guided by the cultural zeitgeist, a few break through, most do not.

In 2012, a bust was finally unveiled in Bloomsbury's Gordon Square to Noor Inayat Khan, the first SOE FANY wireless operative sent into occupied France. She was shot dead in Dachau concentration camp in September 1944. The recent fight for her commemoration spilled into the House of Commons. Today, Noor Inayat Khan is the recipient of the only standalone memorial to a named Muslim woman in the UK. The *Guardian* wondered 'what took them so long?' Likewise, you might ask 'Why only a bust?'.

THE GREATEST GENERATION

She is one of a triptych of female SOE–FANY busts in London. Operative Countess Krystyna Skarbek, the Polish spy who operated out of Britain in World War II, floats on a wooden block inside Kensington's salubrious Ognisko Polskie, the Polish Hearth Club. The representation is arresting, as I imagine Krystyna was. Unveiled in 2019, the sculptor, Ian Wolter, is the husband of Krystyna's accomplished biographer, Clare Mulley. The spy would surely have appreciated their discreet teamwork. But still, it is just a bust. Krystyna, the woman who skied out of occupied Poland with the first plans of Operation Barbarossa under her arm, is not even named on the FANY plaque at St Paul's Church in Knightsbridge. She didn't die during the war, but rather was murdered in 1950s London.

Knightsbridge, Bloomsbury, Kensington: today, cycling between grand commemorative addresses across the capital belies the ruthless danger and anonymity female operatives faced in war. Ironically, the SOE didn't initially want women. It was a shortage of men that saw the war machine succumb to their lethal effectiveness behind enemy lines; recruitment began in 1942. Of the nearly 400 F Section agents working in France, around forty were female. At least twenty were imprisoned and thirteen murdered. None appear to have relinquished sensitive information to the Germans under interrogation.

Commemoration is about scale. Just look at Churchill's reassuring bulk facing down Westminster to understand that. 'There is something almost Freudian about the hardness and permanence of a statue,' one campaigner explained to me. Hero-men crowd our streets, muscling out women's stories, even those who gave their lives.

I cross the River Thames and head east along Albert Embankment. The final SOE bust stares back across the water. As sculpted heads go, it is modern, captivating and defiant. The illustrious Violette Szabo was erected in 2009, half a century after she was immortalised in the 1958 film *Carve Her Name With Pride*. The heady mix of Violette's humble origins (a shopgirl from south London with

LEST WE FORGET

French roots) and a powerful love story – she married a French soldier who was killed fighting in north Africa – were the alchemy for posthumous fame. The emotional gut punch of female widowhood made this young woman easy prey for the SOE.

Given a FANY uniform and some basic training, Violette was parachuted into France on her second mission. She was apparently caught in a German roadblock; unverified accounts claim that Violette successfully fended off the enemy with her Sten gun (she was a good shot) before being captured, tortured and interrogated. Like Lilian Rolfe, she was executed, in Ravensbrück, February 1945.

I recount this story to an Italian family gathered beside the statue. 'She was a beauty,' I add, 'with a wonderful cockney laugh.' The father searches for Violette on his phone; the son is keen to know about the SOE. I want to insist that 'Violette needs more than a bust', but they are so mesmerised by her black-eyed stare, I check myself. And I check the memorial.* Up high on a granite plinth, Violette sits as a first among equals; the monument she heads is to 'all SOE operatives'. This is a sculpture to the agents who fought (and died) behind enemy lines, irrespective of nationality, religion or gender; discreet, unsung and, once in the field, with a life expectancy of just six weeks. Yes, Violette has been recast as a bust, but it is a design that affords more space and attention for broader SOE commemoration on the plinth. A generous, and dare I say it, female gesture.

80. The Bevin Boys Memorial, The National Memorial Arboretum, Alrewas, Staffordshire, 2013

The Bevin Boys, 1943–1948

Philip Robinson is ninety-eight. 'The country has gone to the dogs! I blame that lady. She destroyed the industry.' A former miner, Phil is talking about Margaret Thatcher – but not only her. 'I live near Warrington. We used to have Crosfields here, the big soap people. There's nothing now. And there were hundreds of engineering companies and a foundry. We made the locomotives of the world!' He stops and draws breath; the truth is that Phil 'can't see us being any good at anything anymore'.

This downwards glance at the world is not uncommon in the elderly. Britain has undergone undeniable international slippage in the last hundred years. But, away from the subject of contemporary Britain, Phil is a natural optimist. He had to be; his start in life was not easy. His mother died when he was six, his house was bombed out when he was fourteen and, when finally Phil signed up to fight in 1944 ('Oh, we all wanted to put on a uniform'), he was sent down the pits.

---

* The Albert Embankment bronze bust of Violette Szabo was sculpted by Karen Newman.

LEST WE FORGET

'I had never seen a pit! But there was nowt you could do.' Phil was very disappointed. 'It was a bit stupid not making mining a reserve occupation in the first place.' By 1943, having failed to ringfence miners and facing a chronic coal shortage, the home secretary, Ernest Bevin, resorted to compulsion. Over the next five years, 48,000 men between the ages of eighteen and twenty-five were randomly drafted into mining, Phil included. The Bevin Boys were born. 'It was a ballot scheme and I'll say that for them, they got a good cross-section. In our County Durham billet, we had a lad from Orkney, another from the Isle of Wight, a Cambridge undergraduate and an ice hockey player. We were all very aggrieved.'

On the cusp of manhood and fed up watching war from the sidelines, it's hard to imagine just how much young boys like Phil longed to fight. 'We wanted to be part of it alright. I wanted to join the RAF.' Instead, he was issued with 'a boiler suit, helmet and boots, and assigned to a colliery'.

Phil sighs. During training, he wasn't averse to pulling his weight, lifting iron girders and shovelling heavy minerals. Nor did he mind the underground loading and pony driving once at Pelton Fell Colliery. In fact, Phil discovered he had a penchant for the technicalities of mining; 'it is a very complex industry.' When finally demobbed in 1947, he was summoned by management. 'I'd been to grammar school, they asked me to take up a job in mine-surveying.' Phil qualified from Wigan Mining and Technical College and spent forty years in the industry. 'I had a very interesting job. Lots of geology.' His voice is gruff with pride.

And there is the irony. This disappointed Bevin Boy had a great life overseeing Britain's pits in the post-war period. It was less the wartime work that galled Phil, rather 'the lack of recognition, the lack of uniform'. Mid-war, riding a wave of patriotism, Britain had little truck with men who didn't pull their weight. 'You see, no one knew what we did. They looked at you backwards. I was on leave in Shoreham-by-Sea and at breakfast everyone was staring at us, the only lads without uniform. My friend said we were changing shifts, that we were in the Merchant Navy.' War forefronted male pride. Back home on the Wirral, Phil squirmed. 'I met up with two old friends. One was a squadron leader. He was full of it.'

And on it went: by the 1950s, war heroes were lauded in film, in books and on television. So where was Phil's story? Much later, commemoration became the buzzword for British pride, but the British Legion had little time for men without a uniform. 'They were wicked with us. They asked if we would like to join a military parade. I said "Yes!" but they never called.'

It is this cocktail of compulsion and oversight that is brought to life in four discreet Kirkenny quarry stones in Staffordshire's vast National Memorial Arboretum. They are not flash or large; you might well walk on by. As it was with the Bevin Boys. But look again and they are meaningfully engraved. There is the Bevin Boys' badge and a frank inscription: 'The Bevin Boys were national service conscripts directed to work underground.'

The collection of sculptures looks much as they did on television when unveiled in 2013 by Sophie, then Duchess of Wessex, surrounded by the men for whom it meant so much. She shed a tear; so did they. The flurry of press write-ups was affirming. Phil sends me a bundle in the post, with a photograph of a pit pony and his handwritten notes. And it falls into place. Phil is a proud man, even in old age. He only struggles when he is not able to feel proud. The Bevin Boys monument (and a badge sixty years too late) have set his young self free. But it might take more than a monument to solve his laments about modern Britain.

81. The ATS Memorial, The National Memorial Arboretum, Alrewas, Staffordshire, 2005

The Auxiliary Territorial Service (ATS), 1938–1949

Betty Webb MBE, aged 100, is the living embodiment of war commemoration. Fêted both in Britain (portrait in the National Army Museum, invitation to the coronation, frequent television appearances) and abroad (Légion d'Honneur, front page of *National Geographic*), she is one of the last remaining women who served in World War II. From 1941, Betty worked at Bletchley Park and, by 1945, had been posted to the Pentagon. 'Yes, I suppose it is rather extraordinary, when I look back on it now.'

Betty's phenomenal longevity, her geniality and the unique nature of her military service have seen this former servicewoman fly up the pecking order of World War II veterans in recent years. She pushes a

THE GREATEST GENERATION

piece of A4 paper towards me. Annotated in her own neat hand are the many places which honour Betty's name. The list includes a school classroom in Oxfordshire, the British Embassy in Washington, DC and, of course, Bletchley Park's roll of honour.

Few have worked harder for the memory of Bletchley Park's code-breaking nexus than Betty. In 2015, she was awarded an MBE for her efforts promoting Bletchley Park Trust, the organisation which oversees the museum. She is particularly fond of the Park's red-brick, mock-Tudor mansion: she worked there as a teenager, inputting data on the first floor, and, eighty-two years later, celebrated her 100th birthday in the ground-floor ballroom. Likewise, Betty approves of the Women of World War II memorial in Whitehall, the latter-day anonymous female twin to the earlier Cenotaph.* But neither the museum-mansion nor the monument capture Betty's personal journey during the war.

Instead, she proffers a homespun photograph album. 'I still miss those views,' Betty admits as I leaf through pictures of Shropshire's rolling hills and hedgerows, more specifically the vistas from the village of Betty's birth, Richard's Castle. On the penultimate page, five pictures feature the local church, All Saints, and its wartime rolls of honour. Remembering 'those who fell in the Great War' is a bronze plaque, on which the names of fourteen men are embossed in perpetuity. World War II is commemorated on parchment, behind a glass frame: 'Names of those from the Parish of Richard's Castle on Active Service for their King and Country.' In careful inked calligraphy is Betty's maiden name: Charlotte Vine-Stevens. 'Just one lad did not return home. John Haggart, the gardener's son.' The memorials are an unspoken acknowledgement of how differently the two wars impacted rural communities. The first indiscriminately killed young men; the second conscripted both sexes, but statistically those who did not return home were unlucky. RIP John Haggart.

---

* The Women of World War II monument is Monument 87.

LEST WE FORGET

Betty smiles. The plaque symbolises where she's from, but who did she become in war? She hands me a 100th birthday card featuring a stone figure of an ATS servicewoman. The Auxiliary Territorial Service was a female support service for the British Army, staffed predominantly from conscripts. An early volunteer, Betty's leadership qualities were recognised by the ATS – 'I was promoted to corporal pretty sharpish.' And it was the ATS that ascertained she spoke German, which led to selection for Bletchley Park.

The statue is housed in the National Memorial Arboretum, less than an hour's drive from Betty's home in Wythall in Worcestershire. Among the maze of more than 400 memorials, in a garden dedicated to women in service, sits a petite soldier. She arrived in 2005, after pressure from two veterans, piqued at the failure to recognise World War II's largest female military organisation.

Luminous white, the statue has a Madonna quality; dressed in a neat uniform, legs coyly tucked to one side, hair rolled beneath a cap, the service woman is feminine, modest, discreet – all attributes enhanced by the larger, less graceful WRAC woman standing beside her.* The Women's Royal Army Corps grew out of the ATS after World War II. The few women who chose to remain in military service in the late '40s were 'more hale and hearty', as Betty tactfully puts it, than the 300,000 strong ATS, many of whom were compelled to serve.

Betty shows me her favourite wartime photograph taken in 1945: she has permed hair and wears a lightweight khaki uniform. Freshly spruced for her posting to Washington, DC – where she finished the war paraphrasing Japanese messages – it is a picture of a confident young woman who has grown into adulthood through military service. The similarities between the photograph and the ATS memorial are striking.

As Betty explains, 'It is rather nice to have a statue that looks how you once looked.'

---

* The sculptor of both statues was Andy de Comyn.

CHAPTER 24

BLITZED

By the early twentieth century, the aeroplane had forever changed the conduct of war. In the 1930s, many predicted the next conflict would be won (and lost) in the skies. On the ground in World War II, Germany's early indiscriminate bombing of cities killed record numbers of British civilians, strengthened Britain's resolve and gifted the English language a new verb: to blitz. Retaliation was severe. Disproportionate, even. How do you commemorate winning a war that killed so many innocent victims?

82. New Coventry Cathedral, Priory Street, Coventry, 1962

Air raid on Coventry, World War II, 1940

It was peak Brexit mania, when former prime minister Gordon Brown prowled around the preserved ruins of Coventry's bombed-out cathedral to underline the impact of war, reminding viewers in 2016 that Europe's unprecedented era of peace was best preserved through cooperation, with 'arguments not armaments', and, according to this logic, by the UK remaining in the European Union. The video went viral, a fillip for the Remain cause in an otherwise underwhelming referendum campaign.

The hero of the piece was Coventry's St Michael's Cathedral Church. The sacred building's shell already had form when it came to impactful messaging. In December 1940, just weeks after the most devastating bombing raid ever inflicted on a British city on 14 November, a Christmas service was held in the cathedral's ruins and broadcast around the world. The ravaged church, with its surviving spire, became a symbol for Nazi aggression. That same month, 60 per cent of Americans said they would help Britain, even if it meant being dragged into war.

Early on, a decision was taken to preserve what remained of St Michael's, and alongside the ruins, build back differently – a second chance for a brave new Britain. The new cathedral, designed by architect Basil Spence, was consecrated in the presence of Elizabeth II in 1962. The two adjoining buildings are a spectacular testimony to old and new, medieval and modern, war and peace. Coventry's pride – beneath charred beams and expansive Graham Sutherland

art – is palpable, the messaging evangelical and the mission unequivocal: 'the ruins and the modern cathedral are two halves of one whole, renewal from destruction, love from hate'.

Today, nestled in the corner of the relic church, is a small museum dedicated to Coventry's Blitz. Visitors sit at wartime desks and listen to a brief summation of the city's November 1940 ordeal. The voice-over rattles through horrifying statistics: 4,300 homes flattened, 2,500 shops destroyed and nearly every factory gone, more than 1,000 people missing (568 were killed). Coventry's historic heart gone forever.

And yet viewers were to be under no illusion: the good folk of Coventry defied Hitler with their 'determination' and their 'resolve', a spirit so indestructible the words 'determination' and 'resolve' are repeated twice in a five-minute video. The elderly volunteer smiles. He talks of his grandfather, a firefighter on the night of the attack, who recalled the stench of burning buildings and devastation. The volunteer takes pride in the stories he has heard. More smiles. Pride, resolve, determination, victory: inside a fairy-tale medieval ruin, visitors are soothed with a reassuring ending. Coventry, like a phoenix from the flames, rose again.*

But the city's now higgledy-piggledy, mismatched architecture tells a different tale. With the exception of the cathedral, post-war Coventry was not built back better. As for the population's 'determination' and 'resolve', it was not immediately apparent the morning after an eleven-hour raid that destroyed two-thirds of the city. Tom Harrisson, the anthropologist who set up the Mass Observation Unit, recalled: 'Unprecedented dislocation and depression ... The overwhelmingly dominant feeling was utter helplessness ... there were more open signs of hysteria, terror, neurosis, observed in one evening than during the whole of the past two months in all areas.'†

---

* In 1959, a phoenix was added to the city's crest of arms.

† 'The Coventry Blitz: Hysteria, terror and neurosis', BBC News, 13 November 2015.

LEST WE FORGET

Stories about devastated Coventry reached the airwaves. The government panicked and additional controls were imposed on the BBC; a curb on free speech was the immediate legacy of this horrific attack. The War Cabinet knew Coventry was a special case, the level of bombing eliciting a different, more desperate response than that in other British cities. This knowledge informed the ferocity of later Allied attacks on German cities like Dresden and Hamburg, where 25,000 and 40,000 civilians died respectively. Strategists believed Germany's mistake was not bombing Britain's cities comprehensively enough.

Today, Dresden is twinned with Coventry. The German city has also rebuilt its principal church and gifted its English twin a sculpture that stands in the courtyard of the medieval ruin. In neither case did the flattened cities capitulate. In Germany, it was the army who surrendered, not their civilian population. Today in Gaza, satellite pictures suggest there is no part of the strip untouched by Israel's bombardment, but the people keep on keeping on. The collateral damage of modern warfare – shell-shocked children, women and old folk – are not mindful to be 'determined' and 'resolute'. They are just trying to stay alive.

I leave the museum, walk between the extant ruins, cross the porch and enter Basil Spence's 1960s cathedral. Beyond the soaring nave and hammered concrete altar hangs Sutherland's vast tapestry of a risen Christ. The messaging in this hallowed setting is unambiguous: here is Jesus, the son of God, who went through hell and rose again. 'Thy Kingdom come, thy will be done; on earth as it is in heaven.'

Even the most irreligious visitors must find it hard not to pray for peace in this extraordinary place.

83. RAF Bomber Command Memorial, Hyde Park, London, 2012

Bomber Command, World War II, 1939–1945

Statistically, for those flying in Bomber Command, the most dangerous raids were the first seven and the last seven. Colin Bell, a former flight lieutenant, is 103 years old. A Mosquito pilot during World War II and recipient of the Distinguished Flying Cross (DFC), he flew more than fifty missions over Germany. I meet him in the RAF Club's Cowdray Room in Piccadilly. A buoyant raconteur, Colin still benefits from survivor's good fortune.

'I've been lucky all my life,' he tells me. 'I remember we had a Canadian crew join us in 1944. Their first wartime operation was a raid over Berlin and I could see this man was very nervous. I went over to inject some confidence in him. I had already completed thirty trips. He kept saying "I know I'll not come back. I just know it." I said to my navigator Doug, "You're Canadian, you try and calm him down."'

But Doug had no luck either. The virgin airman was petrified. 'That'll never do,' says Colin and shakes his head. The Canadian crew set off on their night raid to Berlin and were never seen again.

I could write a whole book on Colin. A slight man, around 5 foot 6 tall, he trained in the United States at the beginning of the war and subsequently flew for Bomber Command, mainly over Berlin and mainly at night. 'I was a path finder, out in front.' There were plenty near misses. 'Once a shell exploded beneath us and our engines cut out.' He laughs. Was there anything Colin couldn't handle? 'When the engines kicked back in, I said to my navigator, "You weren't afraid were you?" He said, "No, I was bloody terrified!" We flew at 25,000 ft, about 4 miles above ground. Depending on conditions, after you had fired, you could bank up and look out the side and see the explosions.'

There is no regret. Colin is adamant that the bombing had to continue. Long after it was clear the Allies were going to win the war, he insists: 'we were still enduring a hailstone of missiles from Germany'. He makes reference to the V-3 Cannon, Hitler's unfinished mega-gun. 'They were going to fire those against the City of London.' Colin sits back. 'There is only one winner in war. It would not do to lose.'

He goes on to recall the short shrift that Bomber Command received after the war. 'We were aware of the disapproval. We considered it unfair. We thought we'd done quite a bit to advance victory.' Initially, Churchill thought so too. 'Never in the field of human conflict was so much owed by so many to so few' is the take-away line from his famous speech honouring the fighter pilots during the Battle of Britain. Less well remembered is what he said next: 'We must never forget that all the time, night after night, month after month, our bomber squadrons travel far into Germany, find their targets in the darkness by the highest navigational skill, aim their attacks, often under the heaviest fire, often with serious loss.'

It was after the war when Churchill distanced himself from the carpet bombing which killed more than 400,000 German civilians. By 1944, there was already disquiet in the Cabinet, but Arthur 'Butcher' Harris, head of Bomber Command, didn't relent. 'Harris was a remote, ruthless man,' says Colin, 'but he was a hero to me because he led us to victory.'

Arthur Harris got his statue in 1992. It stands outside the RAF's St Clement Danes Church in London's Strand – a warm-up act for the much bigger Bomber Command Memorial in Hyde Park twenty years later. Before this giant winged edifice was born, there was much hand-wringing on the left and right. Martin Kettle in the *Guardian* later lamented that it was an 'unwanted and objectionable military memorial', while Lord Ashcroft crowed about the £1 million he had donated to the monument's inception. Once complete, surveying its expansive, Portland stone frame, architect critic Rowan Moore considered the staggering number of German civilians killed and concluded that 'owing to a military convention that still applies, death descending from above is considered less terrible than death

that arrives horizontally'.* He lamented the memorial's lack of nuance, just as one might lament his naivety. The German Blitz over Britain killed 60,000 civilians from above and is forever ingrained in our national psyche: war machines prioritise their own dead.

Ex-squadron leader Garry Brown served in Iraq with the RAF. He understands flying, the military and the mindset required: 'There is something very special about going to war. You become singly focused. Nothing else matters.' We meet inside the memorial's white edifice in Hyde Park.† Although not the only monument to Bomber Command, it is much the biggest: built in 2012, at a cost of £12m (including Ashcroft's £1 million and a sizeable contribution from the late Bee Gee, Robin Gibb), this petrification of achievement (and controversy) is defiantly classical and ostentatiously imperial. Ranks

---

* *Guardian*, 24 June 2012, 17 June 2015; *Conservative Home*, 5 April 2011.

† Liam O'Connor was the architect. He also designed the Portland stone Armed Forces Memorial in the National Memorial Arboretum.

of doric columns flank either side of the inner sanctuary and a roof reminiscent of the Vickers Wellington is open to the sky, under which stand seven giants of war.

Of the crew, Garry identifies with the navigator – 'every man had his role'. He explains that 'Bomber Command flattened Germany. They had to stop the Nazis' industrial war machine. The only way to do that was to carpet-bomb.' Around us, visitors ebb and flow; the monument is on active service. One man tells his son that Bomber Command was the Allies' most lethal service and how nearly 50 per cent of the airmen died. Inscribed on the memorial wall is a dedication to the 55,573 who never returned. Of World War II's military services, only German U-boats proved more fatal.

Irene Vaughan is in her nineties now, but she can recall the day her uncle Billy went 'missing in action' as if it were yesterday. Billy's aircraft did not return from a bombing raid over Essen in the Ruhr Valley; the twenty-three-year-old wireless operator was never seen again. The baby boy of the family, Billy's photograph was kept in a locket by Irene's grandmother. She would sit stroking her son's sepia face into deep old age. 'Things were never the same after Billy went missing. Grandmother always held on to the idea that her son would one day find his way home.'

In 2012, Irene attended the unveiling of the Bomber Command Memorial. 'The Queen was there. It was much too hot, but it was very special. The taxi driver wouldn't take a fare off us when he heard about Billy.' She pauses. 'The whole of my puberty was spent in the war and Billy was away for most of it. I wanted to be there at the opening. The memorial felt like an acknowledgement that he was alive, that he did live, that he was here.'

A Battle of Britain memorial sits in Capel-le-Ferne atop the white cliffs of Dover (a solitary pilot looking out to sea) and there is another on London's Victoria Embankment. Uncontroversial war monuments, both were erected long before Bomber Command's, which has been vandalised every year bar one of the last eight (the exception came in lockdown). The attacks are often deliberate assaults against the monumental crew of seven whose outlandish size begs for attention. Five stare skywards (searching for their friends?), two look down (bone-tired? Traumatised?). As intended, the effect is overwhelming. The memorial, when it finally arrived in 2012, was playing catch-up.

George Dunn lives in Brighton. He is another surviving (DFC) pilot who served in Bomber Command. Telephone calls at the age of 102 are hard, but I get the gist. 'We were let down. There was no memorial until 2012 and then almost all the royal family turned up. People thought a bit more about Bomber Command after that.' We sign off; George is a man with places to go. This coming weekend, he's a guest of honour at the annual memorial service held at the Bomber Command Memorial. The venue will overflow with veterans and contemporary service personnel.

Like most war memorials, Bomber Command's tells Britain's side of the story. Look closely and beyond prominent Periclean and Churchillian oratory emblazoned on its walls, a modest inscription rings the interior of the open-roofed structure: 'The memorial also commemorates those of all nations who lost their lives in the bombing of 1939–1945.' The wording was agreed between a British delegation and German representatives from extensively bombed Dresden, but critics weren't placated. 'Those words are hidden away,' insists historian Keith Lowe. 'And why do they only ever mention Dresden? What of the firestorms in Hamburg, Würzburg, Cologne?'

Like most contemporary historians, Keith has not fought a war, but he has spent years analysing its appalling after-effects. 'The Hyde Park memorial gives a very limited point of view. It makes war seem glorious, rather than telling us war is horrendous and yet we still had to do it.'* His truth is very different from that of squadron leader

---

* Keith Lowe is author of *Prisoners of History: What Monuments to the Second World War Tell Us About Our History and Ourselves*, which features twenty-five World War II memorials, including Bomber Command Memorial.

LEST WE FORGET

Garry or World War II pilots Colin and George, whose wars were about service and survival.

First and foremost, the Bomber Command Memorial speaks to them, their fellow airmen and women, and future recruits. It lionises their experience of war. Why would it do otherwise?

CHAPTER 25

WHOSE WAR?

The contemporary assault on much of Britain's colonial history, coupled with criticism of the UK's engagement in more recent conflicts, has underscored the exceptional place occupied by World War II's narrative in the country's wider story. That the Allies' military success in both World Wars was underpinned by Britain's imperial soldiers is irrefutable, but what is up for debate is the extent to which multicultural, modern Britain chooses to associate itself with a war heritage recognised for its colonial roots and military prowess. This tension has played out in differing responses to recent commemorative projects.

More straightforward is women's increased role in World War II, with Britain mobilising proportionally more women than any other belligerent.

84. Commonwealth Memorial Gates, Constitution Hill, London, 2002
Imperial Britain, World Wars I and II

In June 1940, anticipating the fall of France, Winston Churchill remained famously defiant. If fighting on the beaches, and in the streets, proved insufficient, 'then our Empire beyond the seas, armed and guarded by the British Fleet, would carry on the struggle, until, in God's good time, the New World, with all its power and might, steps forth to the rescue and the liberation of the Old'.

The war leader's prophecy came true – in staggering numbers. The British Empire and Dominions raised a total of 8,586,000 men to fight for freedom in the face of fascist forces. In 1945, the Allies emerged victorious. But at what cost? The Indian subcontinent was first to shed its colonial skin and, within two decades, Britain faced the imperial abyss, as 'winds of change' blew across Africa and the Caribbean.

Changed times posed problems for static commemorative forms which spoke to a different era – and, in some cases, an alien imperial order. The young Elizabeth II religiously laid an annual wreath at the Cenotaph on Armistice Day, and Commonwealth high commissioners followed suit, but the connection became increasingly complicated, identity ever more contested. Britain, shorn of its overseas empire, tended towards chauvinistic interpretations of nationhood. The war films of the 1950s and '60s were predominantly white and macho, the Celtic fringes began to challenge a pan-British idea and community tensions followed inward migration from the former empire.

When a fresh wave of commemoration arrived in the wake of the Falklands War, Britain was a very different country. A member of the European Union, multi-ethnic and nominally Commonwealth, memorialisation could no longer rely on a one-stop imperial shop. A reminder of this changed world order and Britain's debt to its former

WHOSE WAR?

colonies, the dawn of a new millennium saw the arrival of prestigious national monuments strategically located in the heart of the old Mother Country. The former dominions – Canada first, then Australia and New Zealand – invested in their own show-piece memorials; the former sits in London's Green Park, the latter two on the high altar of the capital's memorialisation: Hyde Park Corner.

This commemorative huddle that surrounds Wellington's Arch is offset by the Memorial Gates. A contemporary of the above three additions, the Gates are unquestionably more ambitious in scope. They represent the armed forces of the British Empire from Africa, the Caribbean and all five nations of the subcontinent (Bangladesh, India, Nepal, Pakistan and Sri Lanka) that served in two World Wars. While the ex-dominion monuments were designed by their own artists, the Memorial Gates' architect was British stalwart, Liam O'Connor (he of later Bomber Command Memorial fame).* Cue Portland stone pillars that bear a flame on Commonwealth Day, a dome inscribed with the names of those awarded the Victoria Cross and George Cross, two stone slabs and so much more. A closer examination reveals the names of the operational areas where these men fought, a salient reminder Britain relied on troops who were serving miles from their own home.

Today, the Memorial Gates are overseen by a prestigious committee. Its Chairman is Lord Bilimoria of Chelsea, CBE. Karan Bilimoria was born in Hyderabad, India, into a Zoroastrian Parsi family with a distinguished military pedigree: his father was the general officer commanding-in-chief of the Central India Army and led the 2/5 Gurkha Rifles during the Bangladesh Liberation War and his grandfather a squadron leader in the Royal Indian Air Force. Lord Bilimoria took a different route, studying at Cambridge University and subsequently making his fortune founding Cobra

---

* Both carved from Portland stone, Bomber Command Memorial is situated approximately 100 metres north of the Gates and is likewise adjacent to Hyde Park Corner. See Monument 83.

Beer. He has come full circle and, as a deputy lieutenant of Greater London, now occasionally dons a uniform as a personal representative of the monarch.

He engaged with the Memorial Gates from their inception and believes passionately in their mission. 'We have an education committee to get the message out that these 5 million people were volunteers, not conscripts. Had they not fought, served, sacrificed in these two wars, we would not have the freedoms we enjoy today. It's as simple as that. People need to know.'

Lord Bilimoria is viscerally connected to the Gates. He personally knew two of the Victoria Cross recipients named on the pavilion's domed ceiling: Gurkhas Gaje Ghale and Agansing Rai. His is an Anglo-Indian success story, living proof that (for some) the new order people fought and died for works. He refutes the idea that, by trying to talk for all of Britain's former colonies, there is a danger of talking to none, and he insists the monument's location speaks for itself: 'They're right next to Buckingham Palace, next to the Wellington Memorial, the Australian Memorial, the New Zealand Memorial, the Battle of Britain Memorial, the Bomber Memorial. The Household Cavalry ride past them every single day.'

To visit this prime memorial real estate is to accept Lord Bilimoria's logic. Lining the main artery upon which ceremonial London depends, the Memorial Gates intimately bind the sacrifice of Britain's colonies to the present day. Unveiled by the Queen in 2002, carefully synchronised with Wellington's Arch and drawing the hordes onwards to Constitution Hill, in many respects, they are the Cenotaph for a new Britain.

Emblazoned in gold on one pillar are the optimistic words of poet Sir Ben Okri: 'Our Future is Greater than our Past.' Perhaps. But that past has never been more contested.

85. Sikh Troops War Memorial, Victoria Park, Leicester, 2022

British Sikh Military Contribution, World Wars I and II

Raj Mann feels conflicted. 'I like the statue,' he says. 'It is authentic.' His friend, Taranjit Singh, sculpted Leicester's impressive bronze Sikh soldier. Artistically, it is a fine piece of work, exhibiting close attention to detail. Raj directs me to the beard, tucked into the statue's military uniform. 'How to depict it can be controversial,' he explains. 'Orthodox Sikhs have their beards open and flowing, but in the army they're tucked in for practical reasons, so they don't get caught in machinery.'

However, while instrumental in getting the Sikh project off the ground, Raj was no longer on the committee when their plans finally bore fruit. He shrugs. 'My heart was no longer in it. I thought it was feeble to have a statue in among all the other war memorials in a park. I wanted it in the city centre, in a more prominent position like Jubilee Square, where white working-class boys can see it and say "Hey! What is a Sikh solider doing here?"'

Instead of standing among shoppers and vapers in Leicester's city centre, the Sikh soldier is dwarfed by Edwin Luytens's landmark Arch of Remembrance in Victoria Park, also known as War Memorial Park. Elsewhere, there is a stone commemorating the American World War II D-Day efforts; Sikh sacrifice alongside Anglo–American sacrifice, in a compare-and-contrast exercise. Raj believes that, for those actively remembering in this space, Sikh military prowess is already common knowledge.

As if on cue, when looking for the memorial, I meet an elderly NHS worker, Balbir Kaur Jabbal. Bursting with pride, she leads me straight to the Sikh solider and, sitting beneath his manful silhouette, proceeds to tell me all about her late father, Harman Singh, who fought with the British Indian Army in Burma against the Japanese. Singh stood for out for his bravery as a tank gunner during the campaign. Balbir sheds a tear of joy for a father she still misses and whose legacy she is deeply proud of.

Everything Balbir shares about the late Harman Singh conforms to military stereotypes associated with Sikh soldiering since the bloody Anglo–Sikh wars in the 1840s. Revered as a 'martial race' whose brotherhood of men was guided by courage and discipline, Sikh forces were heavily relied upon by imperial Britain after the Punjab was finally annexed in 1849. Raj refuses to shy away from this broader historical context. 'So we helped the British during India's First War of Independence.* Better them than another Mughal empire.'

But therein lies the rub. These days, imperial history is heavily contested, not least by other members of Britain's south Asian community. In Birmingham's Smethwick, a war memorial of a Sikh soldier was vandalised within a week of its unveiling in 2018: 'sepoys no more' read the graffiti.† Raj knows the protestor. Meanwhile, in Leicester, he was tipped off that his ambitions for a more central location would upset anti-colonial sentiments within the city. 'They didn't want to glorify the role soldiers played. The turban is perceived as Sikh, but it is also an Indian symbol, so you have the idea of Indians helping in colonial battles, including Muslims and Hindus.' To ensure the soldier is not misunderstood, safer surely to place him among his own military brethren in Victoria Park?

I revisit the BBC News page where I first read about the Leicester statue's unveiling in 2022. 'The Sikh Troops War Memorial Committee said it would complement the existing war memorials already there.' The journalism captures none of the nuance that Raj expresses and instead focuses on the Sikh military contribution behind Britain's twentieth-century World Wars: 'Sikhs made up more than 20 per cent of the British Indian Army at the outbreak of

---

* Also known as the Indian Mutiny.

† A sepoy was an Indian soldier serving under British or other European powers.

WHOSE WAR?

World War I.' And they were only 2 per cent of the subcontinent's population.

Raj is matter of fact. 'I am proud that Sikhs fought in World War II against fascism. I want other children growing up in Leicester to know that our grandfathers were the same.' But separating out different strands of history is complicated; emotions run high. Is it ever possible to please everyone with something as immutable as a statue? Raj is no longer sure. 'These days, I take my ancestors' relics into schools, things like the famous Kohinoor diamond and the Sikh [Khalsa Army] flag. Kids look at them through VR headsets. Let's face it, statues are for a certain demographic.'*

86. Gurkha statue, Princes Gardens, Aldershot, 2021
Gurkha service in British military, 1815–present

'You must have a Gurkha in the book. There is a great memorial in London.'

The Gurkhas have exhibited extraordinary martial prowess and two centuries of military service for the British army, so of course their inclusion is mandatory.

'Perhaps Hari Budha Magar can help?' suggests a friend, pinging me his profile. A former soldier in the Royal Gurkha Rifles, Hari is outstanding, the personification of Gurkha heroism. Injured in Afghanistan, nowadays the double above-the-knee amputee breaks records scaling the world's highest mountains. Meanwhile, the Ministry of Defence comms team offer Captain Tarjan Gurung, also of the Royal Gurkha Rifles, on the proviso that they can read what I write. Or perhaps Major Naren Gurung?

I am mindful of falling for the idea that Nepal's Gurkhas were, and still are, naturally predisposed to bravery and military capability.

---

* For further examples of the digital relics Raj Mann takes on school visits, see www.anglosikhmuseum.com

Several academics have recently concluded this martial race theory is an imperial construct, peddled in the high days of empire and reinforced through the sharing of impressive anecdotes and individual feats. Certainly, after the 1857 Indian Uprising, the Gurkhas' recruitment as the crack troops of empire was deliberately prioritised, most notably by Lord Roberts, a prominent commander-in-chief of the Indian Army.*

It is through the Gurkha Museum in Winchester that I find retired Captain Bishnu Prasad Shrestha. Does he believe Gurkhas are racially predisposed to be great soldiers? 'Yes, I think we carry an innate ability to work in the army, to fight with the enemy.'

'Why?'

'We are quite natural at it.' He laughs. Now seventy-seven, Captain Bishnu is a proud Gurkha Rifles veteran. A manifestation of

---

* And also Punjabi Sikhs.

that pride has been his committed support of Aldershot's arresting Gurkha monument featuring World War I rifleman Kulbir Thapa Magar carrying a wounded soldier from 2nd Battalion, Leicestershire Regiment. 'When we first discovered that £125k would be needed for the statue, I was a bit afraid. But we raised the money. There were 156 donors and each gave £1,000 plus.'*

Born in Nepal in 1947, Bishnu's Gurkha heritage is very important to him. 'I was part of the Newar community. I did not come from the Khas, Magars or Gurung tribes – the leading Gurkha tribes.' As far back as the eighteenth century, the expanding Nepalese state had subordinated its neighbours with an exclusive warring tradition that runs far deeper than imperial Britain's later military recruiting agenda. As a child, Bishnu remembers Gurkha soldiers on leave in Tahoon, his local village. 'I saw the way they dressed, the way they lived. Always smart, clean, neat. Yes, of course they were better off.'

Bishnu's boyhood dream came true when, in 1965 aged eighteen, he joined the 2nd Battalion of the 7th Duke of Edinburgh's Own Gurkha Rifles. 'My regiment was just coming back from the Borneo. We were posted to Malaysia, then to Hong Kong for the disturbance of 1967. I lived in Hong Kong and I went back to Nepal on leave.'

After twenty-five years of military service for imperial Britain, Bishnu retired in 1990. Since 2014, he has been part of the 6,000-strong Nepalese community in Aldershot, arriving in England after Gurkha resettlement rules were revised in the wake of a public campaign spearheaded by the actress Joanna Lumley. The quest for parity is not over. Gurkha veterans like Bishnu, who retired before 1997 and subsequently relocated to Britain, quickly discovered they didn't have pension equality in England. The Gurkha ideal that Bishnu grew up admiring has proved a something of a strawman.

Bishnu is hurt by that. It underscores the Gurkhas' ongoing quest for equal treatment, a journey embodied by Kulbir Thapa Magar's

---

* These donors are named on the plinth of the statue.

striking statue in Aldershot's Princes Gardens.* Bishnu explains: 'In 1915, Kulbir Thapa was the first Gurkha soldier to be awarded a Victoria Cross. Before then, Gurkhas were not awarded VCs.'

Unveiled in 2021, sitting opposite the Airborne Regiment statue and also made by the sculptor Amy Goodman ('the paratroopers had more money than us, so they got theirs finished a year earlier!', Bishnu laughs), Kulbir Thapa's likeness stands as a testimony to Gurkha resilience in the face of both the enemy and, more recently, British intransigence. Bishnu is inspired by Thapa's story and hopes others will be too: at the Battle of Loos, the wounded rifleman saved a soldier from the Leicestershire Regiment and the next day did the same for two fellow Gurkhas.

As the Gurkha community in Aldershot has long recognised, World War I hero Kulbir Thapa is an ideal military role model, which is surely what the martial race theory is really all about.

87. Monument to the Women of World War II, Whitehall, London, 2005

Female service, World War II, 1939–1945

'After the war, we didn't want to belong to any clubs. My Stan said "We've been regimented for so long."'

In 1946, airman Stan swapped his RAF uniform for coppers' blues, and his new wife, ATS corporal Barbara, abandoned khaki for a pinny. 'It's lucky I enjoyed housework 'cos there was a lot of it.' Like the rest of Britain, the Weatherills were moving on with their lives; in 1947 there was a wedding in Bingley Parish Church, followed by four babies in quick succession. It was much later, in widowhood, that Barbara found time to reflect on her years of military service.

She had joined the ATS aged seventeen-and-a-half; driving Bedford trucks on operational gun-sites across Britain defined much

---

* Aldershot has been home to the Gurkha Brigade since 1997.

of Barbara's young adult life. But she was in no doubt about women's second-rate status. 'Fifty-six years after the war, the Royal Artillery Association finally issued us an apology.' Major General Michael Steele said: 'Welcome home. At last you can call yourselves gunners.' The Women of Anti-Aircraft Command always had, but 'gunner girl' was only ever a colloquialism.

After World War II, recognition of women's military service had not been a priority. The status quo meant reverting to standard gender norms. The returning heroes were men, and womenfolk were expected to facilitate their re-entry into civilian life, the more babies the better.

It took until the 1990s for Barbara and her peers to enjoy something of a military reboot. 'We started having reunions. I suppose there were 450 women on my gun-site and others in the ATS.' What began as a local gathering in York mushroomed. 'For our annual service, soon we couldn't fit into St Michael le Belfrey, so they offered

us the Minster opposite. They closed it to everyone else. Not a dry eye in the house!'

It was there, surrounded by comrades inside York's gothic minster, that Barbara found inspiration in the Five Sisters Window, dedicated to the fallen women who served the British Empire in World War I.* She wondered if perhaps her local Royal Artillery Association could approach the minster about a plaque? Something small to acknowledge the women's service?

Barbara, now ninety-nine, pauses. 'But then the local press got hold of it. The whole thing grew. People said, "What about the other female services? What about the nurses?" We had just wanted something for our girls.' But, very quickly, Barbara and her Yorkshire cohort lost control of the project they initiated.

By 2002, House of Commons Speaker Betty Boothroyd was sweating it out in the hotseat of ITV's *Who Wants to be a Millionaire?* as the patron of the Memorial to the Women of World War II fund. She won £8,000.

'In fact, she raised a lot more than that,' says Barbara. 'She went to see some newspaper editor and got £40,000. She was very nice, born not far from me in Yorkshire. After the war, she was a member of the Tiller Girls dance troupe. She was quite well built, though you wouldn't have thought so.'

Barbara respected Betty; she was a straight talker like herself. But when it came to the proposed war memorial, the Commons Speaker was a symptom of a greater problem – its 'celebrification'. 'Jimmy Savile was there at the opening, dancing around in silly red socks with his cigar. I think he donated 50k.' Barbara had wanted something small and specific. Instead, the growth in interest and money insisted on a far more ambitious project: a monument to every woman of World War II – or, as its plaque stipulates, a memorial 'raised to commemorate the vital work done by over 7 million women'.

---

* See Monument 65.

WHOSE WAR?

Barbara is unequivocal. 'The Arts Council was involved. I think the memorial is hideous. We rejected umpteen designs. They were all awful. And there were never-ending discussions about where to put it.' Today, John Mills' 6.6-metre bronze monument straddles Whitehall, its black bulk a striking contrast with the silver grey of the neighbouring cenotaph. 'John, the sculptor, asked me to send him an ATS button so he could copy it. I said I would as long as he sent it back.* That and my friend's cap strap. We are the only two women with a mark on that monument – except for the Queen's name, because she unveiled it.'

The design was not to Barbara's liking: a series of faceless women's uniforms circling the memorial. Far too unspecific for her taste, and nor was she alone in her dissent. But Betty Boothroyd, who just missed wartime service, loved the monument. 'It depicts the women's working clothes and how they quietly took them off at the end of the day, hung them up and let men take the credit.' Mills captured the anonymity that many female veterans, finally enjoying recognition eighty years later, didn't want to be reminded of.

'And it wasn't local. It was meant to be in York and ended up in London costing £1 million.' The memorial to the Women of World War II was unveiled in 2005, but Barbara and her association were not finished. They returned to York Minster and said they still wanted a local memorial to the ATS women who served on gun-sites. 'It cost £2,000. They hung it up in a small dark place, but at least it is there – a plaque to our local ladies.'

Today, in the Minster's north transept, hidden around a corner, there is a shiny wall-hanging: 'To The Women Who Served In The Anti-Aircraft And Searchlight Batteries During World War II From 1941 To 1945.'

A small golden reminder that commemoration, at its most effective, is personal.

---

* John Mills returned Barbara's ATS button.

CHAPTER 26

COLLATERAL DAMAGE

World War II uprooted and dislocated some 55 million people in Europe alone. The voiceless and those without agency were disproportionality impacted as the victims of a conflict they had no hand in; with good reason, women and children have long been seen as the historic catch-all for military vulnerability. Recent shifts and recalibrations in research and priorities have broadened that definition to include animals. Perhaps unsurprisingly, the newest statue featured in this book commemorates the horses of World War I.

88. Kindertransport – The Arrival, Liverpool Street Station, London, 2006

Britain's Kindertransport children, 1938–1939

Of the five children, I have always assumed the smallest girl, perched on a suitcase with a teddy bear in hand, is my neighbour Kate Danziger. Or more precisely, I project an idea of Kate onto the statue. Only Kate did not arrive in London clutching a teddy, but rather a miniature duvet cover, all silky-soft with a floral print. A comforter. 'Yes, and – you know – I still have it today.'

COLLATERAL DAMAGE

We are eating toast and drinking mugs of tea in an old English pub next to Liverpool Street station. I am asking Kate questions about her childhood, and Kate, a well-mannered eighty-seven-year-old, is gently deflecting, insisting 'we have talked quite enough about me'. But occasionally, between mouthfuls, she adds something more. 'If I am honest, the Kindertransport statue doesn't really trigger memories for me. I was only two-and-a-half when I arrived in London.' Born in October 1936, Kate is understated about her transition to Britain because she doesn't remember it. Nor does she recall her life in Breslau,* one of the sixteen places from which Jewish children fled that are highlighted on Liverpool Street station's largest Kindertransport statue. 'My father was a state attorney. As a Jew, he was no longer able to work, but Mum and Dad couldn't get a visa for England. It was only us children.'

Kate's kind face doesn't light up in recognition until the conversation moves to Sanderstead in Surrey. 'My earliest memories are of bright red poppies bobbing in the garden, and a white dog call Pat. It was lovely. A lovely community. I was very happy there.' In early 1939, Kate was one of 10,000 children granted refuge in Britain under a Kindertransport scheme fast-tracked by the Home Office in the wake of Kristallnacht, the Nazis' November 1938 pogrom against the Jews. Strict conditions were placed on their entry, which was presumed to be short-term. Parents could not accompany their children. Two-year-old Kate arrived with her seven-year-old brother, Hans.†

'I wrote to Mummy and Daddy but, to me, Ron and Betty Pilgrim, who I called Uncle and Auntie, felt like parents.' The Kindertransport scheme, which ran for ten months between December 1938 and September 1939, had appealed for foster

---

* Formerly in Germany, now in south-west Poland.

† Called Kathe and Hans in Germany, their names changed to Katie and John on arrival in England. Eventually Katie became Kate, which is how she is known today.

parents on the BBC Home Service. The Pilgrims volunteered. Kate recalls a dear childless couple; Ron was a chartered accountant and Betty was pretty, flirtatious even. Kate and Hans soon became family. There was the local school and a Sunday school (the village didn't have a synagogue), hiding from bombs under the stairs, and two dolls, Margaret and Rosie.

Kate considers herself blessed. To this day she feels a strong affinity with the England that took her in. So too did the Pilgrims gain enormously from the arrival of little Kate in their lives. But the statue, with five parentless children beautifully executed in bright bronze by a former Kindertransport child, Frank Meisler, only tells half the story. Go to Berlin and you will find two statues, likewise set on rail tracks. The children escape west on their liberating trains. The adults head east to their death.

Kate's parents failed to get visas to Britain (which let in one Jew for every ten who applied). 'Instead, they managed to get visas to

Chile. So that is where they went just before war broke out. Dad could not practise law, so he took up a milk franchise in Santiago, and Mum went with him.'

Displaced parents, miles away from everything they knew: their German language, their children, their work, their community. At war's end, Kate, aged nine, left her English life behind and joined her parents in Chile. She spoke English, they spoke German and Spanish; she had another family in England, they had lost most of their family in concentration camps. Adjustment was difficult. Kate did not like her Jewish school, so she moved, and then, quite suddenly, her father died. Much later, she discovered that he took his own life. 'It must have been awful for mother.'

I ask Kate what she makes of the statue at the entrance of Liverpool Street station. She tells me she hasn't decided yet, but is sure she likes it. I reread the plaque: 'In gratitude to the people of Britain for saving the lives of 10,000 unaccompanied mainly Jewish children who fled from Nazi persecution in 1938 and 1939.'

On the number 35 bus home, I ask Kate if she ever feels angry that her parents weren't allowed to accompany her to England. 'I don't feel anger, but I am sad they could not come.'

89. The Children of Calais, Dorset House Garden, Saffron Walden, Essex, 2015

Contemporary Conflicts: Iraq, Afghanistan, Syria, Yemen, Sudan

I post a picture of my neighbour Kate on social media above the caption: 'my amazing, generous, kind, peace-loving neighbour at Liverpool Street station, where she first arrived from Germany in 1939'.

Below the photograph, historian Clare Mulley comments: 'Let me know if Kate would like to see the new Kindertransport memorial in Harwich. My husband, Ian Woltor, is the sculptor.'

LEST WE FORGET

Online, I find pictures of Ian's haunting memorial: six children negotiating a gangplank. It exhibits none of the polished gratitude baked into the London one. Harwich is the Essex port where the majority of Kindertransport children arrived before they went on to Liverpool Street. I show Kate the pictures. 'Ah yes,' she says. 'But I don't remember arriving in Harwich either.' At eighty-seven, she is not immediately enthusiastic about the idea of travelling to Essex, to once more explore a story she only partially remembers and which has been so often retold.

Yet there are glaring omissions in the Kindertransport tale. The children selected required sizeable deposits for safe passage in a scheme that disproportionately favoured families with means. Jewish and non-Jewish organisations worked to ensure no financial burden would be placed on the British public. Today, we celebrate our country's one-time compassion towards (some) Jewish children, while remaining as selective now as we were then about which children of war to save. Public pressure granted 260,000 Ukrainians visas, but as the Calais migrant population suggests, Syrians, Iraqis, Sudanese, Yeminis and (many) Afghans are not so lucky.

At the time Kate and I are discussing Kindertransport statuary, there is breaking news: Sara Alhashimi, a seven-year-old Iraqi girl, has died in a crush of migrants trying to enter a dinghy off the coast of France. 'Stop the boats' is the political mantra of the day, yet the boats keep coming. It is their cargo who don't always make it. Months later, Sara's family are still living in limbo in France; her siblings are not in school, they fear deportation to Iraq, the country they fled, and are plagued with grief, longing and regret. The Alhashimis are trapped in a nightmare. Kate, a woman whose own dislocated childhood informed her later life and work, is deeply disturbed by their story.

Although reunited with her parents in Chile post-war, Kate never lost her yen for England. 'I read Charles Dickens' *David Copperfield* and my mother, who always checked the *Jewish News Bulletin*, said "Oh Katie, something to interest you. In England, there is a new organisation called Amnesty International. All about human rights."' The path back to Britain was not easy – Kate needed money and visas – but the pull of England proved irresistible. By 1960, she was forging a new life in London, volunteering for the Samaritans and, subsequently, Amnesty International.

More than six decades later, it is the combination of contemporary news and Kate's back story that takes us to Saffron Waldon on election day in July 2024. Here, in the centre of a lawn sugared with daisies, beneath the tallest church spire in Essex, is a challenging statue. Inspired by Auguste Rodin's Burghers of Calais, the Six Children of Calais was sculpted by Ian Woltor, the same man behind the Kindertransport statue in Harwich. His two stunning creations book-end the direct implications of a world experiencing the highest number of conflicts since 1945, with children all too often the victims.

Ian is candid; the Calais statue is political. In 2014, he met his local Conservative MP. 'I had an argument with him. The jungle in Calais was in full flow and the MP said "Even if those unaccompanied children in Calais had parents in Britain, or a legal right to come here, they still shouldn't be allowed in. Because if we let any of them in, we will just get more."'

Ian was appalled. 'I found it unbelievable. I could only respond by making this sculpture.' He turns to his resin children, each with their own expression. One 'trudges forward hopelessly, the other throws her hands up in despair. Another, the youngest, is thinking *Why am I here?*

Where once Rodin's six burghers were captured in their own crucible of defeat and sacrificial heroism, at the mercy of enemy England besieging Calais during the Hundred Years' War, the Children of Calais are likewise individuals in flux. Ian explains, 'Just like Rodin's sculpture, none of them look at each other, none of them touch each other. They are all lost in their own pain.'

Kate nods. She is moved. Perhaps it is Ian's vivid charisma or the statues' intensity, but the connection is real. What is she feeling?

'Common cause. The anguish, the despair.' She walks to the nearest child and reassures him as if talking to a real boy: 'You will pull through, my friend. You will pull through.'

Together, we bid our farewells, thanking Ian for his art and hospitality. Home beckons, it is polling day and Kate must cast her vote.

90. War Horse sculpture, Daisy Field, Shirehampton, Bristol, 2023

The horses of World War I, 1914–1918

'I think she looks feminine.'

Diane nods. 'You might be right. Jason Baggs, who made it, calls her Betty.' But my friend Linda disagrees: 'To me, it will always be Joey, out of *War Horse*.' Linda loves *War Horse*. She has read the book and seen the stage play in both Bristol and London.* We stare at and through the quizzical creature and we all see what we want to see. There is an unseasonably cold wind blowing up the River Avon, but everyone has rallied. Diane is holding open a black bin bag; she's not one to waste an opportunity. Richard is scouring the grass with his stick. John stamps his feet (perhaps the shorts were a mistake), but no one regrets being here. This is what their group, Friends of the Lamplighters Marsh, is all about.

'So how did you first find out about the Remount depot?'

'Historians uncovered the story, around the time of the First World War centenary.'

'And Avonmouth Primary School did a lot of work.'

'And locals kept finding horseshoes everywhere – in allotments, when digging out fish ponds. It's been going on for years round here.'

Remount is shorthand for a stock of military horses, including those suitable to 'replace one that is exhausted, injured or has died'.

---

* Michael Morpurgo's classic tale *War Horse* was first published in 1982.

COLLATERAL DAMAGE

Heavy and light haulage duties, transport and pack work, cavalry horses – World War I depended on equine heft. Back then, Shirehampton Remount Depot stretched as far as the eye could see along the Avon, an animal sorting office where foreign horses disembarked to be serviced and trained. Early on, it was clear that, despite Britain's Horse Registration Scheme, supply was horribly inadequate for a war machine that still depended on horsepower. The subsequent trauma of relinquishing animals was felt across the country.

When I met her on Scotland's Isle of Arran, Lady Jean Fforde was deep into her nineties and predictably terrifying. The woman who considered the work of Bletchley Park beneath her and said as much, sat in an armchair decades later, recounting childhood stories and, very briefly, softened. 'It nearly broke my mother's heart when the cavalry came at the beginning of the war and took away twenty-one of her heavyweight hunters. All those lovely horses off to the frontline never to be seen again.'

Shirehampton, with the nearby port of Avonmouth offering access to both the Irish Sea and the Atlantic, received foreign livestock from Canada, the US, Argentina and Ireland. The horse sculpture stands in Daisy Field, the eastern headquarters of a depot that stabled and serviced more than 300,000 imported horses and mules during World War I before they were dispatched to France. Now a north Bristol suburb, it's hard to imagine how it once looked – or smelled.

Frontiersmen arrived here for the 'breaking and training' of thousands of animals. The job was physical and adrenalised. In transit, animals were stacked one deck on top of the other – standing room only, the stench unbearable – sometimes arriving at the rate of a vessel a day. Soon the surrounding meadows were filled with a 'vast mass of partially wild, unbroken horses'. In the few extant letters that recall the Remount, the impression is a heady one before the grim inevitability of war. 'We have often to "throw" the horses before we can get on the bridle and saddle,' writes one groom. 'I like the life very much.'

LEST WE FORGET

Animals do that to you. They lift you out of yourself. Diane is horsey, or at least she's always kept horses, stabled just a few miles down the road. That's how she happened upon the idea of a statue. She knew her friend, the farrier Jason Baggs, did a bit of part-time modelling with horseshoes. 'He'd made a Christmas tree, that sort of thing. So I asked him if he would make a horse. He said, "No, I'm not arty."' The next time Diane saw Jason, he'd modelled a head and leg. The life-size sculpture that stands in Daisy Field is the result of his endeavours; it is made entirely from 380 horseshoes.

Fundraising was involved and planning permission sought. The statue doesn't yet have its four interpretative panels that will recall the history, the unveiling ceremony and even information on Daisy Field – once a local tip, now a reclaimed nature reserve. Unveiled in September 2023, the he/she horse is less than a year old when I visit. Lamplighter member Richard is looking forward to the summer sun setting behind its handsome head. He points to newly planted hawthorn and mentions the friend he lost in the Pandemic. That's when he found sanctuary in Daisy Field and the Friends of the Lamplighters Marsh. We have gone off topic, but the horse doesn't seem to mind. It's absorbing the conversation. Linda is remembering *War Horse* Joey and his capacity for friendship and connection.

I smile at a camera-phone through the horseshoes. You can see from one end to the other. Not any gender or none, I think, but rather a ghost to horses past. Richard reminds us that only 13,000 horses returned here after the war, less than 5 per cent of those dispatched. 'Did Joey in *War Horse* return?' I ask Linda. 'Yes, of course he did. It's a children's story.'

CHAPTER 27

ACCIDENTAL DEATH

In 2017, the Ministry of Defence began publishing the number of service personnel deaths that have occurred since 2000 while training or on exercise. In the last twenty-four years, there have been 162 accidental deaths, twelve of which involved RAF crew in aircraft.

The risks were even more acute in the first half of the twentieth century, when a cocktail of untested technology and the pressures of war singled out service in the RAF as uniquely risky. The most famous of those accidents occurred in the Scottish Highlands in August 1942.

91. Eagle's Rock Cross, Eagle's Rock, Dunbeath, Caithness, 1946

Eagle's Rock air crash, Dunbeath, Caithness, 1942

Meg Sinclair leans on a solitary fence post and points with her stick. Heavy clouds are rolling in, soon to obliterate the view; it is just possible to make out the hills she references. 'Aeroplanes were in the habit of coming up the coast, getting past the Scarabens, Morven, etc, and cutting across Caithness because it's so flat.'

Where we are standing feels like the end of the world; well off the beaten track, on the lip of the North Sea, hours beyond Inverness.

LEST WE FORGET

Awesomely beautiful and darkly unforgiving, Scotland's aesthetic wonder cruelly underscores its capacity as a killing field for men flying slightly off course. 'That hill over there, with the mast on it, is the next highest point. Flying up from Invergordon, you see how easy it would be to say "Oh yes, we are safe now."' Meg stops briefly. 'But how come they didn't hit the ground where the loch is?' Like so many of Dunbeath's locals, Meg tussles with outstanding questions that still plague the Eagle's Rock accident.

We resume our walk across peaty tussocks and purple heather, now fully focused on the ground immediately before us. Although remote, unmarked terrain, this is a route well-trodden. Of all the flying accidents to occur in the north-eastern corner of Scotland during World War II (and there were many), one has caught the public imagination. On 25 August 1942, a Short Sunderland flying boat W4026, *M for Mother*, crashed into the hillside, killing all of its crew, bar one. On board was an air commodore: Prince George, the Duke of Kent, the thirty-nine-year-old brother to King George VI, and father of three young children, including the present duke, then just six years old.

Eighty-three years later and the Duke of Kent remains fully engaged with his father's tragic, premature death. We meet in his ochre dining room in Wren House, adjacent to Kensington Palace, the duke comfortable in a navy checked shirt, a handsome cane by his side. Caithness is a world away in the other corner of the kingdom and yet, across the decades, His Royal Highness has regularly made the trip north, most recently in 2022 for the 80th anniversary of the accident. He sighs. 'The whole story of that crash is a mystery still. Every pilot, every navigator must have been well aware of the shape of the country and the fact it was steep rising ground. And they were flying in very bad weather.'

Many theories have been mooted regarding the cause of the accident: Scotland's volatile climate; the hubris of young men and their flying machines; new technology coupled with human error (much is written about the distance-reading compass fitted in the

ACCIDENTAL DEATH

seaplane).* But none sufficiently conclusive to bridge the gap between mystery and reality. The duke is a pragmatic man, an individual known for his love of fast cars and their mechanical intricacies, and his outstanding questions regarding the crash are focused on practical aspects of the tragedy. Why was a flying boat destined for Iceland risking a path over land, with the North Sea just a few hundred metres away? Later, he will laugh at the persistent conspiracy theories which surround the accident. There's such an abundance it's hard to keep pace, although he does his best. 'You know, almost every year another book appears saying "This is the true story of what happened."' He pauses. 'No one will ever know the full story. The fact is, it was wartime. You knew aeroplanes crashed and killed people.'

Back on the hillside, Meg, who works in the local Dunbeath Heritage Museum, dexterously outlines key features which gave the story legs. Those arriving early at the crash scene were unaware there was a survivor; the later appearance of flight sergeant Andrew Jack, who escaped death when the rear turret broke away on impact, led to questions over how the initial tally of fifteen bodies failed to account for absent Jack. Theories abounded. The airman was later unforthcoming, no doubt silenced (there was a war on). Silks and perfumes littered the scorched hillside alongside the charred fuselage and buckled bits of wreckage. This was not any wartime tragedy; it was a crash involving the brother of the British monarch. At first, estate workers and crofters thought they had found the king dead in the heather. It was the discovery of the deceased's identity disc that confirmed otherwise. 'HRH, the Duke of Kent, The Coppins, Iver, Bucks, England.'

What happened next is well known. The king, residing at Balmoral, was informed of the lunchtime crash later that evening.

---

* One of the most credible theories is that there may have been an error in the magnetic variation setting for the flying boat's latitude, necessary with the new distance-reading compass and inputted by the navigator before the flight.

Profoundly shocked, he returned to Windsor for the funeral before making his own pilgrimage to Eagle's Rock in September, as noted in his diary. 'I motored to Berriedale & walked from there to the site of the Sunderland crash where George was killed ... It hit one side of the slope, turned over in the air & slid down the other side on its back ... I felt I had to do this pilgrimage.'

The king took consolation from the fact that his brother, whose checkered life had found new purpose in war, 'died on Active Service'. According to the current duke, his widowed mother – Marina, Princess of Greece and Denmark – likewise drew comfort from her husband's wartime death. Churchill caught the public mood, intoning on the 'gallant and handsome prince' whose death 'stands out lamentably even in these hard days of war'. But nothing could detract from the inexplicable loss. Now aged 89, His Royal Highness shakes his head, repeating, 'How an experienced pilot and aircrew could fly their aeroplane in bad weather into a mountain doesn't make any sense.'

This senseless hole has been filled with conjecture. Inside Dunbeath Heritage Centre, considerable floor space is dedicated to the Eagle's Rock accident. Visitors are encouraged to leave their own recollections and bloated scrapbooks spill over with newspaper clippings ruminating on the cause of the crash and its fall-out. The duke's glamorous associations are accentuated, his instinct for appeasement (prevalent across much of pre-war Britain) is hooked onto rumours the plane had made a detour to pick up Germany's deputy führer, Rudolf Hess, in Scotland on a 'peace mission' at the time. The secrecy that shrouded the accident is used to push lurid rumours concerning the late duke's private life. Column inches filled the vacuum left by sudden, shocking death on the home front.

'It is complete nonsense, bunkum, that Hess was involved.' The present-day duke is definitive and so are the facts: the seaplane was en route to Reykjavik in Iceland on a 'special mission' where his father, in his capacity as air commodore, was due to inspect the country's RAF sites. Instead, he died in the Highlands with thirteen

ACCIDENTAL DEATH

other airmen, mission incomplete. Rather than occupy himself with 'bunkum', the young, green duke picked his path through life carefully. He found Sandhurst intimidating but persisted, serving in the Royal Scots Greys for twenty years and rising to the rank of lieutenant colonel. He acknowledges his royal status infringed on his capacity to serve. 'I was commander of 100 men and they insisted I withdrew from Northern Ireland on safety grounds after three weeks. It was embarrassing.'

The parallels with young Prince Harry's life are striking, but the similarities end when the two respective men leave the army. Unlike Harry, in 1976 the Duke of Kent dedicated himself fully to royal duties, excelling in the role of commemoration. His title and name pepper memorials that span the globe and cross the country: Normandy, Ascension Island, Staffordshire, Nottingham, Warwick … On goes the list. An honorary field marshal, and still patron of the Dresden Trust, for half a century the duke was president of the Commonwealth War Graves Commission. He marvels at the nature of this work. 'I have always thought it was enormously important. I have covered a lot of cemeteries and memorials around the world. I think it is a matter of remembering what sacrifice means. One of the things that always struck me going around those cemeteries is that many of them had special inscriptions put in by the families. A personal touch.'

Tucked up within a hugely famous family, the premature loss of his own father gifted this unobtrusive man an unsung strength: the capacity to reach those similarly marked by death in war. 'So many of the graves have incredibly touching inscriptions like "Never to be forgotten". Sometimes I find them absolutely heartbreaking to look at.'

In Scotland, the sky clears for the ascent up Eagle's Rock. A single ray of sun picks out the most recent stone dedication to the late Duke of Kent. Promised by the Ministry of Works after the war, in 2005 a granite slab was finally cemented through the heather, marking the spot where the duke's body was discovered, a reminder that this crash had a double resonance. Back in England, a young royal family joined the legions of British children left without a father. 'He was away a lot. I do remember him but I can't give you examples.'

The inscription reads: HIC MORTUUS EST (He died here). A couple of hundred yards beyond this modest square is a large Celtic cross, installed after the war to commemorate all fourteen airmen who perished en route to Iceland. Princess Marina often visited this spot, sometimes alone, sometimes with others. Her eldest son first accompanied his mother as an adolescent in the mid-1950s. 'She never met the survivor Jack Andrew. I sometimes wished she had.'

Silver clouds scuttle across the sky, the light is majestic, fringeing the pale cross with a spiritual glow. It is a fleeting moment before a blanket of rain closes in: Scotland's fatal weather. But the memorial will endure, a point of certainty amidst all the speculation. It has played sentinel to the current duke's progress across a long life, fatherless but no less committed, in the service of his cousin, the late Queen, unveiling memorials around the world, well into his dotage. A vital human stitch in the military fabric of the state. And something more than that: a man who really understands. 'Memorial is important, in the same way you put a gravestone in a cemetery, but this is a memorial to a group of people who were saving their country in a war and they lost their lives doing it. Pure accident. Bad luck. Memorials are very important.'

I thank the Duke and rise to leave. Later, I will send him my thoughts in a letter: 'No man has done more in the service of military commemoration than Your Royal Highness.'

ACCIDENTAL DEATH

92. Memorial Cairn, Glen Loch, Forest of Atholl, Perthshire, 1994

Hercules XV193 crash, 1993

Flight lieutenant Garry Brown was excited. They all were. 'Flying an aircraft is a very enjoyable thing.' But flying a big aircraft like the Hercules at low level through the Highlands of Scotland – 'that's just a wonderful feeling'. At RAF Lyneham in Wiltshire, anticipation was mounting. 'We were off to Scotland for a night stop. That usually means a few beers, a game of golf. There is something great about taking your aircraft away to another airfield for the night and coming home the next day.'

27 May 1993. The engines were running and Garry's golf clubs and bag were down the back of the Hercules XV193. He was walking up the flight deck steps of the plane, when his squadron leader, Stanley Muir, suggested he flew north in a different aircraft. 'Come back tomorrow on this one,' he said. The training flights were about learning to handle heavily laden aircraft at low levels; on the return leg, Garry would have a chance to instruct the dropping of a large load out of the back. The flight lieutenant did what he was told.

It's been a while – almost thirty-one years – but that flight, that day, will never leave him. The standard pre-take-off banter, the fine weather that green-lit their mission, the beat of adrenaline as three Hercules descended over the sea and down into Scotland. 'It involved formation flying, but once we were north of Glasgow, near Loch Lomond, we split into single craft following a single path.'

Up, then down, into the peaks and crags of the remote central highlands where training flights swoop so low the glen reverberates with their thunder. Children run outside to shriek and wave. 'Whoo hooo!' I know, I was one such child. 'Did the pilot see us? Did he wave?' our common refrain. Garry laughs. 'We get so low we could tell if it was white polka dots or pink polka dots on a bikini!'

LEST WE FORGET

In 1993, the end of the first Gulf War informed the military backdrop. But LXX Squadron weren't thinking about war; they were focused on the minutiae of their operation – twenty-eight men and their flying machines. 'Flying in the RAF is a game that by its nature is very high risk. You train to fight. You train so that it is second nature when you are at war, which means you have to go to the limits.'

The crew of XV193 completed the simulated drop of a small cargo pack in the remote expanse of north Perthshire. 'You've got so many things you need to think about. You need to try and out-climb the hill to get to safety altitude, the height above the hills.' A rocky outcrop forced the Hercules to turn left and enter the narrow passage of Glen Loch.

'There is an element called operational flying,' Garry explains, 'when select crews at select times are permitted to take the aircraft into more dangerous situations – flying lower or faster. The closer you are to the ground, the more deadly dangerous it is.' That day, on their reinforcement training mission in Scotland's skies, Hercules XV193 was flying deliberately low. 'But if something goes wrong, if an engine fails …'

I thank Garry for the call. I tell him I'll be in touch when I get there.

I train the binoculars on the sweep of hill rising from Loch Loch. By foot, the walk across the vast stretch of moorland and mountain is eight hours. A local friend gives me a lift part of the way on private dirt tracks, but eventually the path fizzles out.* Save the cry of a curlew, there is no sound, just Perthshire's offering of flood and glen. I am searching for a small cairn, stacked on the southern side of the loch, near the crash site. 'Look for a bald patch, a few hundred metres wide.' The impact was so intense that, three decades on, still no heather grows where the Hercules imploded.

---

* Access permission is required to use this private track. The glen is a Site of Special Scientific Interest.

ACCIDENTAL DEATH

The ancient burial mound, recreated with modern hands, is built from surrounding stones. The Greeks called it a hermaion, the Scots a cairn. For the nine men who died in Glen Loch on 27 May 1993, it is a full stop. A premature end. Garry and the rest of LXX Squadron never played that game of golf. When the alarm sounded at RAF Lossiemouth, a different game was up. The third Hercules was missing.

Garry has notched up more than thirty years of remembering and commemoration. 'It has been very hard' – just as tough as losing an aircraft in the subsequent Iraq war. More shocking perhaps, but statistically no less surprising. Training for war is a dangerous game. Trying to come to terms with what has happened has taken years, decades. It is a process in which the remote cairn plays its lone card, calling in the families, the friends, the survivors. On the 30th anniversary of the crash, the pilgrimage, miles up Glen Loch, morphed into a soft, warm, memory-filled day of unexpected friendship and consolation. A lone piper matched the curlew, note for note. And for Garry, it was a day shot through with the bittersweet note of survival. Three decades earlier, he was told to change aircraft just before take-off. A split-second decision, the difference between life and death.

RIP squadron leader Stanley Muir and your eight brave men.

PART SIX

PEACETIME BRITAIN?

CHAPTER 28

THE TROUBLES

The Troubles: over 3,600 civilian and military personnel dead and thousands more injured. Really? Just 'troubles'? To be honest, it depends who you ask. Former defence minister Lord Robathan argued that 'if it looks like a duck, and it quacks like a duck, it is a duck'. In other words, The Troubles were a war. But, officially, the euphemism stuck, based on the logic that to call it otherwise was to give terrorism legitimacy – and what country wants to admit to armed conflict? Either way, Northern Ireland witnessed the longest continuous deployment in British military history, with the army on active service there for thirty-eight years.

93. Bloody Sunday Memorial, Joseph Place, Derry/Londonderry, Northern Ireland, 1974

Bloody Sunday 1972

Kate Nash was the oldest sister. 'Counting from the top, I was number four. There were nine below me.' Pecking orders in big families matter, especially when the chips are down. 'Mum had had a heart attack on the Wednesday, and one brother was getting married on the Saturday. The hotel and everything was booked, so we decided not to cancel it.' Kate's recall is vivid. She has revisited this particular week many times.

Small and dark with delicious cheeks and an infectious smile, it is easy to imagine twenty-three-year-old Kate holding things together in her mother's absence, organising the siblings, checking in for her shift at the local car-parts factory, taking a clean nightie up to the hospital. And still there was time for fun. 'Me and Willie, we stood at the sitting room door, giggling. My big brother Alan had come back from London for the wedding with an English girlfriend. We were plucking up the courage to say hello.'

Kate was dating an American lad stationed at the nearby US naval base. He was learning to fly a four-seater plane. The day after the wedding, they spent the critical hours of Sunday 30 January 1972 together in the skies over the town. On the streets below, a vast civil rights protest got underway near the Nash home on the Creggan Estate. It wasn't a warzone; it was a march. At least, that's how it started.

The backstory to Bloody Sunday is well known. Buoyed by the American civil rights movement, Northern Ireland's growing Catholic minority found its voice in the face of a system that comprehensively discriminated against them – votes, housing, jobs, on went the list. By the time the British Army arrived on the scene in August 1969, violence had become a hallmark of The Troubles. Initially, it was Catholics who required protection from the thuggish, Protestant-dominated Royal Ulster Constabulary. But, increasingly, the IRA took things into their own hands. Three days prior to Bloody Sunday, two RUC officers were murdered. Tensions were running high. The (outlawed) march on Sunday 30 January was against internment without trial. More than 100,000 local Catholics joined in, Kate's younger brother, Willie, included. They were headed to the Bogside. She explains: 'he went along for the craic'. As you do on a cold winter's day in 1972.

'Willie was tall. He was a strong docker. Surely, he could throw 8-stone bags of potatoes into a boat, no problem.' Nineteen-year-old

THE TROUBLES

Willie Nash was wearing a fancy suit, specially selected for his brother's wedding the day before, with tan boots, a lemon shirt and a lemon-patterned tie. Kate is sure he wore it well, but she doesn't have a photograph of Willie. 'There were no cameras, so very few pictures. There was no money.' But she holds Willie in her mind's eye, in his wedding suit with his lovely teeth. It's funny what you remember.

Nowadays, when Sunday, Bloody Sunday is referenced, the doleful U2 ballad springs to mind, and sepia photographs of guns and barricades. Or maybe the Saville Report on repeat, later to be confirmed as the longest inquiry in British legal history, preceded by the much-derided Widgery Report. It is easy to get lost in the nettles; lawyers' double-speak, appeals and inconclusive trials against nameless paratroopers who shot men dead, some with their backs turned and hands in the air. Or, in the case of Kate's father, Alex Nash, a middle-aged man running to rescue his son behind the barricade. 'Dad joined the march halfway. A neighbour said the bravest thing he ever saw was Alex running into the gunfire to save Willie.' It was too late. Willie was dead.

Kate shakes her head. Events that Sunday left an indelible mark. 'I went straight to the hospital where Dad was. The police stopped us on the bridge. They mocked us. My brother Charlie was an Olympic boxer. I'd never seen him angry before.' A new level of horror greeted Kate at the hospital: broken men she knew, marked with bullets and blood, lined the ward. She found her injured father with his arm in a contraption. He had been shot through the wrist and in the side. '"That looks sore, Dad," I said. All he could say was "Willie is in the morgue."' Alex had seen his dead son thrown into a Saracen van like a lump of meat.

The massacre heralded a fatal upscale in Northern Ireland's Troubles. A stain on the British Army and a potent recruiting tool for the IRA, on Bloody Sunday, thirteen men – six of whom just seventeen years old – were shot dead protesting on the streets of the United Kingdom. But Kate will insist 'what came next was worse.

LEST WE FORGET

'The lies they told.' I sit on her sofa, less than a mile from the Bogside, and hear how this woman's family was subsequently derided in court, their home raided by soldiers, her father slandered in the British press. 'They said he wasn't able to support his family, that he was a criminal, that he didn't know his [dead] son. My dad picked up a chair in the hearing at that accusation. He was so angry.' Anything to belittle the victims of this heinous act, to traduce their value and infer their culpability.

The Widgery Report delivered its verdict just eleven weeks after Bloody Sunday, with Britain's Lord Chief Justice concluding that while the paratroopers' shooting 'bordered on reckless', the soldiers were fired on first. More lies. I shift on the sofa. 'Sorry,' I say. 'Ach, don't be silly. I like the English,' says Kate. 'I lived in England for a while. But I could never make them believe that the British state lied.'

We turn back to the minutiae of that week: Kate's mother in hospital with a heart attack, Kate's father in hospital with bullet wounds, Kate's brother in the morgue. 'They didn't tell Mum about Willie until the day of his funeral. They didn't want to stress her. Eventually, a priest told her when she was sedated. Mum remained silent. Didn't say a word.'

It was only when Kate's mother, Bridget, arrived home and put her foot on the threshold of her house that she screamed 'Willie, Willie, Willie'. Kate pauses, still affected after all these years. Willie was gone. It was Bridget, in the fog of grief, who organised the annual commemorative march with other mothers. By 1974, it was centred around a limestone monument; the 16-foot-high traditional obelisk, dignified in its simplicity, still stands in the Bogside among the residential flats, on the route near where Willie died.* Etched clearly into the base are the names of all the men 'murdered by

---

* The monument was carved by Ballycastle sculptor, Cathal Newcombe, who was interned in Long Kesh (aka HM Prison Maze) at the time of the Bloody Sunday killings.

British paratroopers on Bloody Sunday, 30 January 1972'. The families had to wait another thirty-six years before they heard the British prime minister, David Cameron, conclude the same, saying: 'There is no doubt, there is nothing equivocal, there are no ambiguities. What happened on Bloody Sunday was both unjustified and unjustifiable. It was wrong.'*

Why did it take so long? That's what Kate wants to know. She hugs me tight before I leave and says: 'Nowadays, I'm all about the underdog. Last January, I laid a wreath for the people of Gaza. We have a superpower if we act together. We just don't realise it.'

94. Warrenpoint Massacre plaque, Warrenpoint, County Down, Northern Ireland, last erected 2020

Warrenpoint Massacre, 1979

Warrenpoint in County Down is beautiful. Painfully so. To stand at the water's edge, looking across Newry River towards Ireland's Cooley Mountains at sunset is both breathtaking and complicated. A handsome Elizabethan stone keep on the Northern Irish side of the river speaks to a long military history and, in the foreground, scores of scarlet wreaths mark a far more recent horror story. This remote borderland was the scene of an unprecedented massacre on 27 August 1979, when two IRA bombs killed eighteen British servicemen. It was the deadliest attack on the British army during its thirty-eight years in Northern Ireland, and the Parachute Regiment's biggest loss of life since World War II.

Richard Mckee was born a decade after the attack. He lives 18 miles from Warrenpoint, in Kilkeel where his family have farmed for the last 400 years. 'I would often drive past the site and never thought much about what happened here, but in 2015 I was passing

---

* 'Bloody Sunday: PM David Cameron's full statement', BBC News, 15 June 2010.

and saw two wreaths. One had been broken.' The scene bothered Richard. He pulled over and was struck by the absence of a plaque. 'Narrow Water Castle is just up the road. Travellers coming here would have no idea what had happened in 1979.' Richard measured the small wooden fence and ordered a brass inscribed plate, 30 inches by 10. 'I knew not to make it too big. This is a predominantly nationalist area.'

Richard felt it was important to mark the spot. We are parked up in his car where, forty-five years ago, a hay-trailer sat with an 800 lb fertiliser bomb hidden among its bales. The trailer was being watched from the other side of the border, across the river.

It was the afternoon of the August Bank Holiday Monday. A paratrooper, Anthony Wood, was driving the last lorry in a four-vehicle convoy when the bomb was detonated. The explosion was so intense that every one of the six men in the vehicle died; all that remained of Anthony was a pelvis bone welded to the seat. 'They evaporated him,' explains his brother Terry. 'He joined the paras a boy-soldier aged sixteen. He was nineteen when he died.'

Terry watched his parents blame and counter-blame each other. 'It's Catholic guilt,' he explains. Terry's family came from County Kildare and Country Kerry in the Republic. 'We were an airborne military family. We served in World War II. My brother and I were the first generation born in England.' Terry sighs. Ireland is complicated. It still is. 'The IRA rang my mum, told her "What did she expect?" – her boy in the British Army in Northern Ireland.'

Terry was seventeen when Anthony was murdered. 'I joined the Paratroopers after that. Needed to get the hell out. Wanted to understand my brother's world. I was on the ground in Northern Ireland by 1980. I worked on the basis that lightning doesn't strike twice.'

It struck twice at Warrenpoint on 27 August. Around twenty minutes after the first explosion, as a helicopter took off carrying some of the injured, a second device was detonated and twelve more soldiers, on a clear-up mission at the nearby gatehouse, were killed. The bomb was hidden in a milk keg. The IRA had correctly predicted the army's movements after the first explosion. Among the dead was the commanding officer of the Queen's Own Highlanders, Lieutenant-Colonel David Blair, the most senior army officer killed in Northern Ireland.* Like Anthony, he was also evaporated. All that remained was his epaulettes, subsequently presented to the prime minister, Margaret Thatcher.

Alexandra Nevill was ten years old and watching *The Great Escape* with her younger brother, Andrew, when she discovered her father, David Blair, was dead. He had been her hero, and then he was gone. Some forty-five years later, Alexandra will tell me: 'losing a dad like that makes you grow up pretty quick'. Times have changed, but grief hasn't. David Blair wasn't just Alexandra's hero, he was a war hero, leading his men on a dangerous rescue mission which would claim his life. The stakes that day were doubly high. Just hours before the first explosion at Warrenpoint, Earl Mountbatten of Burma and three companions were blown up while fishing in Donegal Bay. The IRA struck three times that August bank holiday.

Alexandra sighs. 'It was payback against the British Army for Bloody Sunday. I know it was.' Since that fateful day, seven years had passed, all pock-marked with hundreds of terror attacks, but revenge has deep roots. The men who killed Anthony Wood and David Blair and sixteen others at Warrenpoint were never arrested. As Terry dryly explains, 'I can see where my brother's killer lives by looking on Wikipedia.'

When the Good Friday Agreement was eventually brokered almost twenty years after the Warrenpoint massacre, victims from all sides had to swallow hard. For many, what was billed as a peace process felt more like appeasement. Forgiving is a vital, unsung aspect of reconciliation, Alexandra understands this. 'They have won if you continue that cycle of hatred. You are never going to kill your way out of a war.' But forgiving does not mean forgetting.

---

* Of the eighteen men killed that day in Warrenpoint, sixteen served with the Parachute Regiment and two with the Queen's Own Highlanders.

LEST WE FORGET

Remembering her father is a key plank of Alexandra's identity, likewise that of her mother, Anne, and her brother, Andrew. However, where to remember remains complicated. The family had no body. Together, they were involved in the unveiling of a statue to David Blair's regiment, the Queen's Own Highlanders, in the National Memorial Arboretum, but Britain's leading site of military remembrance prohibits the naming of the dead on regimental monuments. This bewildered and upset Alexandra. 'The soldiers after World War I got their names on a memorial. Without names, in years to come that statue will just be an anonymous soldier.'

That leaves Warrenpoint as the location for a memorial. Terry knows the area well. 'I hated serving in Northern Ireland. We were sitting ducks in red berets.' But he cares about where his brother died. What else does he have to remember him by? Alexandra last visited Warrenpoint twenty years ago on the twenty-fifth anniversary of the attack. It was not a pleasant experience; directly after the signing of the Good Friday Agreement, tensions ran high. When she laid her flowers at the site, an IRA sympathiser popped out of a bush and spoke in support of the massacre.

Two decades on, the province is still healing, but testimony to the progress made are the eighteen wreaths that hang, unmolested, on the fence. As for Richard Mckee's plaque, it has twice been defaced and removed, and twice he has ordered a new one, reattaching it to the same spot. Now classified as a hate crime, the penalty for vandalising the site is steep: one man was given a brief custodial sentence. 'That helped,' admits Richard. 'The current plaque has not been removed or damaged for three years. A record.'

I step out of the car and take a picture of the setting sun against the water and the deep red poppies and the tiny shiny plaque. I send it to Terry. 'It's a shit place to die,' says Terry, but he is glad of the picture.

CHAPTER 29

THE FALKLANDS WAR

Lasting just seventy-four days, the Falklands War was a decade-defining conflict. In 1982, Britain, already stretched by NATO commitments, deployed all three of its armed services for the first time since World War II against a numerically superior enemy in difficult terrain. Argentina was defeated, the Falkland Islands were liberated and, back at home, Britain briefly enjoyed a post-imperial hurrah. But for the military involved, the impact is still felt today.

95. The Yomper, Eastney Esplanade, Southsea, Hampshire, 1992

The Falklands War, 1982

Paul Youngman, a former Royal Navy lieutenant commander, completed two tours in Iraq, one in Afghanistan and also served in the Falklands War. Paul is certain: 'The most straightforward was the Falklands. There was a clear start date and an end date. The other conflicts felt like they never really finished. When I left, they were still going on.' Not so in the South Atlantic, where four weeks after Paul's landing in May 1982 a white flag was hoisted over the islands' capital, Stanley. 'On 14 June, we knew the war had finished.'

A leading medical assistant attached to 45 Commando Unit, at the beginning of 1982 Paul had anticipated a quiet year. 'My wife was pregnant and I was looking forward to Easter leave.' And then Argentina invaded the Falkland Islands and suddenly Paul was heading for Portsmouth. 'We didn't think it was real until the sinking of HMS *Sheffield*. Once people had died, that changed everything. There was no going back.'

Part of a highly trained, amphibious invasion force, Paul experienced his own D-Day landing at Ajax Bay. 'We had to secure the beach and set up a regimental aid post, ready to receive casualties. The broader aim was to take Stanley, 50 miles away. The Argentinians were dug into the surrounding mountains. We had to get our kit and go and do it.' At twenty-three years old, Paul was a lump older than many of the lads, and recalls conflicting emotions. 'I was a

soldier until the first casualty and then I was a medic. As a medic, you never want to use your skills, but there's something intensely professional about being able to put them into practice. And an element of comfort – injured Marines were thankful to see me when I arrived.'

Paul's job was to treat and evacuate wounded personnel back to the next level of medical support. In the cold and wet, he treated casualties on the ground, securing airways, administering fluids, preventing haemorrhages. To his peers and friends, Paul was a saviour. 'I got every one of them back to where they needed to be. I was part of a small team with the necessary skills. It was no good breaking down.'

Pumped with adrenaline, fully focused on the job, Paul would later marvel at his lack of emotion in the moment. On high alert, part of a fraught mission to secure the island, it is small wonder that one image from the war stands out.

'It was the picture of the yomper. He was attached to our unit, yomping at the rear, the Union Jack unfurled behind him, approaching Sapper Hill. That photograph signalled the end of the war before the Argentinians had surrendered. We never fought on Sapper Hill.' Paul is referring to the world-famous image of Commando Peter Robinson who, sensing the end, pinned the British flag to his bergan as he walked across the Falklands' forbidding landscape towards Stanley. The iconic photograph, captured by the force's photographer, Peter Holdgate, messaged to the world that Britain had won. The same picture inspired Philip Jackson's three-ton Yomper statue in Southsea, unveiled by Margaret Thatcher in 1992. The commando looks out to sea, pack on his back, gun in his hand, beret on his head.

It never fails to move Paul. For him, the statue sums up both the Commandos' fighting spirit and the impending end of the war. But, like any memorial, it only tells half the story.

'We flew from Ascension Island back to the UK. Landing in the middle of the night, it was raining and there was a train strike.' But at least Paul had made it home. Thirteen of his unit died in the Falklands: peers, comrades, a band of brothers. For the first time since World War I, families were given a choice over the repatriation of their dead relatives. Eight returned home, five remain in the Falkland Islands. Paul went to visit them forty years later in San Carlos. 'Some who had brought home their next-of-kin came too. Once they saw the cemetery in the Falklands, looking across the bay, across from Ajax Beach, they wondered about their decision to repatriate. It's hard to know. I imagined the boys together, the paras and the royal marines, and all their banter.'

Wherever they fell, they were the class of '82.*

96. The Welsh National Falklands Memorial, Alexandra Gardens, Cardiff, 2007

The Falklands War, 1982

'It was hard to turn on the telly in the late '80s and not see me.' Simon Weston laughs. He has a distinct and unapologetic sense of humour. I'm hosting at a literary festival in Orpington, interviewing the Falkland War's most famous veteran. The room is packed. I have prepared extensively – rereading Simon's memoirs, watching interviews he has given down the years. His extraordinary rebuilt appearance is weirdly familiar. I feel like I know him: his Welsh banter, his goddamn resilience, his redemptive qualities and, most of all, his face. I am as star-struck as the rest of the audience.

The Falklands War began with Argentina's impertinent invasion of the islands they call Islas Malvinas and Britain's fulsome response

---

* In total, 255 British military personnel and three civilian islanders were killed during the Falklands War. They are remembered in the Standing With Giants installation in the parade grounds and ramparts of Fort Nelson in Fareham, near Portsmouth.

from an Iron Lady not yet fully formed. For those of us who came of age in the 1980s, certain images have proved enduring: Margaret Thatcher declaring 'Defeat? I do not recognise the meaning of the word'; the *QE2* cruise-liner slipping its ropes at Southampton with 3,000 troops on board; and the Conservatives' subsequent thumping victory in the 1983 general election. It was a couple of years later that Simon's messy, drunk recovery was widely aired on television, in the wake of what he describes as Britain's last 'uncontentious conflict'.

Aged twenty, Welsh Guardsman Simon was on board the QE2 when it departed England that balmy May day. As they left Southampton, a fellow Guardsman held up a banner: 'Mrs Thatcher, thank you for our holiday cruise.' Simon acknowledges that none of the soldiers standing on the deck had ever been 'in a full-scale war'. They were fresh-faced, naïve, focused on 'righting a wrong' committed 8,000 miles away by a military junta in Buenos Aires.

LEST WE FORGET

How do you jump-cut from that downy-cheeked lad on a cruise ship to 'Air-raid Warning Red!' when *Sir Galahad*, an unarmed, undefended supply vessel full of munitions, fuel and soldiers, was attacked in an East Falkland port? After forty years of telling his story, Simon is adept at gear changes. He cracks a joke about the skin on his face coming from his bum. 'You've just kissed my ass!' he laughs. The audience laugh too. I read a section from his memoir: 'Men were mutilated and burning, and fought to rip off their clothing or douse the flames and beat at their faces, arms, legs, hair. They rushed around in circles in the roadway, screaming like pigs. A human fireball crumpled just 10 feet in front of me like a disintegrating Guy Fawkes, blistered hands outstretched as he called for his mum.'*

The audience stop laughing. Simon will cheer them up again. Forty-eight soldiers and crew died on *Sir Galahad* that day, including thirty-two Welsh Guards. But not Simon. He lived. With a melting face and hands, he 'just ran in the right direction' and has subsequently found a way forward through the nightmares and disability. Key to his recovery was meeting the man who dropped the bomb that burned 46 per cent of Simon's body. He is matter-of-fact about the role of Argentine fighter pilot, First Lieutenant Carlos Cachon. 'Carlos was just doing his job, same as we were. It's just that he had greater success on that day.' Of their meeting decades after the event, Simon insists 'there was no saying sorry, and no forgiveness because there was nothing to forgive'. He explains his logic; Carlos wasn't a terrorist, he was wearing his country's uniform. His is a well-trained military response, but also a sincere one. The two men remain friends.

I ask Simon whether, beyond Stanley, where the Falkland Islands' own memorial stands, he has a preferred British monument. He directs me to the five-ton rock that 'the boys brought back from the Falklands' and erected in Cardiff. 'It is for anybody who served in

---

* Simon Weston, *The Complete Story*, Bloomsbury, 1994.

the Falkland' and names all 255 of the fallen military. The transportation of the giant stone reads like an odyssey, involving the navy, the RAF and a Falklands veteran who specialised in reinforced flooring. The result sits in Cardiff's Alexandra Gardens, its uncomely shape a pleasing contrast to the polished proportions of the 1920s National War Memorial.

I visit the pale rock on its handsome, stepped plinth, and imagine Simon's familiar face staring back. I am reminded of our night together in Orpington: the event has ended and a giant queue snakes across the hall. Women touch him and hug him, men slap him on the back and joke about their own bald bits. Simon withstands the assault, wiping his eye that always weeps. He was the most injured man in the Falklands War and subsequently became the most famous man who served there. Re-sculpted for a full and frank adult life, Simon Weston CBE is a monument to survival.

CHAPTER 30

ASYMMETRICAL WAR

Every decade since 1945, the British armed forces have been engaged in military conflict, including the Korean War, the Malaya Emergency, the Borneo Rebellion, the Suez Crisis and onwards to the Yugoslav Wars and the first Gulf War. It was in 1991 that the idea of a national centre of remembrance was first mooted and today the National Memorial Arboretum in Staffordshire is home to more than 400 memorials highlighting the sacrifice involved in serving Britain's military, irrespective of the conflict. From imperial confrontations to the recent asymmetrical wars in Afghanistan and Iraq, Britain's military history is not straightforward; memorialisation has adapted accordingly.

97. Maiwand Lion, Forbury Gardens, Reading, 1886

Battle of Maiwand, Second Anglo-Afghan War, 1878–1880

It's August 2024 and I have selected my 100 monuments. 'But you've got to include the Maiwand Lion.' Matt Allwright is something of a celebrity in his native Berkshire. Reading born-and-bred, he frequently pops up on national television hosting Britain's favourite fare – *The One Show, Watchdog, Rogue Traders*. I met him in a TV studio. Reading is proud of him, and he them. And that includes The Lion.

What lion? You would not ask that question if you came from Reading. A two-minute walk from the town's train station is Forbury Gardens, where the giant cat demands immediate attention. Forget the oak tree planted from a seed found in Verdun, or trooper William Potts's sculpture commemorating his VC at Gallipoli. The Maiwand Lion is Reading's stand-out memorial and most important emblem. Along with everyone else, young Matt drank Guinness beneath great paws, threw snowballs into a roaring mouth and strummed guitar against the outsized plinth. The roaring big cat is Reading FC's badge and mascot; he made front-page news every day in the *Reading Post*. Forbury's lion even boasts an eponymous beer. Locally, he is loved and appreciated. The residents know their statue has form as an icon, both then and now.

As recently as June 2020, three men were murdered in a homophobic terror attack in Forbury Gardens. In the hours that followed,

local people spontaneously gathered beneath the Maiwand Lion, adopted his leonine image and added the defiant hashtag #Readingtogether. Likewise, in his 1880s heyday, this 16-ton monument was a symbol of fortitude and strength: the giant cat was Reading's version of the British lion standing in the passes of the North-West Frontier region, defending India from an enormous advancing Russian bear.

But at what cost? Nowadays, Maiwand is a village in Afghanistan, north-west of Kandahar, where hundreds of the 66 Berkshire Regiment were outnumbered and cut down in 1880. Their names are etched in perpetuity on Reading's enormous plinth, their grizzly fate explicated through Rudyard Kipling's stark prose:

I 'eard the knives be'ind me, but I dursn't face my man,
Nor I don't know where I went to, 'cause I didn't 'alt to see.*

'I've lived in Reading twenty-five years, but I never knew its significance.' So said Helena Tym after her nineteen-year-old son, Cyrus Thatcher, died in Afghanistan in 2009. With fresh eyes, she rediscovered the Maiwand Lion and its 328 dead men. Part of the Second Anglo-Afghan War, the British were routed at the Battle of Maiwand in 1880; six years later, Reading's memorial, with its early inclusion of privates' names, spoke to the shock impact of that dramatic defeat. Helena's face, staring out from a BBC News feature in 2011, suggests we never learned our lesson. Too busy lionising our military (Britain won the Second Anglo-Afghan War), we didn't listen to its roar.

Till I 'eard a beggar squealin' out for quarter as 'e ran,
An' I thought I knew the voice an' – it was me!

---

* 'That Day', Rudyard Kipling, first published in the *Pall Mall Gazette*, 25 April 1895.

ASYMMETRICAL WAR

Look again at the Maiwand Lion and that roar becomes a plaintive squeal. Matt Allwright alludes to associated ideas of pain when he references an urban myth that suggests the sculptor, George Blackall Simonds, killed himself, unhappy with his work. In fact, Simonds lived; it was his only son who died, during World War I. And irrespective of the rumour, the lion's gait, taken from a study of London Zoo's lions, is anatomically correct. But through contemporary eyes, the Maiwand sculpture is a timeless warning against Britain's penchant for 'little wars' in foreign lands.

In a last conversation Helena had with her son, Cyrus talked about the 'very small unsophisticated devices' that the Taliban were using and 'giving the army a terrible problem … because they couldn't find them'.

Rifleman Thatcher, a soldier of great promise, was killed by an improvised explosive device in Helmand Province on 2 June 2009. Another lion of Reading.

98. Camp Bastion Wall, National Memorial Arboretum, Alrewas, Staffordshire, 2015

The Afghanistan War, 2001–2021

We met Jacqui Thompson earlier in this book, elucidating the importance of her husband Gary's return to Britain in the context of the Unknown Warrior.* Senior aircraftman Gary died in Afghanistan in 2008, but unlike the Maiwand 328 he came home. Great emphasis is placed on the ultimate resting place of the fallen. Former Gulf War veteran and prisoner-of-war John Nicol writes that all soldiers want to come home. But before they return, first they must leave. While conscripts have no choice, for centuries professional soldiers and volunteers alike have rushed to answer the call and join the

---

* Tomb of the Unknown Warrior, Monument 50.

colours. Jacqui smiles. 'Now, looking back on it, I think he must've been having a mid-life crisis.'

A family man with five daughters and a loving wife, Gary, who ran his own sheet metal company in Nottinghamshire, had it all. But there was an itch, perhaps something left over from his early days in the RAF, an urge unfulfilled by weekly rugby and banter with the lads at work. Jacqui isn't sure; she wishes she'd asked him, but you don't in the moment. 'Two wars were going on – first Afghanistan and then he was watching Britain's invasion of Iraq in 2003. He kept saying "I should be there". I think he felt guilty.' Gary was forty-eight, just within the age limit, when he joined the Auxiliary RAF in 2005.

'He was a reservist – occasionally they would go away on training exercise at the weekend. He was still working during the week. We laughed that he was Captain Mainwaring in *Dad's Army*.' But, by 2008, what began as a weekend hobby had been upgraded. Now aged fifty-one, Gary passed all the tests and was deployed to Kandahar Province in Afghanistan. 'I remember the night he told the girls. All five of them were there. "It won't be dangerous, will it, Dad?" "No," he said. "I'm just protecting the airbase. I'll be perfectly safe."'

There was no such thing as 'perfectly safe' in a war against the Taliban. Jacqui knew that, but she didn't want a big argument and it was important Gary went, both for him and his squadron. 'He was so calm. In all the years I knew him, he never once lost his temper.' Gary's was just the kind of level head that NATO needed on patrol at Kandahar Airfield.

Jacqui and I meet on a blustery day in July. She has travelled up from Nottingham and together we leave the shelter of Staffordshire's National Memorial Arboretum café and walk towards the Bastion Wall. Motion helps after so much emotion. These days, Jacqui is an old hand at grief, but the story is shocking nonetheless. Gary had been away fewer than two months. It was April 2008 and his leave was pending – perfect timing as daughter Jade would be turning eighteen. Jacqui had made sure the house was spick and span. 'It was late at night, about eleven o'clock. My daughter said, "Why are there two RAF men at the door?" She saw them through the glass panelling.'

'"Mrs Thompson, can we come in please?"

'"Yes, of course. Would you like a cup of tea?"

'"No, thank you. Can we go somewhere to sit down?"

'"I am sorry to tell you your husband Gary has been killed in Afghanistan."

'"Are you sure it's Gary?"

'"Yes. He was identified by someone who knew him."'

Was it at that moment Jacqui looked up through the door at her daughters sitting on the stairs? 'They saw my face and started crying.'

We arrive at the wall. It's a bit like Camp Bastion Wall in Afghanistan – constructed by service personnel to remember their comrades – but not the same; the materials wouldn't travel, nor endure in the British climate. 'There are sections of the old wall inside this central structure.' Jacqui pivots away from the name of Senior Aircraftman G Thompson to a granite plinth topped with a cross fashioned from gun cases. 'My silver locket is in the foundations, with a faded picture of me and Gary.' She smiles. 'I was accompanying the archbishop, Justin Welby, around the arboretum when they were making this. The builder came from Cornwall, as did Gary. What were the chances? So I took off my locket and gave it to him.'

This second British Bastion Wall commemorates the 454 British lives lost in Afghanistan and was opened by Prince Harry, less than a year after the majority of Britain's forces withdrew in 2014, having handed Camp Bastion to the newly trained Afghan military. 'I didn't go into the marquees. I just wanted to be alone. It was a day for me. For Gary.' Grief morphs. And perspectives change. 'I'm heartbroken by what's since happened in Afghanistan. It was hard to watch after so many sacrifices were made.' She is referring to the risible withdrawal of the coalition's final troops in August 2021. The Taliban took back control and the West had never looked so impotent. Just six months later, Putin invaded Ukraine.

The National Army Museum website, funded by the Ministry of Defence, reckons the legacy of the campaign in Afghanistan is difficult to determine. It concedes that 'British strategy was never clear'. But Jacqui is clear. 'Gary wanted to go. I am proud of him. And I believe that when he was in Afghanistan, he made a difference.'

99. Aaron Lewis Close, Hockley, Essex, 2014

Aaron Lewis, d. 2008, The Afghanistan War, 2001–2021

Mark François is standing in the garden. His British-Ukrainian lapel badge winks in the sunlight and a pair of olive trees flank him, two silent sentinels. 'The Lewises are a remarkable couple.' He gesticulates at the bench; no words are needed. Their son, Aaron Lewis, was clearly a remarkable man. We are silent, I am struck by Mark's poise. Best known as something of a political caricature who sits on the right of the Conservative Party, the Essex MP is deeply affected by the Lewis family. That is why we are here, standing in Aaron Lewis Close, a modern housing development centred around a memorial garden.

'It was a stray bullet that killed him. The Taliban let rip a round into the sky and down it came.' I touch the picture of a young, cheery face smiling out from the bench, a commando, an army lieutenant, a rugby player and a son.

His mother, Helen, then a medical secretary, was at work on 15 December 2008. 'I had been feeling out of sorts from the morning. I did my Christmas shopping all wrong. I just wasn't feeling right.' Later, after our conversation, I will consult a map and mark out the distance between Essex and Helmand Province. It's 6,000km. It is hard not to ponder the power of maternal instinct. The gravest violation against Helen's natural order occurred on the other side of the world and she was already feeling unwell long before two men in dark suits arrived on her doorstep. 'I was named as next-of-kin, so when I heard them asking for me on a Monday evening …'

The noise in her head was terrible, an appalling hammering on the cerebral cortex. 'Afterwards, I discovered it was my own screams.' Helen's husband caught her fall. 'I remember the men of doom, but after that I don't remember anything for days, weeks. It was a blur.' Mark recalls meeting Aaron's mother at a series of commemorative services the following Armistice Day. 'She turned up at all of them, clutching her son's green beret. I said, "You've done enough now, Helen."' Perhaps when you lose a child, you can never do enough.

Helen has survived sixteen years without Aaron. 'Time doesn't heal. I find it offensive when people say that. But it does help you manage the pain better. To begin with, you can't get your brain around it. You feel like you're going mad. You're searching for that person.' Her lovely boy, Aaron. His Ministry of Defence profile sparkles with industry, justice and passion: here was 'someone very special … a natural leader … despite suffering a knee injury he showed incredible determination to pass the arduous All Arms Commando Course.' Hence the green beret. Helen explains: 'He was so proud of his beret. He was adamant that he was going to do a Commando course if the men under him were Commandos. He wouldn't ask them to do something he couldn't do himself.'

As a student, Aaron had decided to join the army 'to make a difference' in the wake of the 9/11 al-Qaeda terror attacks on the US. Seven years later, in September 2008, he was deployed to Afghanistan with 29 Commando Regiment. It was his first overseas tour. And his last. Devoted to family and friends, Aaron took the army's advice and wrote letters before departure, in case the worst happened.

'I am so glad he did. Other parents didn't have that. He wrote, "Mum, I know what's happened must've hurt you terribly." I thought *Hurt me terribly, Aaron? You don't know the half of it.*' Helen was floored by a 'very real pain and terrible sadness', but there was no anger. 'Perhaps that had something to do with Aaron's letter. He told me not to blame the government or Afghanistan or the army, that it was his choice to go. It was a truly amazing letter that gave me a balm of sorts.'

In the wake of an inconsolable loss, Helen has grown and changed. I privately wonder at the way she now embodies the qualities most admired in her son. Helen didn't return to work – 'I just couldn't.' Instead, she took up where others led and is a key player in the Aaron Lewis Foundation.[*]

Back in Aaron Lewis Close, MP Mark shakes his head in wonder. 'I can't even begin to imagine how much they have raised.' Helen privately admits she was glad of the break when lockdown came. Public speaking is not easy, but it opens doors and raises money for Aaron's charity, committed to transforming lives for ex-service personnel through sport and community action. '"To remember his monument, look around you." That is what I was told and that is what I do. Sometimes I think to myself, *Thanks Aaron, look what you've got me into!*'

The landscaped garden in Aaron Lewis Close, near to Helen's own Essex home, provides a respite of sorts and a chance to reflect. Mark smiles. 'Just sometimes, local planners get it right.'

100. Basra Wall, National Memorial Arboretum, Alrewas, Staffordshire, 2010

Kingsman Adam J. Smith, d. 2007, Iraq War, 2003–2011

'Honourable age does not depend on length of days, nor is the number of years a true measure of life.' So reads the main inscription on the Basra Wall in the National Memorial Arboretum.

Surrey-born Padre Huw Evans and Liverpudlian Adam clicked. They would josh over Adam's love of Everton FC (the padre was

---

[*] http://aaronlewisfoundation.org.uk/

more a rugby man), share jokes and coffee. 'I have a lot of memories of Iraq,' Huw tells me. 'There was one soldier, Kingsman Adam Smith, I knew him as Smudge. He would come into my ISO container a lot. An ISO? Oh, it was a small metal box, a shipping container. Roasting hot. I had decent coffee – the box had a cafetière – and someone cobbled together some air con.'

Adam was just nineteen. A well-built, cheerful lad with an appetite for life and a cheeky grin, he was exactly the sort of person Huw joined the army to work alongside. 'I felt called to serve with military people. I get on with them best. I like their honesty and their robustness.'

Two men in their desert combats, two decades apart, from different ends of England in a hot box, making friends and talking football. Army life in Basra, Iraq, 2007.

Huw flew out to Iraq on Armistice Day 2006. The war had been on-going for more than three years. Basra was Britain's military headquarters; what began as a liberation mission with the toppling of Saddam Hussein had morphed into a fight against insurgents. Weapons of mass destruction were never found; instead British troops faced down rival militias and their terror tactics. I try to place Huw in a broader geopolitical context, but he won't be drawn. 'I had no choice where I went. I was with 2nd Battalion, Duke of Lancaster Regiment, as battle group chaplain. My primary role was to offer pastoral care, a listening ear. I never carry a weapon. We are there to provide the faith element if soldiers want it. But also to chat, to share concerns and happy moments.'

In the box with Adam, he mainly shared happy moments. 'I'll see you later, Padre' (Huw has the scouse accent down to a tee) and off went blue-eyed Adam, braced for another mission, fuelled on coffee and good cheer. Huw assures me, 'You don't think about the risk. You go out a few times, you trust the equipment will not fail you.'

It was late and the operation was a big one. Huw watched it from the control room until the adjutant told him to go to bed. He retreated to his night-time cocoon, a small cot-bed with a mosquito net. 'I was woken very early, the adjutant telling me "We've lost Jo". That sticks in my mind.' The day hadn't begun, but someone had died.

Huw wonders if perhaps I remember Second Lieutenant Jo Dyer? Or, at least, remember reading about her. She graduated from Oxford University and trained at Sandhurst with Prince William. They were friends. He was 'deeply saddened' by the news. Twenty-four-year-old Jo's sunny face and death made the front pages. The padre knew and liked Jo; they shared a Yeovil connection. She was one of two British servicewomen to die that night. The other was a nineteen-year-old nurse, Private Eleanor Dlugosz of the Royal Army Medical Corps.

And what about Adam? 'Yes, he died too. All five died, including the translator.* It was a massive bomb.' But Huw can't tell me how massive. 'I made a point of not looking at the burnt-out vehicle on screen. We had to trust the Warrior.' And the padre had work to do; this was not a time for introspection. Huw remembers a sense of purpose, others returning from the operation which was company-strength, about a hundred troops. 'No, I can't tell you more. It's probably still classified.'

Where is God in this moment? God is with Huw. 'I turn around to him and say "I can't do this on my own". I basically say to God "I need your help". I have a faith there is a God.' There are prayers, and a liturgy, a written service and a parade. 'Eventually the bodies are loaded onto a Hercules. I led that. The deceased are carried by friends. With Smudge, one of those carrying him was Kingsman Jones.' The padre pauses. 'A month or so later, we were carrying Jones's coffin onto the plane.'

I find a picture of Kingsman Adam Smith on the internet. I am reminded of lads I was once at school with, full of vim and up for life. He looks like he did in 2007. Young. How does the padre square

---

* Corporal Kris O'Neill was the fourth British service death that night. Twelve British service personnel were killed in April 2007.

the circle of death in a contested war like Iraq? His reply is straightforward. 'If we start doubting why we were there, then we don't honour the dead.'

The Basra Wall remembers all 179 British men and women who died in Iraq. The soldiers built it on location. There were complaints about the quality of the commemorative plaques sent from Britain. 'But eventually they just thought "We need to build it".' And then, after the war, they rebuilt it in Staffordshire's arboretum – with different bricks but the same 179 plaques. That is where Huw goes at least once a year. 'My wife knows I need time by the wall. For my job, I have to hold it in. That is not good.'

POSTSCRIPT

The Armed Forces Memorial, National Memorial Arboretum, Alrewas, Staffordshire, 2007

I've found him. Down among the other pavers, dappled in Sunday sunshine: 'Lieutenant Aaron L Lewis, 29 Commando RA, KIA Afghanistan, 15.12.08.' I ask a Commando in service dress if he'd mind taking a picture of me, self-consciously crouched over the brickwork in my jeans, pointing at the paver, another mark that Aaron's truncated life has left on Planet Earth.

As photographs go, it's not bad. I ponder whether to send it to Aaron's mother, Helen. She might be minding her own business, having a day off grief (can you?). Would she want me, a stranger who never knew her son, butting in with a picture? So I pocket it and move away from the stragglers who stay huddled by the Commando Memorial where the commemorative service has just ended, away and through the numerous monuments in the National Memorial Arboretum. Yet I am struck by how affecting I find it, Aaron's name among all the other names.

I am still thinking about the power of a name you recognise, a reccurring theme in this book, when I make another research call. An ex-colonel, Ali Brown OBE served in the British Army for twenty-seven years and was part of the UN Peacekeeping force in Kosovo.

'The Cenotaph is not the one that resonates for me.' Ali's gut response is away from the Big Daddy of commemoration in the capital. She takes me right back to the National Memorial Arboretum and its landmark monument. 'I like the Armed Forces Memorial. It speaks to me. It has the names that I know.' Later that evening, Ali texts me: 'The person I do always remember at the NMA is Major Vanessa Lang. She died in Sierra Leone on 19 October 2021 when a Hind helicopter crashed. Of all those on board, she was the only one to die. Vanessa was a real livewire and an excellent officer and skier.'

I jot down the name Vanessa. I am writing a book about war and I didn't know that Britain's armed forces trained in Sierra Leone. But I did know about the Armed Forces Memorial. On my first visit to the arboretum in Staffordshire, I sat on its ghost-white steps – a stairway to heaven, the golden tip of the obelisk piercing the stone-grey sky and the curved Portland stone walls cresting the earth mound, reminiscent of ancient times. A scene off-set with cylindrical holly oaks, trimmed within an inch of their lives: short, back and sides for the fallen.

But, still at the beginning of my journey, the real symbolism of the monument was lost on me. It was never lost on ex-colonel Ali. 'It just gets me. In the centre of the horseshoe memorial are those very stark statues. The central one is a wounded solider being tended to, which gives it a human touch. And then those sparkling white walls, with all the names.'

Ian Rank-Broadley sculpted scenes near-biblical in their exposition, the meaning offset by thousands of names scrolling up and down the surrounding walls. This monument, the biggest in the arboretum, lists all the servicemen and women who have died in conflict, both training and active service, since World War II. Here are 16,000 glorious dead in our collective lifetime, including those killed in terror attacks.

POSTSCRIPT

It is on my second visit to the NMA that I see things differently. This time, the memorial's architecture is background noise. It is those 'startling white' storyboards of loss that challenge my rude jump-cuts through modern history. The Malayan Emergency – 1,443 dead. I recall the ninety-three-year-old friend I interviewed, Captain Ian de Sales la Terrière, who didn't make the book because he served in Malaysia, not World War II. The Korean War – 1,086 dead; another conflict I skipped over to get to more recent wars. Every inscription taunts that set phrase my generation learned in primary school: 'peacetime Britain'.

And now I find my own names. Among others there is Garry Brown's crew of LXX Squadron, all in a row, under 1993. Kingsman Adam Smith, the padre's favourite scouser who died in Iraq in 2007. And Aaron Lewis, this time his name picked out in Portland stone, under 2008, the year that Jacqui Thompson lost her husband, Gary. They sit in the same column. I take another picture. For Helen perhaps. Or just for me. And I find Ali Brown's Vanessa, all too recent, in 2021.

And beyond the names, yet more white wall space, smooth and nameless. For Ali, 'that is poignant as well, those blank bits. Because in our minds, we know there will be a next time. We know there will be more deaths and more names.'

EPILOGUE

In lofty Victorian prose, the philosopher Thomas Carlyle made a grand pronouncement on the opening page of his 1841 book *On Heroes, Hero-Worship, & the Heroic in History*: 'the history of what man has accomplished in this world, is at bottom the History of the Great Men who have worked here'. Times have changed since Carlyle's day, when the Great Man fetish was extensively replicated across Britain's cities in monumental form. And, as I hope this book has shown, they will keep changing, with static memorials the immutable touchstones to different versions of our past.

Thank you for coming with me on my travels, criss-crossing the UK in search of 100 seminal monuments to war. I quickly realised that those selected here are statistically very likely to exclude the one that means the most to you. I am sorry about that. But hopefully the story's broader arc helps put all monuments to war in context. It took less than 100 years before Carlyle's one-time 'Great Men' – society's 'modellers, patterns, and in a wide sense creators' – had been reduced by the 'general mass' of men thrown unwittingly into a world war they neither modelled nor created.

The ghastly absence of hundreds of thousands of soldiers who did not return home in 1918 still defines Britain's public spaces. There are crosses, cairns and figurative art everywhere you look. And if these monuments no longer resonate in the way they once did, then the personal stories recorded here from Britain's more recent conflicts are a stark reminder of the personal cost of war.

Today, it is hard to comprehend that, in the immediate aftermath of World War II, there was relief that the conflict had not claimed *more* lives. The mitigation of such an enormous loss, around 380,000 dead military personnel, makes sense only when contrasted with a figure greater than twice its size from World War I.*

In Britain's more peaceful present, World War II's death toll has taken on gargantuan proportions, with society's communal sacrifice underscored by the moral imperative of defeating Nazi Germany. Wide-ranging commemoration ties us back to the nostalgic 1940s, when Britain's nations were in lockstep and (almost) everyone was doing their bit. History tells us World War II was the right war to fight, and its increasingly celebrated status helps explain the scramble of remembering in recent years, with recognition shown not just for the dead, but also those still living who served alongside them. Vicariously, we take pride in the very real appreciation elderly veterans derive from finally being acknowledged. That Sophie, the then Countess of Wessex, cried when she unveiled the Bevin Boys monument in 2013 is not surprising. It really mattered to the men who were emasculated by their compulsory civilian war work and subsequently excluded from macho-style war commemoration.

The communal pleasure involved in the unveiling of a war monument before time runs out is a powerful reminder that memorials, at their most effective, are personal. Today's vibrant identity politics find their historic echo in new forms of ownership over the past. Just as I was putting the hundredth monument in this book to bed, Liam Walker, a proud great-grandson, contacted me via Instagram; his ninety-eight-year-old great-grandmother, Joy Trew, had served in the Women's Auxiliary Air Force (WAAF) in World War II. Liam sent me a short video of Joy, in which she explained why she was getting

---

* A further 60,000 civilians were killed in bombing campaigns across Britain.

EPILOGUE

in touch. Having joined the WAAF as a teenager, war work meant a lot to her but, in old age, she felt overlooked. 'No one seems to be very knowledgeable about the WAAF and it makes me feel as though I am talking about something like the Girl Guides. It has hurt me very much as I did enlist and work hard.'

I replayed the message. Initially, it didn't stack up. A sumptuous memorial in WAAF blue was unveiled in the National Memorial Arboretum in 2011 to Britain's Women's Auxiliary Air Force. The press attended and praise was lavished online, with the WAAF Association understandably proud they finally had a memorial in their name and to all their many trades.

So, what about Joy? It turns out that, after the death of her husband, she emigrated to Spain in 2002. Joy had left Britain by the time a spate of memorials to female service, including the World War II monument in Whitehall, were unveiled. She arrived back in England last year and, in a sign of changed times, wondered where her part was in a wider war story so frequently commemorated.

'According to my service book, I enlisted on 7 March 1944 aged seventeen-and-a-half.' She recalls 'being in an invalid chair by VE Day because I was having a rest from listening to Morse all the way from Germany, during 24-hour shifts'. Joy was a wireless operator, otherwise known as a Y-station listener. At the coalface of intercepting enemy communications, she was a vital cog in Britain's giant code-breaking nexus. By implication, that means Joy also belongs to the Bletchley Park Roll of Honour, except, unaware of her elevated veteran status, her name isn't on the Roll. Yet.

Belatedly reassured that her war service has not been forgotten, Joy finally feels seen. In the words of her daughter, Beverley, 'Mum doesn't need a reason to keep living but exploring this has definitely given her another project. She is looking forward to visiting the National Memorial Arboretum and having a bit of fuss made over her.' Lest we forget, Joy Trew served too.

ACKNOWLEDGEMENTS

Writing acknowledgements at the end of a book can appear formulaic. There are a list of obligatory (and heartfelt!) thank yous: agents, publishers, friends and family, all of which, in the case of *Lest We Forget*, have put in considerable time and effort. The sheer physicality of visiting 100 monuments meant a few even incurred expense and risk. (Visiting the battlefield at Culloden resulted in three points on my driving licence – too much animated conversation with my English mother. Did the cameras detect the car belonged to a Sassenach?)

But never before have I been mid-book when not one but two major contributors saw a glorious uptick in their national status. In the case of 103-year-old Mosquito pilot Colin Bell DFC, he was the oldest person named on the king's 2025 New Year Honours. He is now Colin Bell DFC BEM, the latter awarded for services to charitable fundraising and public speaking. About time too. In the same list, I also found my literary agent, the remarkable Caroline Michel at Peters Fraser + Dunlop, now Dame Caroline Michel for services to the literary world. I have indeed been blessed with a stellar team, including my publisher at HarperNorth (Jon – an honour can only be a matter of time!). If this book doesn't fly, it is no one's fault but my own.

LEST WE FORGET

In fact, these pages are replete with heroes. I have spent much of the last year reframing ideas of war and loss through the stories I have heard first hand. Helen Lewis and Jacqui Thompson stand out as two women who so eloquently shared their own battles in the wake of the dreadful news that their next-of-kin had been killed. Their pain helped me better understand how important lasting testimony is – not just bricks and mortar, but something so much more. Both women have touched the void and generously passed on what they have learnt. And their passion pushed me to do the best I could with this book, time permitting. I am forever grateful.

The preceding pages are filled with the names and testimonies of those to whom I owe the most. (My time in Northern Ireland particularly stands out – a great big thank you to all and everyone who met me in that extraordinary province.) However, in some cases it has not been possible to namecheck assistance received in the actual text itself. Among this invisible cast, the input and perspicacity of GCSE students Daisy Wright, Beth Ratcliffe and Mara Luca, and university undergraduate Rory More O'Ferrall, stand out. As well as introducing me to the delights of Harrow School, Oliver Webb-Carter, editor of *Aspects of History* magazine, did more than his fair share of support, moral and otherwise. Please do subscribe to his magazine!

However, history is one of the rare games where the older you get, the better you become, so peak thanks have to go to Bruce Collins, emeritus professor, one-time supervisor of my PhD and, ever since, not just a dear friend but a wise guide, sage, researcher, fellow traveller and proof-reader. As I write this blurb, my book is yet to be copyedited – more thanks to come – but in the meantime, it's been given the once-over by Bruce. He has also fact-checked the text. Obviously all mistakes are my own.

Regrettably, 100 monuments were not nearly enough. In fact, never great at admin, I somehow managed to file 103 monuments. And that was after I had undertaken a brutal edit. Ideally, Edith Cavell would have enjoyed a third memorial: her burial site and new

ACKNOWLEDGEMENTS

headstone at glorious Norwich Cathedral. My day spent there was unforgettable, for which many thanks go to the Reverend Dr Peter Doll. Likewise, gratitude to Mike and Di Levins, who generously gave me a tour of their great city – Worcester. Britain's historic failure to provide its civil wars with commemorative heft (see Monuments 22–24) helps explains why Worcester did not make the cut. Elsewhere, I am grateful for tip-offs that led to unexpected inclusions. A particular favourite is the Chattri Memorial near Brighton, with Yasmin Alibhai-Brown providing vital intel. I am also indebted to Hannah Bower at the Royal Air Force Benevolent Fund for her enthusiasm, recommendations and support.

One of the great pleasures of writing this book was getting to know the National Memorial Arboretum in Staffordshire, where my tireless guide was former English teacher and volunteer, Keith Forster. Always on hand to help with my never-ending enquiries, I am delighted to hear that he has swapped retirement for a job on the Arboretum's events team. Further collaboration is surely pending.

And finally, my thanks to you for reading *Lest We Forget*. Your thoughts, feedback and monuments are always welcome and may just find their way into the paperback edition ...

Tessa Dunlop
Kinloch Rannoch, February 2025

BIBLIOGRAPHY

Lest We Forget is a deliberate fusion of art and oral testimony, location and local heritage. However, it is also a history book and there are some key texts, publications and websites I could not have done without. Those not mentioned in the footnotes are listed below.

PART ONE: OUTSIDERS
Books
Asser (trans: Keynes, Simon & Lapidge, Michael), *Alfred the Great: Asser's Life of King Alfred and Other Contemporary Sources*, Penguin Classics, 1983
Bartlett, Robert. *England Under the Norman and Angevin Kings: 1075–1225*, Oxford University Press, 2000
Bartlett, W. B. *Richard the Lionheart: The Crusader King of England*, Amberley Publishing, 2018
Coltman, Viccy. *Art and Identity in Scotland: A Cultural History From the Jacobite Rising of 1745 to Walter Scott*, Cambridge University Press, 2019
Douglas, David C. *William the Conqueror: The Norman Impact Upon England*, Yale University Press, 1999
Hingley, Richard, and Unwin, Christina. *Boudica: Iron Age Warrior Queen*, Hambledon Continuum, 2006 (new edition)

Hudson, Derek. *Martin Tupper: His Rise and Fall*, Constable, 1949
Jackson, Dan. *The Northumbrians: North-East England and Its People – A New History*, C Hurst & Co, 2019
Linklater, Eric. *The Survival of Scotland: A Review of Scottish History from Roman Times to the Present Day*, Heinemann, 1968
Parker, Joanne. *'England's Darling': The Victorian Cult of Alfred the Great*, Manchester University Press, 2007
Prebble, John. *Glencoe: The Story of the Massacre*, Penguin, 1973
Riches, Samantha. *St George: Hero, Martyr and Myth*, The History Press, 2009

Articles
Keynes, Simon. 'The Cult of King Alfred the Great', *Anglo-Saxon England*, 1999, vol.28, pp.225–356
Powell, F. York. 'The Alfred Millenary of 1901', *The North American Review*, October 1901, vol.173, no.539, pp.518–532
Yorke, Barbara. 'The King Alfred Millenary in Winchester, 1901', *Hampshire Papers Committee*, Hampshire County Council, 1999

Guides
Lindisfarne Priory, Historic England, 2006
The Temple Church: Mother-Church of the Common Law – A Pilgrim's Guide, Temple Church and Jarrold Publishing, 2024

Radio programmes
'Great Lives: Richard the Lionheart', BBC Radio 4, 2021
'In Our Time: Boudica', BBC Radio 4, 2010
'In Our Time: The Norman Yoke', BBC Radio 4, 2008

Websites
https://rssg.org.uk

BIBLIOGRAPHY

PART TWO: WARRING BRITANNIA
Books

Ambler, Sophie Thérèse. *The Song of Simon de Montfort: England's First Revolutionary*, Picador, 2019

Bardon, Jonathan. *A History of Ulster*, Blackstaff Press, 1992

Carpenter, David. *Henry III: The Rise to Power and Personal Rule, 1207–1258*, Yale University Press, 2020

de Cuellar, Francisco (ed: Allingham, Hugh; trans: Crawford, Robert). *Captain Francisco de Cuéllar's Adventures in Connacht and Ulster*, Elliot Stock, 1897

Davies, John. *A History of Wales*, Allen Lane, 1993

Davies, R. R. *Owain Glyn Dŵr: Prince of Wales*, Y Lolfa, 2011

Devine, Tom M. *The Scottish Nation: 1700–2000*, Allen Lane, 1999

Goring, Rosemary (ed). *Scotland, The Autobiography: 2000 Years of Scottish History by Those Who Saw It Happen*, Viking, 2007

Guthrie, Neil. *The Material Culture of the Jacobites*, Cambridge University Press, 2013

Healey, Jonathan. *The Blazing World: A New History of Revolutionary England*, Bloomsbury, 2023

Jackson, Clare. *Devil-Land: England Under Siege, 1588–1688*, Allen Lane, 2021

Jobson, Adrian. *The First English Revolution: Simon de Montfort, Henry III and the Barons' War*, Continuum, 2012

Jones, Dan. *Henry V: The Astonishing Rise of England's Greatest Warrior King*, Head of Zeus, 2023

Jones, Dan. *Powers and Thrones: A New History of the Middle Ages*, Head of Zeus, 2021

Langley, Philippa & Jones, Michael. *The King's Grave: The Search for Richard III*, St Martins Press, 2013

Lay, Paul. *Providence Lost: The Rise and Fall of Cromwell's Protectorate*, Apollo, 2020

Lewis-Stempel, John. *England, The Autobiography: 2000 Years of English History by Those Who Saw It Happen*, Viking, 2005

Lord, Steve. *Walking With Charlie: In the Footsteps of the Forty-Five*, Pookus Publications, 2003

Morton, Graeme. *William Wallace: Man and Myth*, Sutton Publishing, 2001

Perkins, Jocelyn. *Westminster Abbey: Its Worship and Ornaments, Vol III*, Oxford University Press, 1952

Smith, J. Beverley. *Llywelyn ap Gruffudd: Prince of Wales*, University of Wales Press, 2014

Smith, Nicola. *The Royal Image and the English People*, Ashgate, 2001

Starkey, David. *Monarchy: From the Middle Ages to Modernity*, HarperPress, 2006

Stewart, Laura A. M. *Urban Politics and the British Civil Wars: Edinburgh, 1617–53*, Brill, 2006

Stewart, Laura A. M. *Rethinking the Scottish Revolution: Covenanted Scotland, 1637–1651*, Oxford University Press, 2018

Williams, Gruffydd Aled. *The Last Days of Owain Glyndwr*, Y Lolfa Cyf, 2017

Whinney, Margaret. *Sculpture in Britain, 1530–1830*, Penguin, 1964

Williams, Kate. *Rival Queens: The Betrayal of Mary, Queen of Scots*, Hutchinson, 2018

Wormald, Jenny (ed). *The Seventeenth Century: 1603–1688*, Oxford University Press, 2000

Accident or Assassination? The Death of Llywelyn 11 December 1282, The Story, Original Documents and Poems, Abbey Cwmhir Heritage Trust, 2020

Articles

Gold. John R. & and Gold, Margaret M. 'The Graves of the Gallant Highlanders: Memory, Interpretation and Narrative of Culloden', *History and Memory*, Indiana University Press, vol. 19, no.1, 2007, pp.5–38

Rigney, Ann. 'Commemoration by Committee', *Victorian Review*, John Hopkins University, Spring 2018, vol. 44, no.1, pp.1–5

BIBLIOGRAPHY

Scott, Alexander M. 'Notes on the Battle of Langside', *Transactions of the Glasgow Archaeological Society*, vol.1, no.3, 1888, pp.281–300

Van Hensbergen, Claudine. 'Print, Poetry and Posterity: Grinling Gibbons's Statue for the Royal Exchange', *Sculpture Journal*, 9.3, 2020

Guides
Blenheim Palace visitors' guide, Jarrod Publishing, 2006
Cardiff City Hall visitor information guide, 2006
Leicester Cathedral guidebook, 2023

Radio programmes
'In Our Time: Agincourt', BBC Radio 4, 2004
'In Our Time: Owain Glyndwr', BBC Radio 4, 2019
'In Our Time: The Second Barons' War', BBC Radio 4, 2021

Websites
https://www.battlefieldstrust.com/resource-centre
https://courtauld.ac.uk/news-blogs/2021/scientific-study-of-the-tomb-of-the-black-prince
http://www.covenanter.org.uk
https://langsidecommunityheritage.org
https://naseby.com
https://www.westminster-abbey.org
https://www.1745association.org.uk

PART THREE: LAND OF HOPE AND GLORY
Books
Adams, Max. *Admiral Collingwood: Nelson's Own Hero*, Orion, 2005
Bostridge, Mark. *Florence Nightingale: The Woman and Her Legend*, 200th Anniversary Edition, Penguin, 2020
Cannadine, David. *Trafalgar in History: A Battle and its Afterlife*, Palgrave Macmillan, 2006

Cole, Howard N. *The Story of Aldershot*, Southern Books, 1980

Czisnik, Marianne. *Horatio Nelson: A Controversial Hero*, Hodder, 2005

Donaldson, Peter. *Remembering the South African War: Britain and the Memory of the Anglo-Boer War, from 1899 to the Present*, Liverpool University Press, 2013

Forrest, Alan. *Great Battles: Waterloo*, Oxford University Press, 2015

Hoock, Holger. *History, Commemoration and National Preoccupation: Trafalgar 1805–2005*, Oxford University Press, 2007

Longford, Elizabeth. *Wellington*, Weidenfeld & Nicolson, 1982

Rappaport, Helen. *In Search of Mary Seacole: The Making of a Cultural Icon*, Simon & Schuster, 2022

Reed, Michael. *A History of Buckinghamshire*, Phillimore & Co, 1993

Reynolds, Luke. *Who Owned Waterloo? Battle, Memory and Myth in British History*, 1815–1852, OUP, 2022

Roberts, Andrew. *Napoleon and Wellington*, Weidenfeld & Nicolson, 2001

Rodger, N. A. M. *The Command of the Ocean: A Naval History of Britain 1649–1815*, Allen Lane, 2004

Articles

Brockliss, Laurence; Cardwell, John; and Moss, Michael. 'Nelson's Grand National Obsequies', *The English Historical Review*, Oxford University Press, Feb 2006, vol.121, no.490, pp.162–182

Cattrall, Pippa. 'Statues, Spatial Syntax and Surrealism: "History" and Heritagescapes in Public Spaces', *Transactions of the RHS*, 2021, no.1, pp.267–290

Cookson, J.E. 'The Edinburgh and Glasgow Duke of Wellington Statues: Early Nineteenth-Century Unionist Nationalism as a Tory Project', *The Scottish Historical Review*, Apr 2004, vol.83, no.215, Part 1, pp.23–44

BIBLIOGRAPHY

Finucane, Julie. 'Civilian Legacies of Military Nursing', *Health and History*, Australian and New Zealand Society of the History of Medicine, 2004, vol.6, no.2, pp.97–110

Hanna, William. 'Bath and the Crimean War', *History of Bath Research Group*, vol.8, 2000

Howarth, David. '"The Fourth Estate" Commemorating the Duke of Wellington, 1814–1914,' *The British Art Journal*, 2013/14, vol.14, no.3, pp.58–67

Lambert, Andrew. '"The Glory of England": Nelson, Trafalgar and the Meaning of Victory,' *The Great Circle*, 2006, vol.28, no.1, pp.3–12

Macleod, Jenny. 'Memorials and Location: Local Versus National Identity and the Scottish National War Memorial', *The Scottish Historical Review*, April 2020, vol.89, no.227, Part 1, pp.73–95

Sinnema, P. E. 'Wyatt's "Wellington" and the Hyde Park Corner Controversy', *Oxford Art Journal*, vol.27, no.2, 2004, pp.173–192

Ward Jackson, Philip. 'Carlo Marochetti and the Glasgow War Memorial', *The Burlington Magazine*, December 1990, vol.132, no.1953

'The Nightingale Statue', *The British Medical Journal*, 27 February 1915, vol.1, no.2826, pp.384–385

Red Hackle, The Regimental Journal of the Black Watch, 2023

The Duke of Wellington's Statue, Second Letter, From Viator, J Olivier, 1847

Radio programmes

'Florence Nightingale', BBC World Service, 1969

'In Our Time: The Battle of Trafalgar', BBC Radio 4, 2021

'In Our Time: Napoleon and Wellington', BBC Radio 4, 2001

'Mary Seacole', BBC World Service, 1994

'The Boer War: Separating Fact from Fiction in Britain's Forgotten War', BBC World Service, 1999

'Witness History: The Funeral of the Duke of Wellington', BBC World Service, 2018

Websites
https://kingswoodchurches.weebly.com/holy-trinity-church-kingswood.html
https://www.florence-nightingale.co.uk
https://www.newmp.org.uk
https://www.stpauls.co.uk
https://yorkminster.org

PART FOUR: MECHANISED KILLING
Books
Alibhai-Brown, Yasmin. *Exotic England: The Making of a Curious Nation*, Portobello Books, 2015
Borg, Alan. *War Memorials*, Leo Cooper, 1991
Cannadine, David. 'War, Death, Grief and Mourning in Modern Britain', in Whalley, Joachim (ed), *Mirrors of Mortality, Social Studies in the History of Death*, Routledge, reprinted 2011
Cockburn, Cynthia & French, Sue. *Women in Black: Against Violence, For Peace with Justice*, Merlin Press, 2023
Gorer, Geoffrey. *Death, Grief and Mourning in Contemporary Britain*, The Cresset Press, 1965
Nicol, John. *The Unknown Warrior: A Personal Journey of Discovery and Remembrance*, Simon & Schuster, 2024
Orr, Philip. *The Road to the Somme: Men of the Ulster Division Tell Their Story*, Blackstaff Press, 1987
Quinlan, Mark. *British War Memorials*, Authors Online, 2005
Sitwell, Osbert. *The People's Album of London Statues*, Duckworth, 1928
Seldon, Anthony & Walsh, David. *Public Schools and the Great War*, Pen and Sword, 2013
Whittingham, Sarah. *Sir George Oatley: Architect of Bristol*, Redcliffe Press, 2011

Bristol and the First World War, The Great Reading Adventure, 2014
The Story of Norwich Cathedral, Jigsaw Design and Publishing, 2017

Articles
Gough, P. & Morgan, S. 'Manipulating the Metonymic: The Politics of Civic Identity and the Bristol Cenotaph, 1919–1932', *Journal of Historical Geography*, 30, 2004, pp.665–684
Hodgeson, Guy Richard. 'Nurse, Martyr, Propaganda Tool', *Media, War & Conflict*, Saga Publications, August 2017, vol.10, no.2, pp.239–53

Radio programmes
'Anti-Social: Does Britain Need a Muslim War Memorial?', BBC Radio 4, 2024
'Great Lives: Edwin Lutyens', BBC Radio 4, 2018
'Secrets and Spies: The Untold Story of Edith Cavell', BBC Radio 4, 2022

PART FIVE: AN EXCEPTIONAL WAR
Books
Basu, Shrabani. *Spy Princess: The Life of Noor Inayat Khan*, The History Press, 2006
Bradford, Sarah. *George VI: The Dutiful King*, Penguin Books, 2002
Boorman, Derek. *For Your Tomorrow: British Second World War Memorials*, Dunnington Hall, 1995
Cardozo, Major General Ian. *Lieutenant General Bilimoria: His Life and Times*, Centre for Armed Forces Historical Research, United Service Institution of India, 2016
Dunlop, Tessa. *Army Girls: The Secrets and Stories of Military Service from the Final Few Women Who Fought in the Second World War*, Headline Press, 2021
Dunlop, Tessa. *The Bletchley Girls: War, Secrecy, Love and Loss – The Women of Bletchley Park Tell Their Story*, Hodder & Stoughton, 2015

Dunlop, Tessa. *The Century Girls: The Final Word from the Women Who've Lived the Past Hundred Years of British History*, Simon & Schuster, 2018

Dunning, James. *It Had To Be Tough: The Origins and Training of the Commandos in World War II*, Frontline Books, 2012

Escott, Beryl E. *The Heroines of SOE: F Section, Britain's Secret Women in France*, The History Press, 2010

Hawkins, Desmond (ed). *War Report: From D-Day to Berlin as it Happened*, BBC Books, 2019

Helm, Sarah. *A Life in Secrets: The Story of Vera Atkins and the Lost Agents of SOE*, Hachette, 2005

Keegan, John (ed). *Churchill's Generals*, Abacus, 1991

Milton, Giles. *Churchill's Ministry of Ungentlemanly Warfare: The Mavericks Who Plotted Hitler's Defeat*, Picador, 2016

Roberts, Andrew. *Churchill: Walking with Destiny*, Allen Lane, 2018

Seldon, Anthony (with Meakin, Jonathan; Thoms, Illias; Egerton, Tom). *The Impossible Office: The History of the British Prime Minister*, Cambridge University Press, 2021

Articles

Gurung, Tejimala. 'The Making of Gurkhas as a "Martial Race" in Colonial India: Theory and Practice', *Indian History Congress*, vol.75, 2014

PART SIX: PEACETIME BRITAIN

Books

HRH The Duke of Kent & Vickers, Hugo. *A Royal Life*, Hodder & Stoughton, 2022

Mansergh, Nicholas. *The Anglo-Irish Settlement and Its Undoing, 1912–72*, Yale University, 1991

Morpurgo, Michael. *War Horse*, Kaye & Ward, 1982

Petraeus, General David & Roberts Andrew. *Conflict: The Evolution of Warfare from 1945 to Ukraine*, William Collins, 2023

BIBLIOGRAPHY

Weston, Simon. 'Foreword' in *Helmand: Diaries of Front-line Soldiers*, Osprey Publishing, 2013
Weston, Simon. *Moving On*, Piaktus, 2004
Weston, Simon. *Walking Tall: An Autobiography*, Ted Smart, 1989
Whyte, John. *Interpreting Northern Ireland*, Clarendon Press, 1991

Radio programmes
'Drawing a Line Under the Troubles', BBC Radio 4, 2018
'The History Hour: Fifty Years Since Northern Ireland's Bloody Sunday', BBC Radio 4, 2022

Websites
https://thenma.org.uk

General Reading
Baycroft, Timothy. *Nationalism in Europe, 1789–1945*, Cambridge University Press, 1998
Beard, Mary. *Emperor of Rome*, Profile Books, 2023
Bullus, Claire & Asprey, Ronald. *The Statues of London*, Merrell, 2009
Cannon, John & Hargreaves, Anne. *The Kings and Queens of Britain*, Oxford University Press, 2004
Carlyle, Thomas. *On Heroes, Hero Worship and the Heroic in History*, James Fraser, 1840
Chancellor, E. Beresford. *The Lives of the British Sculptors and Those Who Have Worked in England from the Earliest Days to Sir Francis Chantrey*, Chapman & Hall, 1911
Hewitt, Nick. 'A Sceptical Generation? War Memorials and the Collective Memory of the Second World War in Britain, 1945–2000', in Geppert, Dominik (ed), *The Postwar Challenge: Cultural, Social and Political Change in Western Europe, 1945–58*, Oxford University Press, 2003
Hobsbawm, Eric & Ranger, Terence (eds). *The Invention of Tradition*, Cambridge University Press, 1983

Hughes, Bettany. *The Seven Wonders of the Ancient World*, Weidenfeld & Nicolson, 2024

Hughes, Peter. *A History of Love & Hate in 21 Statues*, Aurum, 2021

Ross, Peter. *A Tomb With a View: The Stories and Glories of Graveyards*, Headline, 2020

Von Tunzelmann, Alex. *Fallen Idols: Twelve Statues That Made History*, Headline Press, 2021

Newspapers and journals

Belfast Telegraph
British Medical Journal
The Daily Mail
Dispatches, The Journal of the Commando Association
The Guardian
Illustrated London News
The Independent
The Irish Times
The Telegraph
The Times

Websites

https://britishnewspaperarchive.co.uk
https://www.bbc.co.uk/news
https://www.iwm.org.uk/memorials
https://www.english-heritage.org.uk/
https://www.oxforddnb.com
https://www.nam.ac.uk
https://www.nationaltrust.org.uk

BOOK CREDITS

HarperNorth would like to thank the following staff and contributors for their involvement in making this book a reality:

Sarah Allen-Sutter
Jospeh Barnes
Fionnuala Barrett
Peter Borcsok
Sarah Burke
Alan Cracknell
Jonathan de Peyer
Anna Derkacz
Tom Dunstan
Kate Elton
Sarah Emsley
Simon Gerratt
Lydia Grainge
Monica Green
Natassa Hadjinicolaou
Martin Hargreaves
Emma Hatlen
Jess Haycox
Megan Jones

Jean-Marie Kelly
Taslima Khatun
Holly Kyte
Rachel McCarron
Alice Murphy-Pyle
Adam Murray
Genevieve Pegg
Amanda Percival
James Ryan
Florence Shepherd
Colleen Simpson
Eleanor Slater
Henry Steadman
Hilary Stein
Emma Sullivan
Nige Tassell
Katrina Troy
Daisy Watt
Ben Wright

For more unmissable reads,
sign up to the HarperNorth newsletter at
www.harpernorth.co.uk

or find us on X at
@HarperNorthUK